D0800556

WEST'S LAW SCHOOL
ADVISORY BOARD

CHILDREN AND THE LAW

IN A NUTSHELL

SECOND EDITION

By

SARAH H. RAMSEY
Laura J. and L. Douglas Meredith Professor for
Teaching Excellence and Professor of Law
Syracuse University College of Law

DOUGLAS E. ABRAMS
Associate Professor of Law
University of Missouri-Columbia

THOMSON
＊ ™
WEST

Nutshell Series, In a Nutshell, the Nutshell Logo and West Group are trademarks registered in the U.S. Patent and Trademark Office.

COPYRIGHT © 2001 WEST GROUP
COPYRIGHT © 2003 By West, a Thomson business
        610 Opperman Drive
        P.O. Box 64526
        St. Paul, MN 55164–0526
        1–800–328–9352
Printed in the United States of America

ISBN 0–314–14410–2

TEXT IS PRINTED ON 10% POST
CONSUMER RECYCLED PAPER

To my parents,
Sibyl Street Ramsey
and Robert Weberg Ramsey,
with love and thanks

S.H.R.

To Judge Hugh R. Jones, Mary Lou Crowley and
Martha Willmot,
Valued colleagues during my clerkship
in the New York Court of Appeals (1976-78)

D.E.A.

III

PREFACE

This book explores the status, rights and obligations of children throughout the wide range of American law. We have written with an eye toward an audience with diverse needs for a learning tool, a refresher text or a general reference work. Like our casebook, this text addresses students who seek to learn about children and the law, and perhaps to explore prospects for a career in child advocacy. The text also addresses practitioners who may or may not have taken a juvenile law course, but who are summoned to serve children as retained or appointed counsel, or as participants in law revision efforts. The text also addresses the needs of social services employees, physicians, mental health professionals, and others whose valuable contributions to child advocacy will be more effective with a general understanding of legal doctrine.

Because Nutshells strive to provide a meaningful examination of the law in a succinct format, we examine central legal doctrine with necessary self-imposed limits on extended citations and discussions of particular judicial decisions, legislation, scholarly commentary and statistical analyses. Readers seeking material beyond these limits might refer to the notes and commentary in our casebook, *Children and the Law: Doctrine, Policy and Practice* (2d ed. West Group 2003). To provide interchangeability to facilitate learning and reference, the Nutshell generally follows the casebook's format.

We want to thank Teia L. Johnson and Lisa MacDonald for their effort in preparing the first edition for publication and Christy Ramsdell for her work on the second edition. We are grateful as well to Melissa Gamble for research assistance on the first edition. Chapter 3 contains material reprinted by permission from *Missouri Juvenile Law*, copyright The Missouri Bar (1999, 2001). All rights reserved.

We anticipate treating new developments in this vibrant field of law in future editions. As we look toward the future, we would welcome suggestions from readers who share our enthusiasm for the field and are kind enough to exchange ideas with us.

Sarah H. Ramsey
Douglas E. Abrams
July 2003

OUTLINE

VIII

XVI

XVIII

XXIV

XXVI

TABLE OF CASES

References are to Pages

XXVIII

XXIX

XXX

XXXI

In re E.G., 549 N.E.2d 322 (Ill. 1989), 341-42, 358

Elmore v. Van Horn, 844 P.2d 1078 (Wyo. 1992), 99

Eisenstadt v. Baird, 405 U.S. 438 (1972), 89

In re Eric J.D., 1998 WL 149486 (Wis. Ct. App.), 533

In re Erickson, 604 P.2d 513 (Wash. Ct. App. 1979), 573

Ernst v. Child and Youth Services, 108 F.3d 486 (3rd Cir. 1997), 147

Estate of _____ (see name of party)

In re E.T.C., 449 A.2d 937 (Vt. 1982), 526

Ex parte _____ (see name of party)

United States v. Faasse, 227 F. 3d 660 (6th Cir. 2000), 373

Fare v. Michael C., 442 U.S. 707 (1979), 523-25

In re F.B., 726 A.2d 361 (Pa. 1999), 519

Felix v. State, 849 P.2d 220 (Nev. 1993), 239

Ferguson v. City of Charleston, 532 U.S. 67 (2001), 141

Ferris v. Santa Clara County, 891 F.2d 715 (9th Cir. 1989), 220

Gabin v. Skyline Cabana Club, 258 A.2d 6 (N.J. 1969), 424

In re Marriage of Gallagher, 539 N.W.2d 49 (Iowa 1995), 71, 76-77

XXXIX

XL

XLI

XLIV

XLVI

XLVIII

XLIX

CHILDREN AND THE LAW

IN A NUTSHELL

SECOND EDITION

*

CHAPTER 1

THE STATUS, RIGHTS AND OBLIGATIONS OF CHILDREN

A. AN INTRODUCTION TO THE JUVENILE COURT SYSTEM

1. JUVENILE COURT JURISDICTION

Each state has a trial court devoted to various proceedings relating to children, called the "juvenile court" in most states. In some states, the juvenile court is a distinct trial court; in some states, the general jurisdiction trial court has juvenile jurisdiction; in other states, the juvenile court is a separate division of the general-jurisdiction trial court, such as "the juvenile division of the superior court."

Juvenile courts typically have exclusive original jurisdiction over four major categories of proceedings:

Abuse and neglect (chapter 3). Civil abuse and neglect proceedings determine the state's claims that a parent or custodian (1) has physically, sexually or

emotionally abused the child, or (2) has
failed to provide the child a minimal level
of support, education, nutrition, or
medical or other care necessary for the
child's well-being. (Criminal abuse or
neglect charges against the parent or
custodian, the subject of chapter 5, are
heard in criminal court rather than
juvenile court.) This category of juvenile
court jurisdiction generally confers
jurisdiction to decide termination-of-
parental-rights petitions filed by the state
seeking to permanently sever the parent-
child relationship because of gross abuse
or gross neglect.

Adoption (chapter 6). Adoption generally
terminates the parent-child relationship
between the child and the natural
parents, and creates a new parent-child
relationship between the child and the
adoptive parents. (In an adoption by a
stepparent, however, the spouse's parental rights are not terminated.) A child may
be adopted only if parental rights have
been terminated by consent or court
order, and if the juvenile court approves
the adoption as being in the best
interests of the child. In some states,
adoption jurisdiction is in the probate or

surrogate's court.

Status offenses (chapter 9).   A status offense is misconduct sanctionable only where the person committing it is a juvenile. Prime examples are truancy, running away from home, and ungovernability (that the juvenile habitually resists reasonable discipline from his or her parents and is beyond their control).

Delinquency (chapter 10).   A delinquency proceeding alleges that the juvenile has committed an act that would be a felony or misdemeanor if committed by an adult.

In some states, the juvenile court may also hear and decide various other matters, such as juvenile traffic offenses, guardianship proceedings, commitment proceedings for mentally ill or seriously disabled children, proceedings for consent to an abortion or underage marriage, and paternity and child support proceedings. State appellate codes define the circumstances in which appeals may be taken from juvenile court decisions.

2. UNIFIED FAMILY COURTS

A growing number of jurisdictions have replaced the juvenile court with a unified family court. Family courts enable one specialist judge, working with social service workers and other support personnel, to resolve all matters typically associated with distressed families. The family court's exclusive original jurisdiction includes not only matters within the four major categories of juvenile court jurisdiction, but also an array of matters traditionally heard in general jurisdiction courts. This array typically includes divorce proceedings, paternity suits, support actions, criminal prosecutions charging abuse or neglect or domestic violence, emancipation proceedings, and proceedings for protective orders under child abuse and adult abuse statutes.

Troubled children often come from troubled families, and frequently the juvenile justice system can provide effective relief most efficiently when one tribunal responds to all related domestic dysfunction. Proponents assert that unified family courts can produce consistency that serves the best interests of children, families and courts. Families and the judicial system save time, effort and resources when one decisionmaker remains abreast of the family's circumstances and resolves all family-related matters. Family members are spared the ordeal of appearing in multiple courts that determine frequently interrelated factual and legal issues. Children are spared the discomfort of testifying in multiple proceedings. Consider, for example, the plight of a young child allegedly molested by her father. In a jurisdiction without a unified family court, the child may be forced to endure the embarrassment of testifying about the same or similar events in multiple proceedings if the mother files for divorce, child protective authorities file a civil abuse proceeding to remove the child from the home, and the prosecutor files criminal charges.

Family court critics are particularly skeptical of removing criminal court jurisdiction over domestic violence. They fear that because unified family courts are essentially civil courts, removal would diminish the impact of sanction. An additional concern is that family courts will be underfunded. In 1994, the American Bar Association reaffirmed its commitment to unified family courts. See American Bar Association Policy on Unified Family Courts, 32 Fam. L.Q. 1 (1998) (adopted Aug. 1994).

B.   THE NATURE AND SOURCES OF CHILDREN'S STATUS, RIGHTS AND OBLIGATIONS

1.   INTRODUCTION

For most purposes, the status of childhood lasts until a person reaches the general age of majority, which was twenty-one for most of our nation's history. Nearly all states lowered the age to eighteen in the early 1970s, shortly after the Twenty-Sixth Amendment lowered the voting age in federal and state elections to eighteen. Equal protection requires that the age of majority be the same for boys and girls. See Stanton v. Stanton (S.Ct.1975).

The general age of majority does not determine adult status for all purposes. Some statutes define circumstances in which children first assume adult rights and obligations at an age higher than eighteen. The alcoholic beverage control laws, for example, set the minimum drinking age at twenty-one in all states.

Children assume some adult rights and obligations before they reach the general age of majority. Many states, for example, terminate delinquency jurisdiction and expose a child to adult criminal prosecution before eighteen.

Statutes also frequently permit persons under eighteen to make medical treatment decisions for some diseases, such as sexually transmitted diseases. Before reaching the general age of majority, a child may also gain most adult rights and obligations through a judicial order of "emancipation," which chapter 8 discusses.

The general age of majority, and the statutes departing from it, apply to all persons, regardless of a particular person's maturity. The general age is easy to administer, but ignores individual differences.

Sometimes adult status is conferred by individualized determination, rather than general standard. The court may find a child sufficiently mature to make a particular decision an adult would normally make for him or her. If a court finds a pregnant girl to be mature, for example, the girl may decide whether to have an abortion without parental consent to the procedure. See Bellotti v. Baird, which section D.2 discusses.

The status of childhood thus is a complex concept in our society. The law views children as vulnerable, incapable and needing protection in some circumstances, but as holding consti- tutional rights, decisionmaking ability and personal responsibility in others. A person may

be a child for one purpose, but an adult for
another. A fifteen-year-old, for example, cannot
sign a binding contract but may be tried as an
adult and sentenced to life in prison for a crime.

2. THE PARENS PATRIAE DOCTRINE

Derived from the royal prerogative, the
common law parens patriae ("parent of the
country") doctrine gave the English Crown the
right and responsibility to protect persons deemed
legally incapable of caring for themselves.
Protection of children was normally confined to
those of the landed gentry, with an eye toward
securing financial reward for the Crown itself.

Following the Revolution, states assumed
the parens patriae authority held by the Crown.
American law, however, extended protection of
children beyond the landed gentry. Justice Story's
influential treatise, for example, spoke of children
generally: "[P]arents are intrusted with the
custody of the persons, and the education, of
their children; yet this is done upon the natural
presumption, that the children will be properly
taken care of ...; and that they will be treated with
kindness and affection. But, whenever ... a father
... acts in a manner injurious to the morals or
interests of his children; in every such case, the
Court of Chancery will interfere." Joseph Story,

Commentaries on Equity Jurisprudence § 1341 (3d ed. 1843).

Throughout the nineteenth century, child advocates in the United States sought to invoke the parens patriae doctrine to protect children from abuse, neglect and the adult criminal justice system's harshness. In 1890, the Supreme Court held that the doctrine was "inherent in the supreme power of every state, ... a most beneficent function, and often necessary to be exercised in the interests of humanity, and for the prevention of injury to those who cannot protect themselves." Mormon Church v. United States (S.Ct.1890). The doctrine was a guiding force behind creation of the first juvenile court in 1899.

Today the parens patriae doctrine underlies much public regulation discussed in this book in such areas as abuse and neglect, foster care, adoption, medical decisionmaking, support, protective legislation and delinquency. Regulation generally lasts until the child reaches the general age of majority, but, as discussed above in section B.1, protection may end earlier or last longer for some purposes.

As a practical matter, the parens patriae doctrine's reach may sometimes be affected by the reluctance of public authorities to intervene in family affairs and regulate conduct within the family, including some parental conduct affecting children. Because much child abuse occurs in private, for example, official investigation may be distasteful, or may be hampered by the family's unwillingness to cooperate. Not only that, but if the state investigates the perpetrator and arouses his anger without stopping the abuse, investigation may provoke even greater family violence.

3. THE POLICE POWER

Besides parens patriae authority, states may regulate children and the family under their general police powers. The two sources of authority are conceptually distinct.

Parens patriae confers state authority to protect or promote a particular child's welfare. The police power is the state's inherent plenary authority to promote the public health, safety and welfare generally. "Acting under its parens patriae power, the state may pursue ends that would be impermissible under the police power because they are unrelated to any harm to third parties or to the public welfare. At the same time, however, when the state acts as parens patriae, it should advance only the best interests of the incompetent individual and not attempt to further other objectives, deriving from its police power,

that may conflict with the individual's welfare. ...
[T]he state should seek, if possible, to make its
decisions in the same way that the individual
would were he fully competent." Developments in
the Law -- The Constitution and the Family, 93
Harv. L. Rev. 1156 (1980).

4.   THE CHILD'S DUTY TO OBEY

At common law, children were expected to
obey their parents and heed the biblical command
to "honor thy father and mother." In New
England, for example, a 1641 law provided that "If
any child, or children, above sixteen years old,
and of sufficient understanding shall CURSE or
SMITE their natural FATHER or MOTHER, he or
she shall be putt to death, unless it can be
sufficiently testified that the Parents have been
very unchristianly negligent in the education of
such children: so provoked them by extreme and
cruel correction, that they have been forced
thereunto, to preserve themselves from death or
maiming."

Early in the nineteenth century, Chancellor James Kent said this about children's
obligations to their parents: "The rights of parents
result from their duties. As they are bound to
maintain and educate their children, the law has
given them a right to such authority; and in the

support of that authority, a right to the exercise of such discipline as may be requisite for the discharge of their sacred trust. ... The duties that are enjoined upon children to their parents, are obedience and assistance during their own minority, and gratitude and reverence during the rest of their lives." James Kent, Commentaries on American Law (5th ed. 1844).

The law's expectation that children would obey their parents' wishes is implicit in *Meyer* and *Pierce* discussed below, the Supreme Court's early decisions granting parents a substantive due process right to direct their children's upbringing free from unreasonable government intervention.

C. THE LAW'S EVOLVING CONCEPTION OF CHILDREN'S STATUS, RIGHTS AND OBLIGATIONS

1. THE TRADITIONAL ROLES OF PARENTS AND THE GOVERNMENT

Neither the Constitution nor the Bill of Rights speaks explicitly about the status, rights and obligations of children or parents, and nothing in the proceedings of the Constitutional Convention or the ensuing ratification debates indicates that the Founders or the ratifying states ever considered these matters. The absence of explicit statement is interesting because several colonial charters and bills of rights did address children's legal capacity, their standing in civil and criminal proceedings, their inheritance rights, their treatment by parents, and their education. The debates leading to enactment of the Civil War Amendments similarly yield no evidence that children or parents received any attention.

Professor Homer H. Clark, Jr. advances two reasons why children and parents received no explicit attention when the federal Constitution was drafted. "The most obvious is that it never occurred to the Framers that children, as distinguished from adults, needed constitutional status. The assumption may well have been that common-law parental power and authority over children, reinforced by parental affection and concern, were sufficient to protect the children's interests." He also suggests that silence about the family stemmed from the doctrine that "states, rather than the federal government, should regulate the relationship of parent and child." Homer H. Clark, Jr., Children and the Constitution, 1992 U. Ill. L. Rev. 1.

Throughout most of the nation's early history, children were viewed as legal incompetents in family matters until they reached the age of majority. See, e.g., Morrissey v. Perry (S.Ct.

1890). The law recognized almost absolute parental authority over children, and perceived children almost as the property of their parents, particularly of the father. The property analogy was not altogether inapt because children frequently had economic value to their parents before enactment of child labor and compulsory education laws. The analogy, however, was imperfect because the law allowed parents, for example, to kill or destroy their property but not their children. The property analogy nonetheless helps explain why children remained effectively voiceless in controversies with state authorities.

In other areas, however, particularly in criminal law, children could be treated as adults. By the early twentieth century, psychological thought had begun to question the criminal justice system's prevailing perception of children merely as "miniature adults" deserving of adult punishment. Creation of the nation's first juvenile court in 1899 climaxed decades of efforts by reformers who argued persuasively that children have distinct physical and emotional needs worthy of the law's recognition.

2. *MEYER, PIERCE* AND PARENTAL PREROGATIVES

Two Supreme Court decisions – Meyer v.

Nebraska (S.Ct.1923) and Pierce v. Society of Sisters (S.Ct.1925) -- are landmarks, not only because they gave parents due process protection in disputes with the government, but also because they helped create a doctrinal foundation for ongoing refinement of the status, rights and obligations of children.

Meyer reversed a parochial schoolteacher's conviction for teaching in the German language. The Court held that the statute permitting instruction only in English below the eighth grade violated the due process liberty interest of the teacher to teach in German, and of the parents to hire him to do so.

Meyer recognized a parent's due process liberty interest in "establish[ing] a home and bring[ing] up children." The Court also acknowledged the state's parens patriae authority "to compel attendance at some school and to make reasonable regulations for all schools," and "to prescribe a curriculum for institutions which it supports." *Meyer* held that the parental interest prevailed in this case, but the Court's weighing process made no mention of any interest, constitutional or otherwise, held by the students.

Two years later, *Pierce* struck down a state statute that required parents to send their

children between eight and sixteen to public
school, and not private or parochial school. Again
the Court perceived the dispute as between the
parents' due process liberty interest and the
state's parens patriae interest, without indicating
that the children held any interest of their own.
The Court again acknowledged state authority
"reasonably to regulate all schools," but held that
the challenged statute unreasonably interfered
with the parents' interest to "direct the upbringing
and education of children under their control."

The parents' due process liberty interest in
directing their children's upbringing, recognized
in *Meyer* and *Pierce*, prevails to this day. Courts
frequently call the interest "fundamental," though
the two seminal decisions used "reasonableness"
language now associated with rational basis
scrutiny. Lower courts have ordinarily applied
rational basis, rather than strict, scrutiny to
determine the strength of the state interest in
disputes between a school system and parents
invoking due process. See, e.g., Herndon v.
Chapel Hill-Carrboro City Board of Education (4th
Cir. 1996).

3. *PRINCE* AND THE MOVEMENT TOWARD "CHILDREN'S RIGHTS"

In Prince v. Massachusetts (S.Ct. 1944),

the Court upheld the custodial aunt's conviction for violating the state child labor law by permitting her nine-year-old niece to accompany her and seek to sell Jehovah's Witnesses periodicals on a public street. (The Court's analysis treated the aunt like a parent.) *Prince* marks a turn toward the modern children's rights movement.

The parental due process interest was at stake, as it had been in *Meyer* and *Pierce*. "It is cardinal with us," Justice Rutledge wrote for the *Prince* majority, "that the custody, care and nurture of the child reside first in the parents, whose primary function and freedom include preparations for obligations the state can neither supply nor hinder." *Prince* identified a "private realm of family life which the state cannot enter."

Also at stake in *Prince* were "the interests of society to protect the welfare of children." "Acting to guard the general interest in youth's well being, the state as *parens patriae* ... has a wide range of power for limiting parental freedom and authority in things affecting the child's welfare."

The decision did not end here, however. Unlike *Meyer* and *Pierce*, *Prince* expressly recognized the child's independent interest.

Prince considered "[t]he rights of children to exercise their religion," and acknowledged that "children have rights, in common with older people, in the primary use of highways." But *Prince* subordinated the child's interest to those of the parents and the state: "The state's authority over children's activities is broader than over like actions of adults. ... What may be wholly permissible for adults therefore may not be so for children, either with or without their parents' presence."

4. *BROWN* AND *GAULT*: EXPLICIT RECOGNITION OF CHILDREN'S RIGHTS

A decade after *Prince*, Brown v. Board of Education (S.Ct.1954) unanimously held that racial segregation in the public schools denies equal protection guaranteed by the Fourteenth Amendment. Unlike *Meyer* and *Pierce*, Brown did not concern the rights of parents to provide their children particular courses of study or to send their children to particular schools. *Brown's* named plaintiffs were the school children themselves, suing through their legal representatives. The Court decided the consolidated cases on the express premise that the rights vindicated were held by the children, and not by their parents: "[S]egregation of children in public schools solely on the basis of race, even though the physical facilities and other 'tangible' factors may be equal, deprive[s] the children of the minority group of equal educational opportunities."

Four years later, in Cooper v. Aaron (S.Ct.1958), the Court reiterated that *Brown* had squarely vindicated the rights of the children themselves. *Cooper* rejected efforts by Arkansas' governor and legislature to delay implementing *Brown* amid violence that led the President to send federal troops and then federalize the National Guard to assure safe admission of black students to the previously segregated public high school. In an opinion signed by the entire Court, *Cooper* stated that "delay in any guise in order to deny the constitutional rights of Negro children could not be countenanced," and that "law and order are not here to be preserved by depriving the Negro children of their constitutional rights."

Thirteen years after *Brown*, the Court decided In re Gault (S.Ct.1967) (discussed in chapter 10), its most celebrated juvenile law decision. The juvenile court had adjudicated fifteen-year-old Gerald Gault delinquent for making lewd telephone calls to a female neighbor and had committed him to the state industrial school until the age of twenty-one, unless released earlier. The Supreme Court reversed on the ground that the trial court's adjudicatory procedures did not comport with due process.

Writing for *Gault's* majority, Justice Abe Fortas stated that "neither the Fourteenth Amendment nor the Bill of Rights is for adults alone." By thus holding that children are persons under the Fourteenth Amendment, the Court overcame the Constitution's failure to mention children explicitly. *Gault* held that a juvenile is entitled to several due process rights during the adjudicatory phase of any delinquency proceeding that might result in secure detention.

Gault undermined the state's parens patriae authority to exercise informal discretion in delinquency proceedings, virtually free of procedural guarantees available to adults charged with crimes. Concluding that parens patriae had been "a great help to those who sought to rationalize the exclusion of juveniles from the constitutional scheme," *Gault* imposed due process constraints because "unbridled discretion, however benevolently motivated, is frequently a poor substitute for principle and procedure."

Brown and *Gault* were watershed decisions for reasons that transcend their precise holdings. *Meyer* and *Pierce* had perceived the underlying disputes as pitting the government against the parents. In a child labor prosecution, *Prince* outlined the child's interest. *Brown* and *Gault* framed the disputes as pitting the government against the children named as parties and then vindicated the children's position. *Brown* vindicated the children's substantive constitutional rights, and *Gault* vindicated their procedural constitutional rights.

The Supreme Court has never again questioned the core proposition that a child, like parents and the government, may have rights and interests in matters concerning the child's welfare. In Planned Parenthood of Central Missouri v. Danforth (S.Ct.1976), for example, the Court stated unequivocally that "[c]onstitutional rights do not mature and come into being magically only when one attains the state-defined age of majority. Minors, as well as adults, are protected by the Constitution and possess constitutional rights."

Danforth, however, reaffirmed that "the State has somewhat broader authority to regulate the activities of children than of adults." The Court has articulated three reasons why the constitutional rights of children are not equated with those of adults: "the peculiar vulnerability of children; their inability to make critical decisions in an informed, mature manner; and the

importance of the parental role in child rearing."
Bellotti v. Baird (S.Ct.1979) (plurality opinion).

5. *TINKER* AND THE ZENITH OF CHILDREN'S RIGHTS

a. The *Tinker* Decision (1969)

In Tinker v. Des Moines Independent
Community School District (S.Ct.1969), the Court
upheld the First Amendment rights of three
students to wear black armbands in their public
schools to express their opposition to the Vietnam
War. As in *Brown*, the named plaintiffs were the
students themselves.

Writing for the majority, Justice Abe
Fortas engaged in a weighing process. On the one
hand, "[s]tudents in school as well as out of
school are 'persons' under our Constitution," and
they do not "shed their constitutional rights to
freedom of speech or expression at the
schoolhouse gate." On the other hand, school
officials hold "comprehensive authority ..., consistent with fundamental constitutional safeguards,
to prescribe and control conduct in the schools."
But "[s]chool officials do not possess absolute
authority over their students. Students ... are
possessed of fundamental rights which the State
must respect, just as they themselves must
respect their obligations to the State."

The three students prevailed in their confrontation with school authorities because the record indicated that they had engaged in a silent, passive expression of political opinion, without disorder or disturbance to school operations. But *Tinker* contained broad language sufficient to empower children in disputes with the state outside the First Amendment and public school contexts. By stating that students do not "shed their constitutional rights to freedom of speech or expression at the schoolhouse gate," the Court indicated that children also do not shed other rights at the gate or elsewhere.

For more than thirty years, children's counsel have cited *Tinker* in confrontations with state authority. In retrospect, however, the decision was the high-water mark in children's rights in the Supreme Court, which soon grew uneasy with its apparently resounding language and began limiting the rationale and holding. The remainder of this section explores important post-*Tinker* decisions.

b. Disruption or Violence

As a threshold matter, lower courts have frequently distinguished *Tinker* where school officials restrained the student's expressive activity because they reasonably foresaw the likelihood of disruption or violence stemming from that activity. "School authorities ... are not required to wait until disorder or invasion occurs." Phillips v. Anderson County School District Five (D.S.C.1997) (holding that school officials properly suspended the middle school student who refused to refrain from wearing his Confederate battle flag jacket in school).

c. Hair Length, Dress Codes and School Uniforms

Hair length regulations. Most of the earliest decisions citing *Tinker* concerned grooming and attire standards, particularly hair length regulations in an era when boys wore longer hair than they generally wear nowadays. Challenges to hair-length regulations have sharply divided the courts. See, e.g., Holsapple v. Woods (7th Cir.1974) (holding that regulations violated students' First and Fourteenth Amendment symbolic speech rights); Kraus v. Board of Education (Mo.1973) (upholding regulations). A number of decisions have dismissed these challenges on the ground that school authorities, and not judges, should determine hair length standards. See, e.g., Zeller v. Donegal School District (3d Cir.1975) (en banc).

Dress codes and uniforms. In the 1990s, many public school districts adopted dress codes or policies mandating that students wear uniforms. At least half the states enacted legislation authorizing local school boards to act. See, e.g., Ohio Rev. Code § 3313.665. Courts have also upheld dress codes prohibiting students from wearing apparel determined by school officials to be gang-related. See, e.g., Bivens v. Albuquerque Public Schools (D.N.M.1995). At least where parents may "opt out," courts have rejected constitutional challenges to school uniform requirements. See, e.g., Canaday v. Bossier Parish School Board (5th Cir.2001); Littlefield v. Forney Ind. School District (N.D.Tex.2000). By 2002, official enthusiasm for school uniform policies had faded and many school districts abandoned them because so many parents had opted out, uniforms stigmatized poor students, and teachers found themselves forced to spend valuable class time determining who had opted out and who had not and then meting out discipline.

d. Goss v. Lopez (1975)

In Goss v. Lopez (S.Ct.1975), the Court held that where a state guarantees children a free public education, public school students have a due process property interest in that guarantee and a liberty interest in not having their reputations sullied by suspension for less than good cause. *Goss* also recognized, however, that "[j]udicial interposition in the operation of the public school system ... raises problems requiring care and restraint."

When a student faces suspension for less than ten days, *Goss* requires only "an informal give-and-take between student and disciple-narian." The student must receive "oral or written notice of the charges against him and, if he denies them, an explanation of the evidence the authorities have and an opportunity to present his side of the story." "[A]s a general rule notice and hearing should precede removal of the student from school." Removal may occur before the rudimentary hearing, however, where the student's presence poses "a continuing danger to persons or property or an ongoing threat of disrupting the academic process."

e. Board of Education v. Pico (1982)

In Board of Education v. Pico (S.Ct. 1982), the sharply divided Court grappled with the question whether the First Amendment limits a school board's discretion to remove assertedly immoral books from high school and junior high school libraries. *Pico* highlighted the Court's growing ambivalence toward *Tinker*, with the three-Justice plurality stressing the earlier decision and the dissenters acknowledging it but maintaining a distance.

Justice Brennan's plurality opinion concluded that the school board's removal of library books implicated a First Amendment right of the students to "receive information and ideas." The plurality acknowledged that the right is construed "in light of the special characteristics of the school environment," but concluded that the board denies the right when it acts with intent to deny students access to ideas with which the board disagrees.

To the four dissenters, however, *Pico* turned on "whether local schools are to be administered by elected school boards, or by federal judges and teenage pupils" and "whether the values of morality, good taste, and relevance to education are valid reasons for school board decisions concerning the contents of a school library." "[A]s a matter of *educational policy* students should have wide access to information and ideas. But the people elect school boards, who in turn select administrators, who select the teachers, and these are the individuals best able to determine the substance of that policy."

f. New Jersey v. T.L.O. (1985)

In New Jersey v. T.L.O. (S.Ct.1985), the Court reiterated that the constitutional rights of children in public schools may be more restricted than the constitutional rights of adults. *T.L.O.*, which is discussed more fully in chapter 10, held that under the Fourth Amendment, the validity of a school official's search of a student depends on the search's reasonableness under all the circumstances, and not on probable cause.

g. Bethel School District v. Fraser (1986)

In Bethel School District v. Fraser (S.Ct.1986), the Court upheld a high school student's three-day suspension for delivering a speech laced with "pervasive sexual innuendo" during an assembly attended by about 600 students. The Court found a "marked distinction between the political 'message' of the armbands in *Tinker* and the sexual content" of the assembly speech.

Fraser emphasized that "the constitutional rights of students in public school are not automatically coextensive with the rights of adults in other settings": "The First Amendment guarantees wide freedom in matters of adult public discourse. ... It does not follow, however, that simply because the use of an offensive form of expression may not be prohibited to adults making what the speaker considers a political point, the same latitude must be permitted to children in a public school." "Surely it is a highly appropriate function of public school education to prohibit the use of vulgar and offensive terms in public discourse," and "[t]he determination of what manner of speech in the classroom or in school assembly is inappropriate properly rests with the school board."

Fraser has loomed large in decisions resolving constitutional challenges to suspensions of public school students for wearing clothing featuring messages deemed obscene or otherwise inappropriate. A central issue has been whether the court deemed the message political (as in *Tinker*), or vulgar or obscene (as in *Fraser*). Compare, e.g., Chandler v. McMinnville School District (9th Cir.1992) (applying *Tinker* to overturn suspension of students for wearing buttons reading "Do Scabs Bleed?" and "I'm Not Listening Scab" to support a teachers strike), with Doe v. De Palma (S.D. Ohio 2000) (applying *Fraser* to affirm discipline imposed on sixth-grade male student who wrote "I just smelled your crack" near the crease on a page of a female classmate's yearbook).

h. Hazelwood School District v. Kuhlmeier (1988)

In Hazelwood School District v. Kuhlmeier (1988), the Court upheld the school district's authority to exercise editorial control over the contents of a high school newspaper produced by a journalism class as part of the curriculum. The five-Justice majority distinguished *Tinker.* "The question whether the First Amendment requires a school to tolerate particular student speech ... is different from the question whether the First Amendment requires a school affirmatively to promote particular student speech [in] school-sponsored publications, theatrical productions, and other expressive activities that students, parents, and members of the public might reasonably perceive to bear the imprimatur of the school."

Kuhlmeier held that "educators do not offend the First Amendment by exercising editorial control over the style and content of student speech in school-sponsored expressive activities so long as their actions are reasonably related to legitimate pedagogical concerns." "[T]he education of the Nation's youth is primarily the responsibility of parents, teachers, and state and local school officials, and not of federal judges. It is only when the decision to censor a school-sponsored publication, theatrical production, or other vehicle of student expression has no valid educational purpose that the First Amendment is so 'directly and sharply implicate[d],' as to require judicial intervention to protect students' constitutional rights." Justice Brennan's dissent accused the majority of "abandoning *Tinker.*"

i.   Vernonia School District 47J v. Acton (1995) and Board of Education v. Earls (2002)

In Vernonia School District 47J v. Acton (S.Ct.1995), the Court upheld, against a Fourth Amendment challenge, the school district's policy authorizing random urinalysis drug testing of its interscholastic athletes. The Court found the search reasonable because the intrusion on the students' privacy was "negligible," because the government concern in preventing drug use was "important -- indeed, perhaps compelling," and because the student-athletes had only a "decreased" expectation of privacy.

The Court's privacy analysis reiterated *Tinker's* celebrated dictum that schoolchildren do not shed their constitutional rights at the schoolhouse gate. *Vernonia* emphasized, however, that "the nature of those rights is what is appropriate for children in school" because "the State's power over schoolchildren is ... custodial and tutelary, permitting a degree of supervision and control that could not be exercised over free adults." "Traditionally at common law, and still today, unemancipated minors lack some of the most fundamental rights of self-determination -- including even the right of liberty in its narrow sense, i.e., the right to come and go at will. They are subject, even as to their physical freedom, to the control of their parents or guardians."

In Board of Education v. Earls (S.Ct.2002), the Court reaffirmed *Vernonia's* analysis and upheld a random suspicionless urinalysis drug testing policy for students in all competitive extracurricular activities, including non-athletic activities.

6. *TROXEL* AND PARENTAL PREROGATIVES REDUX

In Troxel v. Granville (S.Ct.2000) (plurality opinion), the sharply divided Court reviewed a Washington state statute that permits "[a]ny person" to petition the trial court for visitation rights with a child "at any time," and authorizes the court to grant visitation whenever "visitation may serve the best interest of the child." Wash. Rev. Stat. § 26.10.160(3). In the paternal grand-parents' suit against the mother for visitation with the two young children, the state supreme court held that the statute, on its face, interfered with the mother's fundamental due process right to direct the upbringing of her children.

Writing for the plurality, Justice O'Connor stated that the Washington statute, as applied, violated the mother's due process right to direct the children's upbringing because it granted her visitation decision "no deference," but rather "places the best-interest determination solely in the hands of the judge." Finding that the law recognizes a presumption that fit parents act in the best interests of their children, the plurality concluded that "there will normally be no reason for the State to inject itself into the private realm of the family to further question the ability of that parent to make the best decisions concerning the rearing of that parent's children." A court reviewing a fit parent's visitation decision "must accord at least some special weight to the parent's own determination."

From a broader perspective, all nine Justices acknowledged that the *Meyer-Pierce-Prince* line of decisions confers on parents a substantive due process right to direct their children's upbringing, which the plurality called "perhaps the oldest of the fundamental liberty interests recognized by [the] Court." Six Justices (the four-Justice plurality and concurring Justices Souter and Thomas) concluded that the state supreme court correctly found unconstitutional interference with that right in the case under review. Six Justices (the plurality and dissenting Justices Stevens and Kennedy) concluded that third-party visitation cases require a case-by-case weighing of interests, which left

the lower court's facial invalidity order constitutionally flawed.

Justice Stevens stressed that the
weighing process must consider the child's
interest in "preserving relationships that serve her
welfare and protection." Visitation disputes "do
not present a bipolar struggle between the
parents and the State over who has final
authority to determine what is in the child's best
interests. There is at minimum a third individual,
whose interests are implicated in every case to
which the statute applies -- the child."

Lower courts have rejected efforts to
invoke *Troxel* to strengthen parents' positions in
disputes concerning children generally, such as
public school curricular decisions or the child
labor laws. *Troxel* may strengthen the parent's
hand in disputes concerning family intimacy, but
would not upset operation of the abuse and
neglect laws and other regulatory statutes.

7. SYNTHESIZING THE CASE LAW

Decisions determining the status, rights
and obligations of children frequently defy neat
synthesis. "To date, neither legislatures nor
courts have developed a coherent philosophy or
approach when addressing questions relating to

children's rights. Different courts and legislatures have been willing to give some new rights to children, while denying them others, without explaining the difference in outcome." Michael S. Wald, Children's Rights: A Framework For Analysis, 12 U.C. Davis L. Rev. 255 (1979). Difficulties continue because of the tensions among children's rights, children's vulnerability and parental prerogatives.

8. NON-CONSTITUTIONAL SOURCES OF CHILDREN'S STATUS, RIGHTS AND OBLIGATIONS

a. Statutes, Administrative Regulations and Court Rules

Thus far this chapter has concerned the profound effect of constitutional litigation on the status, rights and obligations of children. As statutes and their attendant administrative regulations have come to play a more dominant role in American life, these sources too have profoundly affected the place of children in American society. A much invoked and widely litigated statute, for example, is the Individuals with Disabilities Education Act (IDEA), which "assure[s] that all children with disabilities have available to them ... a free appropriate public education which emphasizes special education and related services designed to meet their unique needs." 20 U.S.C. § 1400(c).

Juvenile and family court rules also affect proceedings in those courts. On matters not covered in those rules, general civil practice and procedure rules (and in delinquency proceedings, general criminal rules) may apply. General jurisdiction courts may also have civil and criminal rules applicable to children in those courts.

b. International Law
The United Nations Convention on the Rights of the Child is the first international instrument to comprehensively cover children's civil, political, economic, social and cultural rights. The U.N. General Assembly unanimously adopted the Convention on November 20, 1989, and it was opened for signature on January 26, 1990. Sixty-one nations signed the Convention on the first day, a greater first-day response than any other international human rights treaty had ever received. The Convention entered into force when the twentieth nation ratified it only seven months later, more swiftly than any other human rights convention.

The Convention has been ratified by all but two nations recognized by the United Nations, the most widely ratified human rights treaty in history. Somalia (which does not have a recognized government capable of ratifying a treaty) and the United States are the only holdouts. After considerable delay, the United States on February 23, 1995 became the 177th nation to sign the Convention, but the Senate has not considered it for ratification because of strong opposition from political and religious conservatives.

The Convention continues along the path blazed by the Geneva Declaration of the Rights of the Child, which the Assembly of the League of Nations accepted in 1924, and the U.N. Declaration of the Rights of the Child, which the U.N. General Assembly adopted in 1959. The two brief declarations are nonbinding, but they express general principles to guide national aspirations.

The first legally binding provisions protecting children's rights appeared in two covenants the U.N. adopted in 1966. The first, the International Covenant on Civil and Political Rights, provides that "[e]very child shall have, without any discrimination as to race, colour, sex, language, religion, national or social origin, property or birth, the right to such measures of protection as are required by his status as a minor, on the part of his family, society and the State." 999 U.N.T.S. 171 (entered into force Mar.

23, 1976). The second, the International Covenant on Economic, Social and Cultural Rights, provides, among other things, that "[s]pecial measures of protection and assistance should be taken on behalf of all children and young persons without any discrimination for reasons of parentage or other conditions." 993 U.N.T.S. 3 (entered into force Jan. 3, 1976). The United States has signed both covenants, but has ratified only the first. Several dozen other international instruments also carry provisions relating to children.

Under the federal Constitution's Supremacy Clause, a ratified treaty becomes the "supreme law of the land," with authority equal to a federal statute. The treaty would thus override inconsistent state and local law as well as prior federal law. See, e.g., Edye v. Robertson (S.Ct.1884). The 1989 Convention's potential effect would be greatest on state and local jurisdictions because most of its articles cover rights regulated by state rather than federal law. Commentators have described the Convention's covered rights as the three P's: participation of children in society and in decisions affecting their own future; protection of children against discrimination, neglect and exploitation; and provision of assistance for children's basic needs.

The United States might blunt or avoid the legal effect of particular provisions by ratifying the Convention with reservations, understandings or declarations (RUDs) that particular articles or provisions would not create rights, claims or defenses in federal or state civil or criminal proceedings. (To avoid effects on domestic law, the United States has attached "RUDs" to a number of other human rights treaties the Senate has ratified.) Otherwise persons could presumably allege government noncompliance as a claim or defense in domestic courts.

Discussion of the Convention does not necessarily end the story. International law has two basic sources: international agreements ("conventional law") and customary law. The Convention is an international agreement, which creates law for the nations that ratify it, subject to any valid RUDs attached by a ratifying nation. Customary international law "results from a general and consistent practice of states followed by them from a sense of legal obligation," and binds nations that have not dissented from the rule while it was developing. Restatement (Third) Foreign Relations Law of the United States § 102 & cmt. d.

The United States is not bound by the Convention, which the nation has not ratified.

The question would remain, however, whether any of the Convention's articles would hold the status of binding customary international law. The Supreme Court long ago held that customary law is "part of our law, and must be ascertained and administered by the courts of justice of appropriate jurisdiction, as often as questions of right depending upon it are duly presented for their determination." The Paquete Habana (S.Ct. 1900). Under the Supremacy Clause, customary international law would supersede inconsistent state law or policy. Restatement, supra § 115 cmt. e.

The juvenile death penalty, discussed in chapter 10, has directly implicated customary international law. In Stanford v. Kentucky (S.Ct. 1989), the Court held that executing a defendant who was sixteen or seventeen at the time of the crime does not constitute cruel and unusual punishment in violation of the Eighth Amendment. The majority concluded that such executions do not violate "evolving standards of decency" because a majority of the American states permitting capital punishment authorize it for crimes committed at age sixteen or older. The Court firmly rejected a role for customary international law: "We emphasize that it is *American* conceptions of decency that are dispositive, rejecting the contention ... that the sentencing practices of other countries are relevant."

D. MAY CHILDREN ARTICULATE THEIR OWN INTERESTS?

1. THE GENERAL QUESTION

To identify three interests (parent, government and child) is one thing. A related, yet conceptually different, question also arises: May the child articulate his or her own interests in disputes implicating those interests, or must the child be heard through the adults (the state and the parents)? The question has potentially wide ramifications because many court proceedings affect a child's interests even when the child is not a named party.

Justice William O. Douglas' dissent raised the question in Wisconsin v. Yoder (S.Ct.1972). Three Amish parents were convicted and fined $5 each for violating the state compulsory school attendance statute, which required them to send their children to public or private school until the age of sixteen. The parents had agreed to send the children until the end of the eighth grade, but not afterwards.

Yoder held that the convictions violated

the parents' rights under the First Amendment free exercise clause. On the strength of uncontradicted expert testimony concerning the Amish record of "three centuries as an identifiable religious sect and a long history as a successful and self-sufficient segment of American society," the Court held that the parents' interest in terminating their children's formal education at the eighth grade outweighed the state interest in regulating the duration of basic education. The Court stressed that "[t]he history and culture of Western civilization reflect a strong tradition of parental concern for the nurture and upbringing of their children."

Justice Douglas argued that the *Yoder* children themselves had a constitutional right to a hearing to determine whether they wished to attend school past the eighth grade. The majority rejected the argument on the ground that the parents' prosecution did not depend on proof that the children wished to attend school, and thus did not implicate the children's interests or wishes. The school-choice decision belonged to the parents, not the children.

In matters concerning a child's welfare, claims of the child's constitutional right to be heard are not successful because, as in *Yoder,* the law assumes children are adequately represented when an adult is making choices for them. In a few circumstances, statutes or court rules may provide that older children's preferences must be considered and the children may even have an express right to be heard. Cf. Mass. Ann. Laws ch. 210, § 2 ("A decree of adoption shall not be made ... without the written consent of the child to be adopted, if above the age of twelve"). Generally, however, the child has no control over the court's decision, which is made in the child's best interests.

At common law, minors lack capacity to bring or defend civil lawsuits in their own names. In disputes in which a minor is a party (such as disputes related to the minor's property, contracts or torts), the minor must have adults representing him. Traditionally a next friend, or prochein ami, was appointed to represent a minor plaintiff and a guardian ad litem was appointed to represent a minor defendant. The distinction between these terms frequently has not been maintained, however, and their meaning, particularly of "guardian ad litem," has become ambiguous. The term "guardian ad litem" can refer to a lawyer for the child, or to a non-lawyer representative. The term is also used to refer to a lawyer serving as both the representative and lawyer for the child, without regard to whether the child is a plaintiff, a defendant, or the subject of an action such as an abuse or neglect proceeding. Rule 17 of the Federal Rules of Civil Procedure, which provides for appointment of representatives for children, has been interpreted to require the court to insure that the minor is adequately represented.

2. THE MATURE-MINOR DOCTRINE

a. Introduction

In recent years, the "mature minor" doctrine has sometimes empowered older children to make their own decisions when a court determines that a child appears capable of articulating a reasoned preference on a matter important to the child's welfare. The doctrine may offer some flexibility in matters relating to children below the general age of majority, the age at which persons become adults and ordinarily can make decisions for themselves.

b. Constitutional Decisions

In Parham v. J.R. (S.Ct.1979), discussed in chapter 7, the Court indicated that where a parent opposes the child's wishes, the court should ordinarily give great weight to the parent's preference. The Court presumed that parents act in their children's best interests and that most children are not capable of making sound decisions about important matters such as medical care.   In Bellotti v. Baird (S.Ct.1979), however, the four-Justice plurality staked out a relatively narrow constitutional zone of privacy for "mature" children. The issue was the constitutionality of a state statute regulating unmarried pregnant minors' access to abortions. The plurality determined that where a state requires a minor to obtain the consent of one or both of her parents to an abortion, the state must permit the minor the opportunity, if she desires, to seek court approval directly without first consulting or notifying her parents. "If she satisfies the court that she is mature and well enough informed to make intelligently the abortion decision on her own, the court must authorize her to act without parental consultation or consent. If she fails to satisfy the court that she is competent to make this decision independently, she must be permitted to show that an abortion nevertheless would be in her best interests. If the court is persuaded that it is, the court must authorize the abortion. If, however, the court is not persuaded by the minor that she is mature or that the abortion would be in her best interests, it may decline to sanction the operation."

Courts have occasionally broadened *Bellotti's* constitutional zone of privacy in favor of mature minors. See, e.g., In re Lori M (N.Y.Fam.Ct. 1985) (mature fifteen-year-old may make decisions concerning her sexual orientation and related matters).

c. Statutes and Common Law Decisions

Statutes may shape the mature minor doctrine's influence. The legislature may provide that children can get medical care in some areas without parental consent, for example, or may mandate a voice for mature minors in areas such as adoption, custody and guardianship. Conversely the legislature may preclude invocation of the doctrine. Because alcohol control laws establish a minimum drinking age of twenty-one, for example, a seventeen-year-old charged with consuming alcohol may not avoid liability by establishing that he can drink in a mature fashion.

As discussed in chapter 7, in cases involving medical decisionmaking, courts may consider a mature minor's wishes in the absence of express statutory authority, and may even find the minor's medical care choice determinative.

CHAPTER 2

DEFINING THE CHILD-PARENT RELATIONSHIP

The concept of "parent" is key to identifying the persons who hold parental rights and obligations that are grounded not only in constitutional law, but also in the statutes, administrative regulations, and court rules that have come to dominate our legal landscape. Parents have a substantive due process right to direct the upbringing of their children free from unreasonable government intrusion. (See chapter 1.) This right includes the authority to exclude others from having custody or contact with their child, but this power to exclude may be tempered by state intervention when someone else has assumed a parental role.

Many children are reared by their married, biological parents in what is termed the traditional nuclear family and the parents' identity and whereabouts are readily determinable. As the Supreme Court recognized in *Troxel*, however, "[t]he demographic changes of the past century make it difficult to speak of an average American family." Identifying or locating a parent may sometimes be a threshold issue central to fashioning the rights and obligations of parent and child alike. Sometimes the issue may strain traditional legal doctrine because of developments in reproductive technology.

A. ESTABLISHING PATERNITY OR MATERNITY

1. THE IMPORTANCE OF MARRIAGE

Historically, nonmarital children (that is, children born to unmarried parents) were saddled with the pejorative labels of "bastards" or "illegitimate," and were denied most legal rights for life. Early in the nineteenth century, Chancellor James Kent stated the harsh common law doctrine this way: "A bastard being in the eye of the law *nullius filius* [child of no one], . . . he has no inheritable blood, and is incapable of inheriting as heir, either to his putative father, or his mother, or to any one else, nor can he have heirs but of his own body." Kent, Commentaries on American Law (5th ed. 1844). The unmarried parent's rights were different from those of married parents as well. An unmarried father, for example, had no legal right to custody as against the claim of the mother.

The status, rights and obligations of
nonmarital children are central to the fabric of our
contemporary society. From 1980 to 1997, the
annual percentage of American children born out
of wedlock increased from 18 percent to 32 percent,
but the increase has slowed. In 2002, about 33
percent of births were to single mothers. Some
statutes and decisions persist in using the cruel
language of "bastard" and "illegitimate" to describe
nonmarital children, but the past generation has
seen constitutional and statutory law depart from
the punishment the common law imposed on these
children.

a.   Nonmarital Children and the Constitution

In Levy v. Louisiana in 1968, the Supreme
Court held for the first time that nonmarital
children are "persons" within the meaning of the
Fourteenth Amendment's Equal Protection Clause.
Levy held that equal protection prohibited states
from denying these children the right, granted by
statute to marital children, to recover for the
wrongful death of their mother on whom they were
dependent. In the years since *Levy,* the Court's
equal protection jurisprudence has prohibited
states and the federal government from denying
nonmarital children a variety of benefits available
to marital children, such as child support (Gomez
v. Perez, S.Ct. 1973) and social security benefits
(Jimenez v. Weinberger, S.Ct. 1974). The Court's

decisions establish two core propositions. First, the
parents' marital status may remain relevant to
determination of the child's rights and obligations.
To establish entitlement to a benefit available to
marital children, for example, a nonmarital child
may have to meet special requirements – such as
providing proof of dependency on a wage earner as
a condition for receipt of Social Security insurance
benefits (Matthews v. Lucas, S.Ct. 1976) – that
exceed requirements imposed on marital children.
Second, however, the Court upholds the
constitutionality of a distinction based on parents'
marital status only on a showing that it advances
an important state interest. The state's desire to
influence adult sexual behavior by sanctioning
nonmarital children is not a justification that
survives the intermediate level of scrutiny the
Court applies in these cases.

The Supreme Court's intestate succession
decisions provide an excellent example of the
contemporary equal protection approach. In
Trimble v. Gordon in 1977, the Court struck down
an Illinois Probate Act provision that permitted
marital children to inherit from both their mothers
and fathers, but permitted nonmarital children to
inherit by intestate succession only from their
mothers. *Trimble* gave little credit to the state's
assertion that the probate provision served a
legitimate state interest by helping promote

legitimate family relationships. "A state may not attempt to influence the action of men and women," Justice Powell wrote for the majority, "by imposing sanctions on the children born of their illegitimate relationships."

Trimble did recognize a legitimate state interest in maintaining an accurate, efficient method of property distribution that avoided the difficulties of proving paternity and the related danger of spurious claims. The Court nonetheless stuck down the Illinois statute, because its blanket prohibition failed to recognize that "[f]or at least some significant categories of illegitimate children of intestate men, inheritance rights can be recognized without jeopardizing the orderly settlement of estates or the dependability of titles to property passing under intestacy laws."

By contrast a year later in Lalli v. Lalli, the Court upheld a New York statute that permitted nonmarital children to inherit from an intestate father only on proof that a court had entered a filiation order during the father's lifetime. (S.Ct.1978). The plurality found the requirement "substantially related to the important state interests the statute is intended to promote," namely the need "to provide for the just and orderly disposition of property at death." The Court agreed that the state could constitutionally ignore other evidence of paternity, such as the father's acknowledgement and support of the child during his lifetime, and insist on a formal filiation order.

Intervening scientific advances in paternity determination suggest a need to liberalize *Lalli*'s insistence on a filiation order, and indeed the Uniform Probate Code (§2-108) would permit intestate succession where paternity is established after the father's death. (The New York statute itself is also now less restrictive, see Estates, Powers & Trusts L. § 4-1.2.)

Paternity establishment after death has been allowed even after a long passage of time. A recent Mississippi decision, for example, permitted establishment of paternity even though the nonmarital father had died in 1938. Estate of Johnson (Miss.2000). The decision concerned blues singer Robert L. Johnson who died indigent at age twenty-seven, but whose estate was opened fifty-one years later when his musical recordings began earning royalties. His nonmarital son established paternity by clear and convincing evidence despite the absence of genetic testing.

A new challenge to the law is the status of posthumously conceived children. Some states have conferred intestate succession inheritance rights on these children. See, e.g., Woodward v. Commissioner of Social Sec. (Mass.2002). Other states, however, have not been as inclusive. See, e.g., Gillett-Netting v. Barnhart (D.Ariz.2002) (holding that twins born as the result of in vitro fertilization with the deceased husband's sperm were not the husband's children under state intestate succession law, and hence were not eligible for federal social security survivors' benefits because state law determines social security eligibility).

The Supreme Court recently rejected an equal protection challenge to a statute that applied more difficult citizenship rules to a nonmarital child born abroad when the citizen parent was the father than when the citizen parent was the mother. The statute provided that when the mother was an American citizen and the father was a noncitizen, the child was an American citizen if the mother met a minimal residency requirement. If the mother was a noncitizen, however, the statute required the citizen father to take one of several specified affirmative actions before the child reached eighteen. Petitioner Tuan Anh Nguyen was born out of wedlock in Vietnam to a Vietnamese mother and a United States father. Even though Nguyen became a lawful permanent resident at age six and was reared by his father in the United States, the Immigration and Naturalization Service found him deportable when he pleaded guilty to a felony when he was twenty-two. His father obtained an order of parentage from a state court while the deportation proceeding was pending; this order would have met the requirements had the father obtained it before Nguyen turned eighteen, but the father was too late. Justice O'Connor's dissent, (joined by Justices Souter, Ginsburg and Breyer) characterized the statute as "paradigmatic of a historic regime that left women with responsibility, and freed men from responsibility, for nonmarital children.... The majority ... rather than confronting the stereotypical notion that mothers must care for these children and fathers may ignore them, quietly condones the 'very stereotype the law condemns.'" Nguyen v. Immigration and Naturalization Service (S.Ct.2001).

b. Statutory Reform

Statutory reform has also improved the status of nonmarital children. In 1973, the National Conference of Commissioners on Uniform State Laws (NCCUSL) adopted the Uniform Parentage Act (UPA), which sought to "provid[e] substantive legal equality for all children regardless of the marital status of their parents." By 1997, the Act had been adopted wholly or in part by eighteen states. In July, 2000 NCCUSL adopted a substantial revision of the Act, which incorporated the Uniform Putative and Unknown Fathers Act (1988) and the Uniform Status of

Children of Assisted Conception Act (1988).
Additional amendments were approved in 2002.

The 2002 UPA, like the 1973 UPA, seeks to
achieve legal equality by mandating that "[a] child
born to parents who are not married to each other
has the same rights under the law as a child born
to parents who are married to each other." UPA §
202 (2002). The Comment to this section notes,
however, that "the broad statement according
equal treatment to a nonmarital child regarding
his or her parents is not to be construed as
eliminating all possible distinctions in all aspects
of the lives of the nonmarital child and parents."
The Comment calls attention to Uniform Probate
Code provisions restricting some class gift
recipients to nonmarital children who lived in the
parent's household. These provisions may have a
disproportionate effect on nonmarital children, but
"the disparity is not based on the circumstances of
birth, but rather on post-birth living conditions."
Section 203 of the UPA states that "[u]nless
parental rights are terminated, a parent-child
relationship established under this [Act] applies for
all purposes, except as otherwise specifically
provided by other law of this State."

In states that have not enacted the
Uniform Act, the Supreme Court's equal protection

decisions nonetheless enforce general legal equality between marital and nonmarital children. Rather than impose a lifetime of punishment on children for their parents' conduct, the evolving constitutional and statutory law together recognize that "there are no illegitimate children, only illegitimate parents." Estate of Woodward (Cal.Ct.App.1964).

c. Surnames

By custom and law stemming from the husband's authority over his wife and control over marital property, children born to married parents have been given their fathers' surnames. In the United States the paternal preference has reflected both the long-standing English tradition and the unequal statuses of men and women. Until relatively recently, the assumption that children would bear their fathers' surnames was a matter of common understanding rarely questioned or challenged. When challenges did arise, courts have usually denied petitions to change the marital child's surname from the father's if the father objected.

Nonmarital children, however, presented different considerations. At early common law, a nonmarital child was considered to be the child of no one, had no surname at birth and acquired a surname later in life based on reputation rather than lineage. As the law began to give nonmarital children a right to inherit from their mothers and to give mothers custody and support obligations, however, children began to receive their mothers' surnames.

In recent years, these gender-based assumptions have been discredited. Gubernat v. Deremer (N.J.1995) is typical of current gender-neutral decisions holding that where the parents, married or otherwise, disagree on the child's surname, the court will decide the surname based on the best interests of the child: "[I]n contested cases the surname of the custodial parent — the parent primarily charged with making custodial decisions in the child's best interest — shall be presumed to be consistent with that child's best interests, a presumption rebuttable by evidence that a different surname would better serve those interests."

What role should the child's preference play in the choice of his or her surname? The common law permits a person to adopt a new name, without any legal proceeding, provided the name does not defraud innocent third parties. The common law right applies to minors, without the "ordinary disabilities attendant upon minority." Hall v. Hall (Md.Ct.Spec.App.1976). Some commentators suggest that the legal effect given to the child's preference should depend on the child's age, maturity and capacity to articulate a reasoned preference. In fact, however, a father's objection to a child's name change has frequently controlled and prevented children from exercising the common law right.

2.   WHO IS A "FATHER"?

a.   Unwed Fathers

Paternity establishment used to be a cumbersome and difficult process. The combined efforts of state and federal government, however, have made paternity establishment a quick, routine administrative proceeding. The change came about because identifying, locating, and collecting child support from fathers of nonmarital children became high priorities for the federal government and the states.

Because the rise in welfare costs was attributed in part to the widespread failure of noncustodial fathers to pay child support to single mothers, Congress assumed an active role in paternity establishment and child support enforcement in the mid-1970s. In 1975, Congress passed Title IV-D of the Social Security Act, which established the Office of Child Support Enforcement as a cooperative federal agency to assist the states in recovering child support

payments from noncustodial parents. Paternity
and child support programs thus are frequently
referred to as IV-D programs. Because domestic
relations laws traditionally are state rather than
federal, Congress used an indirect method to
impose federal rules. States were not eligible for
federal welfare and child support enforcement
funds until they had amended their laws to meet
the Title's requirements.

Congress passed a number of amendments
that improved child support enforcement and in
1993 the Omnibus Budget Reconciliation Act
substantially amended Title IV-D to take
advantage of scientific advances in identifying
biological parents, especially DNA testing. Under
current federal law, when genetic tests show a
defined level of probability of paternity, state law
must presume that paternity is established.
(Section 505 of the UPA (2002) provides for a
presumption when the probability of paternity is at
least 99.0% and the combined paternity index is at
least 100 to 1.)

The Personal Responsibility and Work
Opportunity Reconciliation Act of 1996 (PRWORA)
imposed additional requirements on the states,
including a requirement that state law consider a
signed voluntary acknowledgement of paternity to
be a legal finding of paternity (with limited rights

of rescission). 42 U.S.C. § 666(a)(5)(D)(ii). States must give full faith and credit to acknowledgements of paternity from other states. Id. § 666(a)(5)(C)(iv). Jury trials are no longer allowed in paternity suits. Id. § (a)(5)(I).

The federal child support enforcement program now requires states to permit paternity establishment at any time before a child reaches eighteen. Id. § 666(a)(5)(i). The Supreme Court had previously struck down, as denying equal protection to nonmarital children, overly restrictive statutes of limitation for paternity suits. See Mills v. Habluetzel (S.Ct.1982) (one year); Pickett v. Brown (S.Ct.1983) (two years); Clark v. Jeter (S.Ct.1988) (six years). (Under the UPA, when the child has no presumed, acknowledged or adjudicated father a paternity proceeding may begin at any time, even when the child is an adult. UPA § 606 (2002).)

Federal law requires that as a condition for receiving welfare benefits, the mother must cooperate with the state in establishing paternity and must assign child support payments to the state to reimburse it for welfare payments she receives. 42 U.S.C. § 649(29). The cooperation requirement carries "good cause" exceptions designed to protect mothers who might otherwise be forced to identify fathers whose general bad character or negative responses to paternity might lead them to commit violence against the mother or child. A mother who does not seek government aid is not required to identify the father.

b. Marital Presumptions
A married woman's husband is presumed to be the father of her children. This presumption stems from Lord Mansfield's 1777 ruling that neither husband nor wife could testify to non-access by the husband except in very limited circumstances, which left it almost impossible to rebut the presumption. Today, states generally permit the husband or wife to attempt to rebut the presumption, at least within a short time after the child's birth, but the Supreme Court has held that states may constitutionally restrict the ability of others to rebut.

In Michael H. v. Gerald D. (S.Ct.1989), the sharply divided Court upheld a California statute that presumed that a child born to a married woman, living with her husband who was not impotent or sterile, was a child of the marriage. Only the husband or wife could rebut this presumption, and only in limited circumstances.

Carole (married to Gerald D.) began having an adulterous affair with Michael H., became pregnant and gave birth to Victoria D. in 1981. The birth certificate listed Gerald as the father, and he always held Victoria out as his daughter. Blood tests, however, revealed a 98.07 percent probability that Michael was Victoria's father. In the first few years of Victoria's life, she remained with Carole and they sometimes lived with Gerald or Michael. Victoria lived with Michael for a total of about eleven months. In 1984, Carole and Gerald reconciled.

The *Michael H.* four-Justice plurality rejected Michael's procedural due process claim (seeking a right to an evidentiary hearing on his paternity claim) on the ground that the state's marital presumption was a substantive rule of law based on a legislative determination of social policy, namely that challenges to the child's paternity would harm family integrity and privacy. The plurality also rejected Michael's substantive due process claim (seeking an order recognizing his parental relationship with the child) on the ground, hotly disputed by the four dissenters, that historically the law has accorded a protected liberty interest only to the marital family.

Finally the plurality concluded that Victoria had no due process liberty interest in maintaining a relationship with both Michael and Gerald. Regardless of any psychological benefit the child might derive from such a dual relationship, "the claim that a State must recognize multiple fatherhood has no support in the history or traditions of this country." Finally the plurality rejected the child's equal protection challenge on the ground that California law did not label her "illegitimate," but rather entitled her (like other children) to maintain a relationship with her legal parents.

Shortly after *Michael H.,* California amended its statute to join about two-thirds of the other states, which give putative fathers at least a time-limited right to rebut the presumption that a child born during marriage is a child of the marriage. States typically grant the husband and wife rights to rebut the presumption, sometimes with no time limit. The mother may want to rebut to prevent her husband from getting custody, or the husband may want to rebut to avoid a child support obligation.

As a practical matter, however, estoppel and other equitable doctrines may prevent rebuttal of the presumption by recognizing continuing rights and obligations in a spouse who has maintained a relationship with the child despite the lack of a biological tie. Further, when genetic testing indicates that the presumed father is not the child's biological father, some jurisdictions permit rebuttal only when such action would be in the best interests of the child. See, e.g., N.A.H. v. S.L.S. (Colo. 2000); In re Gallagher (Iowa 1995).

c. Errors in Paternity Establishment

Concerns have been expressed about whether new procedures for establishing paternity might sometimes compromise the due process rights of putative fathers, but the availability of genetic tests has diminished these concerns by substantially reducing the likelihood that the wrong man will be identified as the father. The standard of proof required for establishing paternity is a preponderance of the evidence. See Rivera v. Minnich (S.Ct.1987). The state must pay for paternity testing for an indigent man who wishes to dispute paternity. See Little v. Streater (S.Ct.1981).

Some men will not ask for a genetic test, however, because they mistakenly believe they are the child's father. Unmarried men may admit paternity without a genetic test, for example. By statute a married man may be presumed to be the father of his wife's children. Setting aside a declaration or presumption of paternity, however, may be difficult. Under the UPA, a proceeding to adjudicate the parentage of a child with a presumed father must be commenced not later than two years after the child's birth, unless a court determines that the mother did not live with

the presumed father or engage in sexual
intercourse with him at the probable time of
conception; and the presumed father never openly
held out the child as his own. UPA § 607 (2002).

Further, § 608 of the UPA authorizes a
court to refuse to order genetic testing in a
paternity action if testing would be inequitable; if
a father should be estopped from denying
paternity; or the mother should be estopped from
denying the father's paternity. In addition to
estoppel, the equitable doctrine of laches may also
bar presumptive fathers from disavowing
paternity.

In a change from UPA (1973), UPA (2002)
does not make the child a necessary party to a
parentage proceeding, but does require the court to
appoint a representative for the child if the child is
a party, or if "the interests of the child are not
adequately represented." § 612(b). Failure to join
the child, however, may allow a child to collaterally
attack the judgment of paternity, unless the child
was represented or the paternity determination
was consistent with genetic testing. § 637(b).

3.   WHO IS A "MOTHER"?

Identifying a child's birth mother is usually easier than identifying the father because the mother is present at birth and typically is named by witnesses or hospital records. New reproductive technology, however, has raised complex issues concerning the definition of "motherhood." Disputes over a woman's parentage have arisen with such techniques as egg donation, traditional surrogacy (where the surrogate is both the gestational and the genetic mother), gestational surrogacy, and ooplasmic transfer.

The issues frequently defy easy resolution. Many states have not legislated at all with respect to surrogacy and new reproductive technology, and states with legislation disagree on what should be the proper outcome. For example, only about half the states have statutory or case law on surrogacy agreements, with about half recognizing them and about half refusing to enforce them on public policy grounds. (UPA, Article 8, prefatory comment.) Recognizing the need for uniform rules about reproductive technology, Article 8 of the UPA (2002) provides for enforcement of gestational agreements, but only those validated under the Act's requirements, which include court review similar to the review required as a condition for adoption.

An early, highly publicized decision on the validity of traditional surrogacy agreements was In Re Baby M. (N.J.1988), which invalidated such agreements as inconsistent with public policy. The court granted custody to the biological father based on the best interests of the child, but voided the termination of the biological (surrogate) mother's parental rights and adoption of the child by the father's wife. The case was remanded to determine the biological mother's visitation rights with the child.

Another decision illustrating the complexity of gestational surrogacy is Johnson v. Calvert (Cal.1993). The Calverts, a married couple, wanted to have a child. The wife was unable to carry a child, though her ovaries could produce eggs. The couple entered into a surrogacy agreement with Ms. Johnson who would carry the embryo created by the husband's sperm and the wife's egg, and then would relinquish all parental rights to the child. Conflicts arose, however, before Ms. Johnson gave birth to the child, and each side sued claiming parental status. Under California law, the mother-and-child relationship could be established by either a genetic relationship or giving birth. The court held that when these two means do not coincide in one woman, the woman who intended to procreate the child (that is, who intended to bring about the child's birth and raise the child on her own) was the "natural mother" under California law. The mother who donated the egg thus won, and the court avoided the gestational mother's constitutional claims by declaring that she was not the mother. *Johnson* is contrary to the UPA, which would recognize the gestational mother as the legal parent, absent an enforceable agreement.

Errors by fertility clinics, such as implanting a fertilized egg into the wrong recipient, have also resulted in complex cases. See, e.g., Perry-Rogers v. Fasano (N.Y.App.Div.2000). The last chapter has clearly not yet been written in the law concerning the definition of motherhood in the fast evolving field of reproductive technology.

B. QUESTIONING THE DEFINITION OF "PARENT"

As the *Meyer* and *Pierce* line of decisions discussed in chapter 1 demonstrates, a fit parent's substantive due process right to direct the upbringing of his or her child free from unreasonable state interference is not easily overcome. Usually a person's status as a child's parent, with all its attendant rights and obligations, is not disputed. Difficult questions may arise, however, when the person claiming a right of "parenthood" is classified by law as a nonparent, but has nonetheless fulfilled a parental role (such as a stepparent, kinship caretaker, foster parent or prospective adoptive parent), or when the claimant has a biological claim (such as Michael H.). Suits by such claimants (sometimes called third-party claimants) seeking visitation or custody may implicate the relative weight of the child's rights and the biological parents' rights, and the role of the biological parents in the child's life.

Some states are more restrictive than others in defining "parent," or in awarding visitation, custody, or other rights and responsibilities to persons who are not legal parents. Generally claimants must first establish that they have standing to be heard, and then they must establish entitlement to an award. A person who claims parental status, but is not a legal parent under state law, may assert status as a de facto parent, a parent by estoppel, an equitable parent, a psychological parent, or a person in loco parentis. These terms do not necessarily have precise meanings, even within one state. A court might use the terms "de facto parent" and "psychological parent" interchangeably, for example, while using estoppel to protect these claimants. Rubano v. DiCenzo, (R.I.2000). See sections 1-3, below.

Under the common law doctrine of in loco parentis ("in place of a parent"), a person who assumes parental obligations is treated as a parent for some purposes. Whether an in loco parentis relationship exists is determined on a case by case basis. Where a person claims in loco parentis status, the court examines the person's conduct and statements to determine whether the person intentionally assumed parental responsibilities. A person in loco parentis may be considered a parent for some purposes, but not others. Stepparents, for example, may be accorded the same treatment as biological parents in the areas of workers compensation and parental-child tort immunity, but not inheritance. Unlike a parental relationship, the in loco parentis relationship can be terminated at will. Hence the doctrine has been used more to sort out past obligations, than to impose future obligations, such as an ongoing support obligation. Courts have sometimes invoked the doctrine to justify prospective parental claims, however, such as giving a stepparent visitation rights after divorce from the custodial, biological parent because of the stepparent's in loco parentis status. Carter v. Brodrick (Alaska 1982).

Claimants seeking to invoke one or more of these doctrines might argue that they fit within the definition of "parent" in a custody or visitation statute (*Alison D.*, infra), or that they should be given parent-like status even though they do not meet that definition (*In re Gallagher*, infra). Other courts have invoked equitable doctrines such as estoppel to award rights to a non-legal "parent". E.g. Rubano v. DiCenzo, supra (biological mother equitably estopped from objecting to her former partner's visitation with child they brought up together; mother had previously entered into consent order granting visitation).

1. VISITATION

Because visitation intrudes less on parental authority than custody, courts usually grant visitation to third parties more readily than custody awards. Some states' visitation statutes define the potential claimant class so broadly that standing would not typically be at issue, except in a constitutional challenge similar to that in *Troxel*. E.g., Haw. Rev. Stat. Ann. § 571-46 ("Reasonable visitation rights shall be awarded ... any person interested in the welfare of the child in the discretion of the court, unless it is shown that rights of visitation are detrimental to the best interests of the child.") Other states, however, view visitation as a substantial intrusion on parental authority, and thus restrict the categories of persons who may petition.

Most visitation statutes limit standing to parents, grandparents and sometimes siblings, without a broad "any person" category like the Hawaii statute quoted above. Some courts interpret the term "parent" in these statutes to confer standing on biological and adoptive parents only. In Alison D. v. Virginia *M.* (N.Y.1991), for example, Alison and Virginia, a lesbian couple, agreed that Virginia would be artificially inseminated, and that they would share jointly all rights and responsibilities of rearing the child. For the first two years of the child's life, both women cared for and made decisions regarding the child. Shortly thereafter, they ended their relationship but agreed to custody of the child with Virginia and a visitation schedule for Alison. Virginia terminated all contact between Alison and the child after four years, however, and Alison sought visitation rights under a statute that granted such rights to "parents."

The New York Court of Appeals held that Alison was not a "parent" within the meaning of the statute. The court concluded to allow third-party visitation with a person who, like Alison, could claim only status as a de facto parent or parent by estoppel would necessarily impair the natural parents' right to custody and control of the child.

Other courts, however, have defined "parent" more broadly. The New Jersey Supreme Court held that the term "parent" in the state's custody and visitation statute includes not only biological parents, but also "psychological parents." V.C. v. M.J.B. (N.J.2000). For a third party to be a psychological parent, "the legal parent must consent to and foster the relationship between the third party and the child; the third party must have lived with the child; the third party must perform parental functions for the child to a significant degree; and most important, a parent-child bond must be forged."

V.C. sought to allay fears that the decision would invite easy invasion of the biological parent's substantive due process right to raise the child free from undue outside interference. Visitation with the psychological parent was in the best interests of young V.C. only because of "the volitional choice of a legal parent to cede a measure of parental authority to a third party; to allow that party to function as a parent in the day-to-day life of the child; and to foster the forging of a parental bond between the third party and the child." In these circumstances, the court concluded, "the legal parent has created a family with the third party and the child, and has invited the third party into the otherwise inviolable realm of family privacy. By virtue of her own actions, the legal parent's

expectation of autonomous privacy in her
relationship with her child is necessarily reduced
from that which would have been the case had she
never invited the third party into their lives. Most
important, where that invitation and its
consequences have altered her child's life by
essentially giving him or her another parent, the
legal parent's options are constrained."

Broad and restrictive nonparent visitation
regimes alike now must confront the Supreme
Court's due process holding in Troxel v. Granville.
On the one hand, by indicating that a nonparent
visitation statute must give some deference to the
parent's right to decide who may associate with the
child, *Troxel* places broad visitation statutes in
constitutional jeopardy and assures close judicial
scrutiny of visitation claims under narrower
statutes. On the other hand, at least six Justices
(the four-Justice plurality and Justices Stevens
and Kennedy) stated that the parent's visitation
decision is subject to a case-by-case weighing
process that does not render third-party visitation
orders per se unconstitutional. The four-Justice
Troxel plurality recognized a presumption that fit
parents act in the best interests of their children,
but clearly envisioned the presumption as
rebuttable when it concluded that a court
reviewing a fit parent's visitation decision "must

accord at least some special weight to the parent's
own determination."

2. CUSTODY

State statutes also differ in their
willingness to authorize awards of child custody to
persons who have fulfilled a parental role but are
not legal parents. Some states take a restrictive
approach, permitting such awards only on a
showing that the biological parent is unfit or
unable to care for the child. In re A.R.A., for
example, concerned a custody dispute between the
biological father and the stepfather following the
death of the natural custodial mother, whose will
had named the stepfather as the child's guardian.
(Mt.Sup.Ct.1996.)

The trial court used a best-interests-of-the-
child standard and granted the stepfather custody
of A.R.A. The state supreme court reversed on the
ground that a court may determine best interests
only after a showing of dependency or abuse and
neglect by the natural parent; to grant custody of a
child to a nonparent in the absence of such a
showing would violate the biological parent's
constitutional rights.

In addition to stepparent claims, many
other sympathetic fact situations occur in these

cases. A husband may believe a child born of the marriage is his or may treat the child as his with his wife's assent and encouragement. The wife may then seek to deny him the status of father on divorce. A biological mother may seek to deny her lesbian partner's parenthood upon separation. Third-party claimants may also be relatives or others with whom the parent has left the child for a substantial time.

Some states, taking an approach less restrictive than Montana's in *A.R.A.*, recognize equitable doctrines (*Gallagher*) or a showing of extraordinary circumstances (Bennett v. Jeffreys, N.Y.1976) as bases for custody awards to non-parents. The Iowa Supreme Court, for example, endorsed the equitable parent doctrine in In re Marriage of Gallagher (Iowa 1995). In *Gallagher*, John and Amy were married and living together as husband and wife when Riley was conceived and born in 1991. John believed the girl to be his and developed a parental relationship with her. In 1993, John and Amy filed for divorce. Three weeks before trial, and after a home study recommended John as the custodial parent, blood tests confirmed Amy's announcement that John was not Riley's natural father. John asked the court to recognize the equitable parent doctrine or, in the alternative, to equitably estop the mother from denying that he was the child's father. Unlike the husband in

Michael H., John was not protected by a presumption that the child born in wedlock is a child of the marriage.

   Gallagher held that a man may establish equitable parenthood by demonstrating (1) that he was married to the mother when the child was conceived and born, (2) that he reasonably believed he is the child's father, (3) that he established a parental relationship with the child, and (4) that judicial recognition of the relationship is in the child's best interest. The court found it significant that John supported the child and sought a continued support obligation. "Willingness to support the child, though an incomplete test of a child's best interest, is surely a crucial consideration in the determination." John met the first three factors needed to establish equitable parenthood, and the court remanded to determine whether the adjudication John sought was in the child's best interest.

   Gallagher demonstrates a court's willingness to allow a child to have two fathers, but the decision's full implications are unclear. The court noted, for example, that neither the child nor her biological father would be bound by the court's order. The ambiguity is one reason other states have rejected equitable doctrines as a basis for non-parent custody. In Cotton v. Wise, for example, the Missouri Supreme Court noted that "[t]he problem with a court-fashioned 'equitable parent' doctrine is that the court has to improvise, as it goes along, substantive standards and procedural rules about when legal custody may be modified, what terms and conditions may be set, and other matters that already had well-charted passageways under state statutes and related court decisions." (Mo.1998).

States may also use a more liberal standard when the child has lived with the "parent", and not with the biological parent claimant, for a significant period. The Delaware Supreme Court, for example, has upheld the constitutionality of a statute that "effectively gives a stepparent the same status as a natural parent, for purposes of deciding custody, if (i) the child is residing with the stepparent and a natural custodial parent, when (ii) the natural custodial parent dies or becomes disabled." Tailor v. Becker (Del.1998).

As with visitation, a few states have extremely broad third-party custody statutes. See, e.g., Conn. Gen. Stat. Ann. § 46b-57,-59 (allowing "full or partial custody, care, education and visitation rights" to "any interested third-party ... upon such conditions and limitations as [the court] deems equitable"); Ore. Rev. Stat. § 109.119 ("any person...who has established emotional ties creating a child-parent relationship or an ongoing personal relationship with a child" may petition for custody, visitation, guardianship, "or any other generally recognized right of a parent or person in loco parentis...").

These statutes would also be susceptible to constitutional challenge under *Troxel*, particularly because custody is even more intrusive than visitation on parents' due process right to the care and custody of their children. *Troxel* does not foreclose the possibility that custody could be awarded to a nonparent over the objections of a fit legal parent, but the connection between the child and the nonparent would have to be very strong to overcome the parent's custodial status, and perhaps would require a showing that the child would suffer detriment should the nonparent be denied custody.

3. DEFINING "PARENT" FOR CHILD SUPPORT

States may allow more than two adults to hold parental status for purposes of imposing a child support obligation, but may also leave unclear the implications of the expanded parental status. Louisiana, for example, uses a concept of dual paternity that permits imposition of child support

obligations on two "fathers." In Louisiana a child
born to a marriage is conclusively presumed to be
the child of the mother's husband if he does not
disavow paternity in a limited time after the child's
birth. A paternity and support action may
nonetheless be maintained against the biological
father because the presumption of legitimacy was
not intended to shield the biological father from
support responsibilities. The biological father and
mother would be responsible for support and the
legal father might also be required to share the
support obligation. The child would continue to be
the legitimate child of the mother's husband, but it
is not clear what rights and responsibilities the
biological father might have other than the support
obligation. See, e.g., Smith v. Cole (La.1989).
Equitable doctrines such as estoppel may also be
used to impose support obligations on nonparents.
See chapter 8.

4.   REFORM PROPOSALS–THE AMERICAN
LAW INSTITUTE

The American Law Institute (ALI) has
proposed legislation that would provide clearer
rules to define the rights and obligations of
parenthood. The Institute's Principles of the Law
of Family Dissolution: Analysis and
Recommendations Governing the Allocation of
Custodial and Decisionmaking Responsibility for

Children defines three categories of "parent"-- a legal parent, a parent by estoppel, and a de facto parent. Principles § 2.03.

A *legal parent* is one who is defined as such under state law. Decisions that turn on who fits the state definition of legal parent, such as Michael H. v. Gerald D., would not be affected by the Principles. Consequently, Gerald, the husband, would be a legal parent. A biological father in Michael's position might be able to achieve a parent by estoppel or de facto parent status, but only if he met the stringent requirements for one of these categories (discussed below).

The *parent by estoppel* category prevents a legal parent from denying parental status to a person who has acted as a parent of the child. The Principles specify four ways to achieve parent by estoppel status: by being liable for child support; by living with the child for at least two years and having a good faith belief that one is the biological parent; by entering into a co-parenting agreement before the child's birth and living with the child since the child's birth; or by living "with the child for at least two years, holding out and accepting full and permanent responsibilities as a parent, pursuant to an agreement with the child's parent (or, if there are two legal parents, both parents), when the court finds that recognition as a parent is in the child's best interests." § 2.03(1)(b)(iv).

A person is entitled to *de facto parent* status only if he lived with the child for a significant period, not less than two years. Whether a period is "significant" depends on a number of factors, including "the age of the child, the frequency of contact, and the intensity of the relationship." § 2.03, cmt. c (iv.) In addition, during this period, for reasons not based primarily on financial compensation, the claimant must have performed a majority of the caretaking functions, or at least a share least equal to the share assumed by the legal parent with whom the child primarily lived.

As with the category of parent by estoppel, the legal parent's consent is a prerequisite to forming a de facto parent relationship. Consent can be implied, but requires a clear demonstration that the legal parent intended to share parenting responsibilities. If the legal parent maintains control over discipline or other matters related to the child's care, the legal parent typically has not consented. Asking a partner to baby-sit, for example, does not establish consent to a de facto parent relationship.

De facto parent status can also be established without a legal parent's consent, if no legal parent is able or willing to perform caretaking functions as, for example, when a legal parent abandoned a child or was institutionalized. De facto parent status is inferior to legal parent and parent by estoppel status. A de facto parent, for example, typically would not be allocated primary custodial responsibility when a legal parent has also been taking an active parenting role.

Generally a person not a "parent" under any of these categories would not be allocated any parental rights. In other words, the ALI's principles recognize no equivalent to a broad visitation statute. A "grandparent or other relative" may be allocated responsibility, but only in a very narrow range of cases. § 2.18(2). This lack of recognition "reflects the societal consensus that responsibility for children ordinarily should be retained by a child's parents, while recognizing that there are some exceptional circumstances in which the child's needs are best served by continuity of care by other adults." § 2.18, cmt. a. The Principles further provide that a person not qualifying as a legal parent, parent by estoppel, or de facto parent would not have standing to bring an independent action, although in exceptional circumstances a court could grant permission to intervene in an ongoing action.

Time will tell whether the state's current diverse approaches will move toward the ALI Principles, which are less stringent than some states and more restrictive than others. Further the Principles clearly define the different categories of parent and the legal rights and responsibilities of persons in these categories.

In the meantime, *Troxel* leaves the Principles constitutional breathing space because, as discussed above, at least six Justices (the four-Justice plurality and Justices Stevens and Kennedy) concluded that the presumption in favor of a natural parent's due process rights is rebuttable and must be weighed against the interests of other persons holding a strong relationship with the child, and perhaps also against the child's interest in maintaining the strong relationship.

C. GUARDIANSHIP AND THE GUARDIAN'S ROLE

A guardian (also called "guardian of the person") has a parent's duties and responsibilities with regard to the minor's custody, care, education, health and general welfare, but the guardian is not responsible for the minor's financial support. The guardian's role is distinct from that of a conservator (also called "guardian of the estate"), who is responsible for managing the minor's estate, although the same person may perform both functions.

Usually a guardian is needed when the minor's biological or adoptive parents are unavailable due to death, disease, prolonged absence, or termination of parental rights. If the legal parents are available, their obligation to support the child continues and they retain a right to visitation and to give or refuse consent to an adoption. Before the guardian is needed, the parents may appoint a guardian by will or through a stand-by guardian procedure that allows the parents to designate a person who will become the guardian upon the happening of a triggering event, such as the parent's incapacity due to illness. The AIDS crisis that resulted in the incapacity and death of relatively young parents demonstrated the need for stand-by guardianship statutes, which allow the parent to care for the child as long as possible, with a prearranged transition to the guardian when necessary. To continue to serve, the standby guardian typically must be approved by the court within a relatively short period of time. Depending on the child's needs and

circumstances, the court may choose a different
guardian than the one appointed by the parent.

Ideally the parents should arrange
guardianships, but sometimes a third party seeks a
guardianship of a child over the legal parents'
objections. A celebrated case is *Guardianship of
Phillip B.*, which involved a Down's syndrome child
whose parents had placed him in an institution
when he was an infant (Cal.Ct.App.1983). A couple
who volunteered at the facility where Phillip lived
gradually took on a parental role, providing the
boy with love, care and home visits with their
family. Several years of disagreements with
Phillip's parents over medical care and other issues
led the volunteer couple to petition for
guardianship of Phillip, which the trial court
granted.

Relying on the psychological parent
concept, the appellate court affirmed on the ground
that custody of a child may be awarded to a
nonparent without a parent's consent if clear and
convincing evidence demonstrates that awarding
custody to a biological parent would be detrimental
to the child, and that an award to a nonparent
would serve the best interests of the child. The
appellate court explicitly noted that detriment was
not proved by Phillip's institutionalization alone,
but by the biological parents' calculated decision to

remain emotionally and physically detached from him, depriving him of any substantial benefits of a true parent-child relationship.

CHAPTER 3

CHILD ABUSE AND NEGLECT

A. INTRODUCTION

1. CONSTITUTIONAL AND STATUTORY FRAMEWORK

Abuse and neglect laws rest on a delicate balance grounded in due process and other constitutional guarantees, which protect parents from unreasonable state interference but also authorize state intervention to protect children from harm. On the one hand, the Supreme Court has conferred on parents a substantive due process right to direct their children's upbringing, which parents may invoke to prevent unwarranted state intervention. Chapter 1 discusses the foundational due process decisions—Meyer v. Nebraska (S.Ct.1923) and Pierce v. Society of Sisters (S.Ct.1925)—and the recent decision of Troxel v. Granville (S.Ct.2000) (plurality opinion), in which all nine Justices reaffirmed the parental due process right. The Court has also invoked privacy doctrines to sustain the integrity of family decisionmaking. See, e.g., Roe v. Wade (S.Ct.1973); Eisenstadt v. Baird (S.Ct.1972); Griswold v. Connecticut (S.Ct.1965).

On the other hand, parental prerogatives do not have boundless constitutional protection. Prince v. Massachusetts (S.Ct.1944), also discussed in chapter 1, posited a balancing test in parent-state disputes concerning child welfare. Building on the balancing test announced in *Prince* and applied by the Court ever since in such disputes, Stanley v. Illinois (S.Ct.1972) specifically recognized "[t]he state's right – indeed, duty – to protect minor children through a judicial determination of their interests in a neglect proceeding."

Courts are clear that where an abuse or neglect finding is based on sufficiently serious danger to the child, the state's parens patriae authority to protect the child prevails over any constitutional interest asserted by the parents. Reasonably anticipated harm as well as actual harm can be a basis for intervention, because the state does not have to wait until the child is actually injured before it can act. In an appropriate case, the state may remove a child from the abusive or neglectful parents' custody, temporarily or permanently.

In both abuse and neglect cases, the propriety of official intervention may require fine line-drawing. At one end of the spectrum, intervention and removal seem clearly appropriate when a parent has severely beaten or maimed a child. At the other end, however, authorities have sometimes sought to remove children from their parents on little more than a conclusion that the parents follow an immoral lifestyle or have insufficient income to provide a "proper" home. Beyond constitutional and statutory doctrine, the decision whether to intervene, and perhaps remove the child, is made yet more difficult because children too often receive woefully inadequate state-provided care. They may be placed in long-term foster care, for example, with multiple placements and minimal services, resulting in little physical or emotional support throughout childhood and adolescence.

2. THE CHILD PROTECTION SYSTEM

Three major systems regulate families in the context of abuse and neglect. The first system is the criminal law (see chapter 5), which since the 1600s has prosecuted parents for abusing or neglecting their children. The second is the welfare system (see chapter 8), which used child protection as one justification for intervening in poor families.

Early in our nation's history, the poor laws, modeled on the Elizabethan poor laws, authorized overseers of the poor to remove children from their families and bind them out as apprentices or send them to poorhouses or asylums. The modern welfare system is not as intrusive, but government aid to the poor still includes oversight and regulation of family life. The third major system of regulation, applicable regardless of the family's financial circumstances, is the civil child protection system, the focus of this chapter.

The civil child protection system reportedly began in New York City in 1874, in response to the case of Mary Ellen, a child severely beaten by her stepmother. Because no child protection system existed, her case was brought to court by the President of the New York Society for the Prevention of Cruelty to Animals, who argued that even if Mary Ellen had no rights as a human being to be free of physical abuse, she at least deserved the same protections against abuse that other animals had. In response to her case and growing public concern about child abuse, the New York Society for the Prevention of Cruelty to Children was established and New York and other states enacted child protection statutes. The Society and similar groups in other states took active roles in investigating abuse and neglect and placing children in institutions and foster care. When the juvenile court system began in 1899, child protection cases became a major part of the caseload.

In the early 1960s, child abuse attracted the attention of the media, the public, the medical profession, and lawmakers because of reports on the "battered child syndrome," which is discussed in detail below. Responding to widespread public concern, states enacted laws that required physicians to report suspected child abuse to the state. In 1974 Congress enacted the Child Abuse Prevention and Treatment Act (CAPTA), which provided funding to the states for child abuse and neglect programs, established standards for child abuse and neglect reporting and investigation, required appointment of guardians ad litem for children in abuse and neglect cases, and established the National Center on Child Abuse and Neglect.

In 1990, the U.S. Advisory Board on Child Abuse and Neglect called child abuse and neglect a "national emergency" as reported incidents continued to increase, partly because of drug use by parents, the stresses of poverty, and improved reporting. In 2001 child protection agencies received an estimated 2.7 million referrals

concerning approximately five million children.
Sixty-seven percent of these reports were
investigated, with close to 60 percent of the
investigations finding that the maltreatment was
not substantiated. An estimated 826,000 children
were determined to be maltreated. Fifty-nine
percent of the maltreated children were neglected;
19 percent were physically abused; 10 percent were
sexually abused; and 7 percent were emotionally
maltreated. An estimated 1300 children died from
maltreatment. Parents were the main
perpetrators. See U.S. Dep't of Health and Human
Services, Child Maltreatment 2001, at http://
www.acf.dhhs.gov/ programs/cb/publications.

Child maltreatment occurs at all
socioeconomic levels and in all racial and ethnic
groups, but the child protection caseload has a
disproportionably large representation of low-
income and minority families. There is
disagreement about whether this disproportionate
representation is due to a greater incidence of
maltreatment in these families, or whether these
families are more likely to be subjected to intrusive
interventions that are culturally, racially, and
class biased. There is general agreement, however,
that services for children are significantly underfunded.

The complex child protection system can
involve multiple agencies, courts, professionals,
and laws. States have four sets of laws dealing
with abuse and neglect – reporting statutes, child
protective statutes, criminal statutes, and social
services statutes. Definitions of abuse and neglect
may differ somewhat in each statute because the
statutes serve distinct functions. In addition, since
CAPTA, Congress has exercised extensive control
over state child protection and child welfare
systems by requiring states to comply with various
mandates as conditions for receiving federal funds.
Thus lawyers and courts may need to interpret and
apply state laws and regulations in the context of
federal law.

An abuse or neglect case might begin with
a telephone call to the state's central "hot line"
number reporting suspicious circumstances or with
an emergency call to police. The reporter may be a
teacher, physician or neighbor. After child welfare
authorities or police investigate the report, the
matter may be closed because no intervention is
needed or because authorities might consider the
parents' voluntary acceptance of services sufficient
to remove risk to the child.

If more intensive intervention and
oversight are needed, however, or if the parents

refuse to accept services voluntarily, the case may be referred to the juvenile or family court for an order mandating services or removing the child from the home. When the abuse or neglect is severe, the criminal justice system may prosecute the perpetrators. The civil case alone might end up involving not only social workers, physicians, psychologists, lawyers and judges, but also service providers in such fields as daycare, education, health care, housing assistance, benefit programs, drug and alcohol counseling, foster care, and probation.

Effective treatment of the family and child thus requires a coordinated response that depends on extensive cooperation and communication among these diverse professions and services, whose distinctive approaches may be affected by differences in training and objectives. Not surprisingly, this cooperation and communication are often lacking. The child's lawyer can play an important role in advocating for the child's interests, encouraging cooperation, and bridging gaps in communication.

B. REPORTING STATUTES AND INVESTIGATION

1. STATUTORY STRUCTURE

The identification of the battered child syndrome in 1962 was a catalyst for laws requiring physicians to report suspected child abuse to child welfare authorities or law enforcement. By 1967, all states had adopted such mandatory reporting laws. Within a few years, states had expanded the "mandated reporter" class to include other professionals—such as teachers and social workers—who have regular contact with children and are likely to be trained in the duty to report. Partly because of federal requirements, states have also expanded the kinds of maltreatment that must be reported. State laws still vary, however, concerning who must report, what must be reported, what agencies (social services or law enforcement, or both) receive mandatory reports, what penalties may be imposed for failure to report, and what civil liabilities may arise from reporting or failing to report. In all states, reports may also be made by persons who are not mandated reporters. Reporters may act anonymously by hot line telephone call.

2. THE CENTRAL REGISTRY

Very few abuse and neglect reports actually reach the juvenile court because they are screened out or dealt with in some manner short of adjudication. Nationwide only about 30 percent of reports receive any significant intervention, and less than one-third of these proceed to adjudication. Even when no significant intervention occurs, however, reports may remain in a confidential central state registry to identify abusers and patterns of abuse.

Registries are typically accessible by government entities such as law enforcement, departments of social services and the judiciary. Specified private entities, such as day care centers or youth sports programs and other organizations that engage employees or volunteers to work with children, may also be allowed access to screen potential applicants. Where state law permits such private access, the law in effect creates a duty to investigate because failure to do so may help establish the entity's negligence in a later damage action by the victim of abuse committed by the employee or volunteer.

The standard for retaining a person's name in the registry may be so broad as to raise constitutional concerns. In Valmonte v. Bane (2d Cir.1994), for example, the mother was reported as an abuser for slapping her daughter in the face with an open hand. The county child welfare agency found that the mother had engaged in excessive corporal punishment, and the family court dismissed proceedings against her on the condition that the family receive counseling. Despite the dismissal, the mother's name remained in the state Register, which identified persons accused of abuse or neglect and communicated their names to potential child care employers.

Valmonte held that the Register implicated the mother's due process liberty interest in her reputation and provided insufficient safeguards to protect that interest. The risk of erroneous listing was too great because the Register retained reports supported merely by "some credible evidence." The listed person could hold the state department of social services to a higher standard of proof, namely a fair preponderance of the evidence, only after being deprived of an employment opportunity solely because of inclusion in the Central Register. (In response to Valmonte, New York law now provides that disclosure to a potential employer may be made only after the listed person has had an opportunity for an administrative hearing and a showing that the report is relevant to the prospective employment. N.Y. Soc. Serv. Law § 422.

3.   REPORTERS' LIABILITY

Reporting laws grant immunity to mandated reporters and others who report suspected abuse. Some states provide qualified immunity only for reports made in good faith, while other states provide reporters a greater measure of protection. See, e.g., Elmore v. Van Horn (Wyo.1992). California, for example, grants mandated reporters absolute immunity, even for false and reckless reporting, against state law claims and 42 U.S.C. § 1983 claims alike. See, e.g., Thomas v. Chadwick (Cal.Ct.App.1990). Immunity otherwise conferred by the reporting act may be denied if a mandated reporter discloses suspected abuse to a private party rather than the public authorities identified in the act. See, e.g., Searcy v. Auerbach (9th Cir. 1992) (no immunity for psychologist who reported suspected abuse to child's father).

A mandated reporter who fails to report suspected abuse may be held criminally or civilly liable under the state's reporting law. In some jurisdictions, failure to report may also be a basis for tort liability, but Landeros v. Flood (Cal.1976) demonstrates the difficulty of proving a claim. To establish that the defendant physician's failure to report serious abuse constituted negligence, *Landeros* required the child plaintiff to show that the defendant "in fact observed her various injuries and in fact formed the opinion that they were caused by other than accidental means." Violation of the reporting act was a misdemeanor, but *Landeros* held that the criminal violation did not per se establish a civil cause of action. The court was concerned that creating tort liability might result in over-reporting. A Michigan case, however, resulted in a $900,000 verdict for a failure to report that proximately caused the child's death. Williams v. Coleman (Mich. Ct.App.1992).

Mandatory reporting acts can conflict with professional ethics codes mandating client confidentiality. State law, for example, may mandate reports from therapists and researchers, who may feel ethically bound to remain silent even though failure to report may result in a criminal violation. Generally state reporting laws do not abrogate the attorney-client privilege and require attorneys to report, although lawyers in limited circumstances may be able to reveal child abuse under an exception in a state's confidentiality rules. See, e.g., Rule 1.6 (b) of the American Bar

Association Model Rules of Professional Conduct (A lawyer may reveal information to the extent the lawyer believes necessary "to prevent the client from committing a criminal act that the lawyer believes is likely to result in imminent death or substantial bodily harm").

4. INVESTIGATIONS

To help determine whether a child is at risk, child protective authorities may seek to make a warrantless inspection of the home. Statutes normally authorize law enforcement officials or physicians to take an evidently abused or neglected child into immediate protective custody in an emergency.

A government official's entry into the home during an abuse or neglect investigation constitutes a Fourth Amendment search. See, e.g., State v. Boggess (Wis.1983). Officials, however, may conduct a warrantless search in an emergency or in circumstances otherwise reasonable. The federal courts of appeals disagree on what Fourth Amendment test should apply to a social worker's "visual search of a child's body cavities." According to Roe v. Texas Dep't of Protective and Regulatory Services (5th Cir.2002):

The Seventh Circuit has held that a child protective services worker need only satisfy the lesser special needs test and not the more rigorous probable cause requirement. The Third, Ninth, and Tenth Circuits have rejected the Seventh Circuit's approach and apply instead the traditional Fourth Amendment standard to juvenile strip searches. The Second Circuit has taken an intermediate position: Even if social workers need not satisfy the probable cause and warrant requirement in all cases, they must obtain prior judicial approval when doing so would not threaten the child's well-being. [The] social worker must demonstrate probable cause and obtain a court order, obtain parental consent, or act under exigent circumstances. Id. at 407-08.

Before telling the accused abuser to leave or removing the child, however, the investigator need have only an "objectively reasonable suspicion of abuse" See, e.g., Croft v. Westmoreland Co. Children and Youth Services (3d Cir. 1997).

Where a search by or on behalf of child protective authorities is held unreasonable, courts in child protective proceedings have refused to apply the exclusionary rule because application would endanger children's safety without affecting the rule's ordinary application in parallel or later criminal proceedings. See, e.g., State ex rel. A.R. v. C.R. (Utah 1999). "[B]ecause a child protective proceeding itself is not punitive in nature and the deterrent effect of the exclusionary rule will be adequately served by precluding use of the evidence in any related criminal proceeding, the State's interest in protecting its children mandates the admissibility of relevant evidence seized during an illegal search." In re Diane P. (N.Y.App.Div.1995).

C. LIMITS ON INTERVENTION

1. GROUNDS FOR INTERVENTION

As noted at the beginning of this chapter, the state's parens patriae authority to intervene in family life to protect children is limited by the parents' constitutional rights to direct their children's upbringing and to family integrity. Identifying the boundaries of these limits, however, can be quite difficult in the context of particular cases. Two recurrent issues are the degree of actual or threatened harm the state must show before it may intervene, and the level of

assistance the state must provide to help the
family resolve the risk before removing the child.
(For special rules applying to Native American
Children under the Indian Child Welfare Act, see
chapter 4, section G.1.) The Supreme Court has not
directly addressed these issues, but state and
lower federal courts have done so.

Both of these issues were addressed in In
re Juvenile Appeal (Conn.1983), which concerned a
mother of six children who was a welfare recipient
known to the department of social services. When
her youngest child, a nine-month-old infant, died of
unknown causes, the department removed the
other children on an emergency basis. At an ex
parte hearing two days after the death, the court
granted the department temporary custody of the
children to safeguard their welfare.

The state supreme court remanded with
orders to set aside the temporary custody order
because it found post-emergency intervention and
removal unsupported by the requisite compelling
state interest. The state's interest in intervention
is compelling only when the children face serious
physical illness, injury or immediate physical
danger. At the ex parte custody hearing, the state
failed to show that the infant's death was caused
by abuse; indeed an autopsy report completed after

the hearing exonerated the mother. Further the court held that removing the children from the home should be a remedy of last resort, used only when necessary to insure their safety. The court concluded that "[e]ven where the parent-child relationship is 'marginal,' it is usually in the best interests of the child to remain at home and still benefit from a family environment."

Where the grounds for state intervention in abuse or neglect appear tenuous, the right to intervene may sometimes be limited by the due process void-for-vagueness doctrine, which is discussed more fully in chapter 5. Statutes and regulations often define abuse and neglect broadly in an effort to effectuate their child protective purposes, but breadth has its permissible limits.

Courts tend to reject vagueness challenges where the parent's conduct would appear clearly abusive or neglectful to reasonable persons, but vagueness challenges sometimes succeed where the abusiveness of a parent's conduct is open to fair question. In Roe v. Conn (M.D.Ala.1976), for example, the statute defined "neglected child" as "any child, who, while under sixteen years of age ... has no proper parental care or guardianship or whose home, by reason of neglect, cruelty, or depravity, on the part of his parent or parents, guardian or other person in whose care he may be, is an unfit or improper place for such child." The court held that the statute was unconstitutionally vague because the definition of neglect was circular and "was couched in terms that have no common meaning. When is a home an 'unfit' or 'improper' place for a child? Obviously, this is a question about which men and women of ordinary intelligence would greatly disagree. Their answers would vary in large measure in relation to their differing social, ethical, and religious views."

Relatively tight definitions of abuse and neglect, which balance parental rights and the state's parens patriae interest, are possible. A consent decree following a successful challenge to Kentucky removal practices, for example, contained these definitions: "'Abused or neglected child' means a child whose health or welfare is harmed or threatened with harm when his parent, guardian, or other person who has the permanent or temporary care, custody, or responsibility for the supervision of the child: inflicts or allows to be inflicted upon the child physical or mental injury to the child by other than accidental means; commits or allows to be committed an act of sexual abuse upon the child; willfully abandons or exploits such child; does not provide the child with adequate care and supervision, food, clothing and shelter, education, or medical care necessary for the child's well-being." Siereveld v. Conn (E.D.Ky.1983).

2. OTHER CONSTITUTIONAL LIMITS ON INTERVENTION

Does the Fourth Amendment permit child protective authorities to make periodic inspections of the home as part of a treatment plan or court-ordered disposition in an abuse or neglect action? The Supreme Court's decision in Wyman v. James (S.Ct.1971) provides helpful instruction. *Wyman* held that a welfare department caseworker's visit to a recipient's home did not concern "any search by the ... social service agency in the Fourth Amendment meaning of that term." The Court also concluded that even if the Fourth Amendment were "somehow" implicated, the proposed home visit was reasonable and thus lawful where it was made by a caseworker, was not permitted outside working hours, and did not involve forcible entry or snooping. *Wyman* stressed that "[t]he focus is on the ... child who is dependent. There is no more worthy object of the public's concern. The dependent child's needs are paramount, and only with hesitancy would we relegate those needs, in the scale of comparative values, to a position secondary to what the mother claims as her rights."

The Fifth Amendment privilege against compulsory self-incrimination, which Fourteenth Amendment due process applies to the states, may sometimes hamper abuse and neglect investigations by permitting the alleged perpetrator to remain silent, at least where he or she is not presently subject to a court order relating to the child. In Baltimore City Department of Social Services v. Bouknight (S.Ct.1990), the juvenile court placed the child under its continuing oversight by asserting jurisdiction over the mother on a finding that she had committed serious recurring acts of physical abuse against her infant son. Shortly afterwards, the mother regained custody after signing a court-approved protective supervision order, which she later violated in nearly every respect. After reports of further serious abuse, the juvenile court ordered the mother to produce the child or reveal his whereabouts.

The Supreme Court assumed, without deciding, that the limited testimonial assertion inherent in producing the child would be sufficiently incriminating to trigger the Fifth Amendment privilege, but concluded that the

challenged production order fell within the
"required records" exception to the privilege
because the mother was the subject of the existing
protective supervision order. The Court left open
the possibility that in later criminal proceedings
against the mother, the privilege might limit the
state's ability to use the testimonial aspects of her
act of production. In a later civil abuse or neglect
proceeding, however, the court may draw a
negative inference against a party invoking the
privilege, provided some other evidence supports
the inference. See Baxter v. Palmigiano
(S.Ct.1976).

D.   PATTERNS OF ABUSE AND NEGLECT

This section identifies major categories of
abuse and neglect, a discussion that will continue
in the chapters on criminal abuse and neglect and
medical decision-making. The section distinguishes
between "abuse" and "neglect" because state laws
and reporting statistics frequently draw the
distinction, even though cases frequently contain
elements of both. For example, In re S.T.,
discussed below, concerned malnourished children
living without adequate medical care in a filthy
home (indicia of neglect), but these children also
suffered from bruises, cuts, bumps and burns

(indicia of abuse). Symptoms of neglect also may precede physical abuse. Because abuse and neglect overlap in so many cases, some authorities prefer a broader term, such as "maltreatment syndrome," to encompass all forms of "hurt" to a child. See Vincent J. Fontana and Douglas J. Besharov, The Maltreated Child (5th ed.1996).

1. NEGLECT

a. The General Concept

Neglect is the subject of a high percentage of maltreatment reports, and of most cases in which children are removed from their homes and placed in foster care. A majority of neglect removal cases involve low-income families. One study, for example, found that homelessness was a factor in over 30 percent of foster care placements. See U.S. General Accounting Office, Foster Care: Parental Drug Abuse Has Alarming Impact on Young Children (1994). Unfortunately, the child protective services system does not always have sufficient resources to maintain the increased caseload and demand for services from poor, multi-problem families. Such families may receive either no services or services inappropriate to their needs, and cases can drag on for years, with the children drifting in and out of foster care.

The parents' poverty no longer is a per se basis for a neglect finding. Statutes may specify that a neglect finding may be predicated on the parents' not providing adequate food, shelter, or clothing, but only if the parents are financially able to provide these necessities or have been offered state assistance. The risk remains, however, that neglect may be found even though the parents' deficiencies stem primarily from financial distress rather than from intentional denial of their children's needs. Low income parents often live in substandard housing and their diets often fall short of recognized nutritional guidelines, for example. Where no clinic is available, the hospital emergency room is the primary health care facility used by low income households; repeated appearances frequently arouse suspicion of neglect or abuse. If a low-income family receives public assistance, the family's regular required contacts with the social services agency give the parents a higher profile with state authorities, and thus may make them more susceptible to identification as neglectful or abusive.

In re S.T. (Utah Ct.App.1996) demonstrates the ambiguities and uncertainties that persist in many neglect cases involving parents in evident poverty. After investigating the family following a

1989 abuse/neglect referral, authorities found several problems that continued until parental rights to the four young children were terminated six years later. The initial investigators found that the children were malnourished, lacked adequate medical care, did not attend school and lived in an extremely dirty house; the "[f]loor was covered with food and soiled diapers, and dirty dishes, with aged, crusted food, ... piled in the kitchen."

On a second visit in 1989, the worker found that the home situation had not changed and that the four-month-old baby still appeared "lethargic and very thin." In two visits later that year, investigators found that living conditions had improved slightly, but that the parents had not heeded the worker's instructions to obtain medical care for the baby. After several failed promises, a social services worker took the baby to the doctor, who diagnosed her with "failure to thrive" because she had only gained three pounds since birth. The children were placed in foster care and drifted in and out of foster care over the next several years.

After another referral in 1991, investigators visiting S.T.'s home reported a burn on another child's palm that precisely and clearly spelled "IF." The parents claimed the child was burned on the stove while a babysitter was with the children, but the babysitter knew nothing of the burn. Investigators also reported that the children, dressed only in diapers and underpants, had an offensive odor about them. The apartment was unsanitary and smelled because, according to the parents, their pet messed and urinated on the floor. While noticing food and garbage on the floor, investigators observed two of the children picking a stale piece of bread and a cookie off the floor and putting them in their mouths.

Several times, the social services agency offered the parents services, including a vacuum and cleaning supplies, access to a twenty-four-hour crisis nursery and other daycare, counseling, parenting classes, homemaking services and assistance with getting medical care for the children. The state finally moved to terminate the parents' parental rights in 1994, and the court ordered termination in 1995. The court of appeals in 1996 found ample evidence to support the findings that the parents were unfit, neglectful, unable or unwilling to change the conditions requiring removal of their children, and unable to meet the children's physical, emotional and educational needs.

Like many neglect cases, *S.T.* is troubling in two respects. First, it is not clear that the state provided the family appropriate or adequate services. The parents were diagnosed with occasional physical illnesses, chronic fatigue, depression and anxiety, but the court's opinion contained no indication that the state had ever helped them obtain medical treatment. Nor was it clear why the children were persistently malnourished and living in a filthy home. If adequate food was unavailable, the state might have helped the parents apply for food stamps or other public assistance. If the parents needed assistance to maintain their home, the record indicated only that the agency had provided cleaning supplies and had required the father "to find meaningful employment," even though his aptitude test "resulted in a score within the range of borderline intellectual functioning." The state continued to offer services, such as parenting classes, that apparently did not work, without better tailoring its services to the parents' distinct needs.

On the other hand, perhaps the state should have terminated parental rights even sooner. Six years of pre-termination delay may have consigned S.T. and the three other children (between six and nine years old when the appeal was decided) to adolescence in foster care, because children become considerably more difficult to place for adoption as they grow older, particularly when they are members of a sibling group that courts try to keep together where possible. It is not clear why the state felt it needed to give the parents so many opportunities to become minimally adequate parents while the children suffered from continual malnutrition, lack of medical care, educational neglect, physical abuse and various other harms.

The *S.T.* children exhibited a number of conditions that appear frequently in neglect cases. Common conditions include (1) skin manifestations in infants, such as severe and persistent diaper rash or other skin breakdown secondary to poor hygiene; (2) sunburn, frostbite, or ongoing diseases such as recurrent respiratory infections, which may indicate inadequate clothing or shelter; (3) malnourishment; (4) physical growth and mental developmental lags, which may be due to inadequate diet; (5) inadequate medical care, such as failure to obtain necessary drugs for the child and sometimes failure to give children prescribed drugs, or failure to get necessary immunizations; (6) physical appearance indicating prenatal neglect from fetal alcohol syndrome, or physical deformity from drug use; and (7) failure to provide education.

b. Failure to Protect

Parents are responsible for protecting their children from harm when they are able to do so. A parent who fails to intervene to protect a child (or who takes insufficient protective action) can be adjudicated neglectful, even though the parent was not the actual abuser of the child. "Failure to protect" is a type of neglect, but usually arises in abuse cases. Parents who fail to protect a child can have the child removed from their care, and may even have parental rights terminated when the abuse is severe.

The state frequently alleges failure to protect when a mother does not intervene when her children are abused by their father or another male partner. In In re Craig T. (N.H.1999), for example, a mother was adjudicated neglectful because she did nothing to protect her three-year-old son from an assault by his father in a shopping mall parking lot and denied the assault occurred. No evidence indicated that she was afraid to intervene, and the court concluded that she was complicit in the attack. She also failed to protect her five-year-old daughter from witnessing the attack, which was so severe that it horrified witnesses.

In In re T.G. (S.D.1998), the court upheld termination of parental rights of a mother who did not physically or sexually abuse her daughters, but allowed them to travel with a known sexual abuser. Further she knew that the children's stepfather had been convicted of child molestation and that he was abusing the daughters, but nonetheless chose to live with him and expose the girls to him. She even tried to stop the children from discussing the abuse with authorities.

Associating with known abusers can also be a basis for state intervention. In In re Joshua M. (Neb.1997), for example, the court terminated the mother's parental rights because of her associations with the man who fathered her oldest daughter when he was thirty-six and she was fifteen, and with a man who was imprisoned for abusing her oldest daughter and was the father of her three other children.

Where a battered woman, herself a victim, does not remove herself and the children from the batterer, she generally can be held responsible for failing to protect the children. Children are psychologically harmed by exposure to domestic violence and are at risk of being physically harmed as well. Women domestic violence victims have successfully argued, however, that removing

children from their others' care and placing them
in foster care is not an appropriate remedy, but
that rather the state should assist the mother in
her efforts to escape the violence. See, e.g.,
Nicholson v. Williams (2d Cir.2002). Some courts,
also, have allowed a mother to use a battered
woman syndrome defense when the state seeks to
terminate her rights for failure to protect. See, e.g.,
In re Betty J.W. (W.Va.1988).

Because civil abuse proceedings focus on
the child's condition, the court may act even
without allegation of the identity of the person who
inflicted the violence. In In re D.L.W.
(Mo.Ct.App.1975), for example, the court found
abuse despite the parents' contention that a
babysitter, and not the parents, was responsible
for the child's injuries. The court held that to
sustain jurisdiction, "[i]t was not necessary to
prove, as in a criminal case, whether the parents
actually inflicted the injury or whether such injury
was inflicted by someone else .... The sole question
for determination is whether or not the
environment of this child was injurious to its
welfare."

Parents may also be found neglectful, and
may even suffer termination of parental rights,
when failure to cooperate with the state in an

abuse investigation leaves the perpetrator unidentified and the child at risk of future harm. See, e.g., In re Jeffrey R.L. (W.Va.1993) (upholding termination of parental rights to three-month-old infant who suffered from battered child syndrome and could not safely be returned home because perpetrator was unknown).

2.   PSYCHOLOGICAL MALTREATMENT

a.   The General Concept
        Psychological maltreatment may be coupled with physical neglect or abuse, or may occur separately. State statutes may not distinguish among emotional neglect, emotional abuse, and the emotional harm caused by physical neglect or abuse, including inappropriate discipline. An emotional neglect case also may be brought under more general statutory language such as "an environment injurious to the child's welfare." Acts of physical violence toward the child, including acts inflicted during efforts at discipline, may also support an emotional abuse finding. In some jurisdictions, a threat of emotional harm without a showing of actual harm is sufficient. In re Matthew S. (Cal.Ct.App.1996).

        Statutes that do specifically address psychological maltreatment may focus on the

condition of the child. See, e.g., Minn. Stat. §
626.556(9) (neglect means "a pattern of behavior
which contributes to impaired emotional
functioning of the child which may be demonstrated
by a substantial and observable effect in the child's
behavior, emotional response, or cognition that is
not within the normal range for the child's age and
stage of development, with due regard to the child's
culture"). Statutes may also focus on parental
behavior, such as persistent negative or belittling
parental communications and interactions with
children.

b. Failure to Thrive

"Failure to thrive," one of the allegations
against the *S.T.* parents, supra, can be caused by
emotional neglect. Failure to thrive, or growth
deficiency, is a condition in which the child's weight
and linear growth have fallen below standard
measures or have significantly dropped without a
physical cause. Children not treated can suffer
permanent physical, cognitive, and behavioral
problems. Early studies identified maternal
deprivation and neglect as causes of failure to
thrive. Later the importance of family, social, and
economic stresses was identified. More recently,
studies have identified child behavior and
temperament as important "failure to thrive"
factors. Parents may feel incompetent when dealing

with a child's unusually demanding physical or mental problems.

c. Expert Testimony

Evidence of emotional abuse or neglect may be elusive because such conduct usually consists of a pattern of behavior, without physical injury or an identifiable specific act or precipitating incident. The effects of emotional abuse or neglect may be incremental and cumulative for months or years. Even where a clear pattern of emotional maltreatment appears, a causal relationship between the maltreatment and resulting psychological harm may be difficult to establish. Causation may be demonstrated by documenting the dates and times of the alleged abusive acts and by identifying who was present each time. Psychiatric and psychological evaluation and testimony may be required. Because of difficulties of proof, some juvenile officers do not file an emotional abuse petition unless expert testimony will support it.

Expert testimony typically is used to establish "failure to thrive" as well. The physician first provides testimony that establishes "failure to thrive" symptoms and then rules out medical causes for the child's delayed development.

3. ABUSE

a. The General Question of Proof

To sustain allegations of physical abuse, generally medical evidence must establish that the child's injury was not accidental. Even where the parties present no eyewitness testimony concerning the acts of abuse, a physician's testimony (accompanied by photographs and x-rays when appropriate) demonstrating that the injuries were nonaccidental may constitute substantial evidence of abuse.

Several common pathological conditions tend to suggest that the child's injuries were intentional and unlikely to have been self-inflicted. These conditions include, for example, patterned abrasions consisting of marks or bruises whose shape, size, and severity suggest they were produced by objects such as belts, cords or sticks; patterned burns suggesting the child was held in scalding water or burned with cigarettes or other objects; and spiral fractures, particularly in young children, of the upper arm or leg indicating a twisting motion unlikely to have occurred without intent.

Physicians can also give expert testimony about the means used to inflict the injury and

whether the explanation given for the injuries is
reasonable. A parent, for example, may give an
explanation that in fact is unlikely to have caused
the injury (e.g., that the child fell from a chair
causing multiple, fatal injuries); or is implausible
(e.g., that an infant climbed up to and turned on a
hot water faucet); or that conflicts with the
explanation given by the other parent. See John E.
B. Myers, Evidence in Child Abuse and Neglect
Cases (3d ed. 1997).

b. The Battered Child Syndrome

Unfortunately some parents not only
neglect their children's needs, but also beat, maim,
tie up, torture or even murder their children. To
cite only one example, in Deborah S. v. Superior
Court (Cal.Ct.App.1996), the five-year-old child
had old and new bone fractures, scars and other
eye injuries, missing teeth, multiple bruises and
scars in various degrees of healing, and healed
scalp lacerations. All these injuries had been
inflicted on him by his mother, who had also
periodically confined the boy to his room, to a crib,
and to a closet, and had tied his wrists and ankles
together with a sock in his mouth to prevent him
from screaming.

Particularly when the child is young and
has suffered multiple injuries over time, the child

may fit the "battered child syndrome," a condition
identified in an influential article by Dr. C. Henry
Kempe and his colleagues in 1962. See C. Henry
Kempe et al., The Battered Child Syndrome, 181
JAMA 17 (1962). The battered child syndrome
"may occur at any age, but, in general, the affected
children are younger than three years. In some
instances the clinical manifestations are limited to
those resulting from a single episode of trauma,
but more often the child's general health is below
par, and he shows evidence of neglect including
poor skin hygiene, multiple soft tissue injuries, and
malnutrition. One often obtains a history of
previous episodes suggestive of parental neglect or
trauma. A marked discrepancy between clinical
findings and historical data as supplied by the
parents is a major diagnostic feature of the
battered child syndrome."

The battered child is often admitted to the
hospital during evening hours and often has had
multiple visits to various hospitals. Parents
frequently appear reluctant to give the physician
or medical staff information about the child, the
history or the present injuries. The parents may
react inappropriately to news of an injury's
severity, such as by appearing relatively calm to
the diagnosis of a fractured femur. Significant
inconsistencies between parents' explanations of

injuries and the diagnosed condition, gaps between the estimated time of injury and the date of treatment, and an unusually confused social history also suggest a dysfunctional family. The child may have previous injuries in various stages of healing. Where no new injuries occur while the child is hospitalized or in a protective environment, this change may also demonstrate that past injuries were products of abuse. Especially in cases of serious abuse, the child appears frequently withdrawn, noncommunicative, and developmentally far below chronological age. Speech, language, and behavior patterns appear retarded and not age appropriate.

In both criminal and civil cases, the syndrome has become a well-recognized medical diagnosis that can be established through expert testimony, which indicates (without identifying the perpetrator) that the child's injuries were not accidental

c. **The Shaken Baby Syndrome**
The "shaken baby syndrome," identified in the early 1970s, is caused by a person who severely shakes an infant, resulting in whiplash type injuries. The typical case involves shaking by a parent exasperated by an infant who will not stop crying or soiling his diapers. No external injury is

seen, but the shaking can cause blindness from internal eye damage, severe brain injury, and even death. The syndrome is an accepted medical diagnosis, but identifying the perpetrator can be very difficult, because typically there are no witnesses to the shaking and identifying the time of the incident may be difficult.

d. The Target Child

Some parents single out one child for abuse while leaving other children in the household unharmed. Social workers investigating abuse may see the unharmed children and either remain unaware of the presence of the "target child" or assume the child is safe because the other children appear well. Proper training for social workers would emphasize the necessity for careful attention to all children in a household. Two recent notorious New York City cases fit this tragic pattern.

Elisa Izquierdo's mother tortured and beat her to death in 1995 and was sentenced to fifteen years to life in prison. Her five other children were not physically abused. Elisa's case made national news, perhaps because she had come to the attention of a prince and was characterized as a fairy-tale princess. She was born addicted to crack and was placed in the custody of her father, who

was devoted to her and enrolled her at age one in a
Montessori preschool. She and her father were
favorites of the Montessori staff, and when her
father fell behind on tuition payments, the staff
brought her to the attention of Prince Michael of
Greece, a benefactor of the school, who described
her as a "lively, charming, beautiful girl" and
eventually promised to pay her full private school
tuition through 12th grade.

When Elisa visited her mother on
weekends, however, she was abused by her mother
and stepfather. Her father's efforts to limit the
mother's access were unsuccessful and when he
died of cancer, Elisa's mother was given custody
despite allegations of abuse. Elisa then endured
more than a year of horrifying beatings, sexual
abuse and torture, until her mother killed her
when she was six by throwing her against a
concrete wall. While she was in her mother's
custody, child protective services received at least
eight reports of abuse. Because of allegations that
the City had reacted improperly to multiple
reports of abuse, Elisa's death resulted in laws
designed to make New York child protective
services records more open and agencies more
publicly accountable.

Five-year-old Daytwon Bennett's mother beat and starved him to death. When he died in 1997, he weighed only thirty pounds and had scars all over his body, even though his four siblings living with him in a well-kept, immaculately clean apartment were unharmed. His family was involved with the social services department because of prior abuse of Daytwon, and a caseworker had visited the home thirteen times in the nine months before the boy's death.

4.   CORPORAL PUNISHMENT

a.   The General Concept

Abuse may result from misguided efforts to discipline a child. Commentators continue to disagree about the efficacy of corporal punishment amid changing social mores, but both criminal and civil law have traditionally found reasonable corporal punishment of children justified and thus not abusive. Many parents thus seek to justify abuse by characterizing their conduct as necessary and appropriate discipline. (For a discussion of efforts to raise cultural defenses, see chapter 5.)

The Restatement (Second) of Torts provides that a parent "is privileged to apply such reasonable force or to impose such reasonable confinement upon his child as he reasonably believes to be necessary for its proper control, training, or education." § 147. The Restatement considers the following factors in determining the reasonableness of punishment: whether the actor is a parent; the child's age, sex and physical and mental condition; the nature of the child's offense and his apparent motive; the influence of his example upon other children of the same family or group; whether the force or confinement is reasonably necessary and appropriate to compel obedience to a proper command; and whether it is disproportionate to the offense, unnecessarily degrading, or likely to cause serious or permanent harm.

A child protection act's definition of abuse may be critical to determining whether corporal punishment exceeds the bounds of reasonableness. A statute might require a showing of actual harm. E.g., Raboin v. North Dakota Department of Human Services (N.D.1996) (corporal punishment administered by the parents with a wooden or plastic spoon or belt that caused slight bruising on the children's buttocks did not yet demonstrate "serious physical harm or traumatic abuse as a result of the parents' spankings"). By contrast, other jurisdictions find abusive discipline on proof of a substantial risk of serious injury, without the need to show substantial injury itself.

b. The International Picture

Corporal punishment is viewed more negatively in some countries and in international law than it is in the United States. In 1979 Sweden outlawed parental corporal punishment. The law carries no penalties, but relies on public education to achieve compliance with the law. A number of other countries, including Norway, Denmark, Finland and Austria, have also prohibited parental corporal punishment. Corporal punishment in schools had been banned much earlier. The Committee on the Rights of the Child, which supervises implementation of the United Nations Convention on the Rights of the Child, has condemned corporal punishment in both families and institutions. (As chapter 1 discusses, the United States has signed but not ratified the Convention.)

c. Public Schools

Public schools in the United States may use reasonable corporal punishment. In Ingraham v. Wright (S.Ct.1977), the Supreme Court considered whether corporal punishment constituted cruel and unusual punishment in violation of the Eighth Amendment and, if not, whether due process required prior notice and an opportunity to be heard. The Court concluded that the Eighth Amendment does not apply to the public schools and that notice and a hearing are not required. The Court indicated that common law remedies are adequate where punishment is excessive.

In more recent challenges to school authority, *T.L.O., Vernonia* and *Earls* (see chapter 1), the Supreme Court did not back away from *Ingraham,* though it noted that public schools' authority is more limited than that of private schools. When parents place their children in private schools, the teachers and administrators stand in loco parentis over the children. In public schools, however, the exercise of authority is not directly analogous to parental authority, but rather is subject to constitutional restraints applied to state actors. Nonetheless, *Vernonia* concluded that the public schools have "custodial and tutelary" authority, "permitting a degree of supervision and control that could not be exercised over free adults."

The trend in public schools has been away from the use of corporal punishment, which was explicitly permitted in a vast majority of states as late as 1974 but is now prohibited in more than half the states. See, e.g., Leonard P. Edwards,

Corporal Punishment in the Legal System, 36
Santa Clara L. Rev. 983 (1996).

d. Domestic Violence Statutes

Children have occasionally been successful
in using domestic violence statutes to secure court
orders of protection against abusive parents. In
Beermann v. Beermann (S.D.1997), for example,
the court granted a protective order to a fourteen-
year-old girl who wanted to continue to visit her
father, but wanted him to stop his abusive
behavior during her visits. The court noted a
number of advantages to using the domestic
violence statute rather than the child protection
statute, including that the domestic violence victim
could fill out the standard forms herself and could
get immediate relief.

5. SEXUAL ABUSE

Child sexual abuse was not acknowledged
as a serious problem until the 1970s, when the
women's movement and CAPTA raised public
awareness. Sexual abuse cases comprise a
relatively small percentage of the overall child
protective services caseload, but surveys of adults
have indicated that as many as a million children
may be victimized each year. Diana J. English, The
Extent and Consequences of Child Maltreatment, 8

The Future of Children 39 (Spring 1998). Because of the shame and embarrassment involved, sexual abuse is underreported by child and adult victims alike.

The term "child sexual abuse" reaches a wide range of acts. Legal and research definitions of child sexual abuse generally require two elements: (1) sexual activities involving children and (2) an "abusive condition" such as coercion or a large age gap between the participants, indicating a lack of consensuality. See David Finkelhor, Current Information of the Scope and Nature of Child Sexual Abuse, 4 The Future of Children 31 (Summer/Fall 1994). Sexual abuse may include offenses such as exhibitionism that do not result in contact with the child. Most sexual abusers of children are men known to the victim before the attack. Girls are at higher risk of sexual abuse, but boys may be less likely to report because of the shame of being a victim and concerns about being labeled homosexual.

a. Proving the Case

Even in a civil case (where the burden of proof is lower than the criminal beyond-a-reasonable-doubt standard), child sexual abuse is often difficult to prove because of a lack of physical evidence or of adult witnesses other than the perpetrator (or at least none willing to testify). Requiring a child to testify can be very traumatic, even if the court permits the state to use a child witness protection statute (described in chapter 5). Some jurisdictions have amended their evidence rules to facilitate the use of a child's out-of-court statements because the child victim called to testify might be unwilling to give accurate information, might not be found competent, or might make a poor witness.

In New York, for example, the child victim's unsworn out-of-court statements, if corroborated, will support an abuse or neglect finding. In In re Nicole V. (N.Y.1987), the court held that corroboration may include any other evidence tending to support the statements' reliability, such as proof that the parent abused another child; that the injuries were of the type that would not ordinarily be sustained but for the parent's acts or omissions; or that the parent abuses drugs or alcohol sufficiently to create a stupor, unconsciousness, intoxication, halluci-nation, disorientation, incompetence or irrationality. Also sufficient corroboration would be hospital or agency reports suggesting the parent committed the act or omission, or evidence regarding the parent's emotional health, admissions by the parent even if later recanted, evidence that the child was afflicted with a sexually transmitted disease or evidence that the child had become pregnant.

Corroboration can also include expert testimony on the characteristics of sexually abused children. Nicole V.'s therapist testified that among the symptoms manifested by children who are sexually abused in an intrafamilial setting are age-inappropriate knowledge of sexual behavior that is manifested verbally, in play activities, or through drawings; enuresis in a toilet trained child; regressive behavior and withdrawal; and severe temper tantrums or depression inappropriate for children of their age. Chapter 5 discusses the child sexual abuse accommodation syndrome's role in criminal trials.

In the end, evidentiary difficulties may lead the juvenile court to base its decision on other grounds, such as parental unfitness, even when evidence of sexual abuse exists. See, e.g., Adoption of Quentin (Mass.1997).

b. Repressed Memories of Sexual Abuse
In the past decade or so, numerous adults have alleged that they were sexually abused as children years earlier, but that they had repressed memories of the abuse and had recalled it only

shortly before filing suit. These claims of childhood sexual abuse present particularly vexing statute of limitations issues. Typically the claims (for such torts as assault, battery, or negligent or intentional infliction of emotional distress) carry limitations periods ranging from only one to three years. Facing dismissal for untimeliness, some plaintiffs have sought to invoke provisions which toll the statute of limitations while a would-be plaintiff suffers from mental disability that deprives him of capacity to sue. Other plaintiffs have sought to invoke discovery rules, which would postpone commencement of the limitations period until the plaintiff discovered, or should reasonably have discovered, the abuse, the injury, or the causal relationship between them. In the absence of a statute specifically tolling or postponing commencement of the limitations period for claims alleging repressed memories of childhood sexual abuse, plaintiffs have met with mixed results in the courts.

California's attempt to statutorily authorize prosecution by enacting a new statute of limitations where the prior limitations period had expired was held to violate the Ex Post Facto Clause. The statute required that prosecution be begun within one year of the victim's report to the police. In Stogner v. California, the Supreme Court held that "a law enacted after expiration of a previously applicable limitations period violates the *Ex Post Facto* Clause when it is applied to revive a previously time-barred prosecution." (S.Ct. 2003) (four justices dissented).

The scientific community remains divided on the questions whether memories can truly be repressed and, if so, whether repressed memories are likely to be accurate in suits alleging childhood sexual abuse that occurred years or decades earlier. Nevertheless about half the states have enacted discovery statutes that permit plaintiffs to allege such abuse within a specified period after recalling the abuse or the injury, regardless of the time that has passed since the abusive acts themselves. Suits filed decades after the alleged acts may thus be timely. After *Stogner* these statutes might be suspect if they are applied to revive a prosecution that had been time barred.

To complicate matters further, some states with discovery statutes also have general statutes of repose, which establish an outer limit on the time within which suits may be brought even under a discovery provision. The question may arise whether these general repose provisions affect the operation of specific discovery statutes relating to alleged childhood sexual abuse.

6.   NEWBORNS WITH A POSITIVE TOXICOLOGY

Babies are more likely to be born healthy if their mothers have prenatal medical care, receive good nutrition, and abstain from alcohol, tobacco, and controlled substances such as cocaine. As discussed in section B of this chapter, reporting statutes require medical personnel to report suspected abuse or neglect. Several states also require health professionals attending the birth of a child to report positive toxicology tests results on the newborn to child welfare agencies. See, e.g., Okla. Stat. Ann. tit. 10, § 7103 ("alcohol or a controlled dangerous substance").

In the child abuse and neglect context, much attention has focused on pregnant women's use of illegal drugs. Some states explicitly define neglect to include prenatal exposure to a controlled substance, but not alcohol and tobacco, even though alcohol and tobacco may be as harmful as a controlled substance. Minnesota, for example, provides that "[n]eglect includes prenatal exposure to a controlled substance ... used by the mother for a nonmedical purpose, as evidenced by withdrawal symptoms in the child at birth, results of a toxicology test performed on the mother at delivery

or the child at birth, or medical effects or
developmental delays during the child's first year
of life that medically indicate prenatal exposure to
a controlled substance." Minn. Stat. §
626.556(2)(c). In other states, however, a positive
toxicology for a controlled substance alone does not
prove abuse because it fails to establish that the
infant will be at substantial risk; a positive
toxicology report in conjunction with other
evidence, however, may support a neglect finding.
See, e.g., In re Dante M. (N.Y.1995)

Even when a positive toxicology is coupled
with a neglect finding, the mother may be allowed
to take the child home from the hospital because
the dispositive question is whether the mother can
care for the child. See, e.g., In re Dante M. (child
allowed to be home with supervision); In re J.W.
(Ill.App.Ct.1997) (mother's alcohol abuse, coupled
with her lack of permanent housing or a telephone,
made it unlikely that she could provide the special
medical care the child needed).

The issue of whether the child protection
system should regulate the conduct of pregnant
women has grown in importance in the past
decade, particularly in response to the nationwide
crack cocaine epidemic. The National Institute on
Drug Abuse estimates that 45,000 mothers inhaled

or ingested cocaine at least once during pregnancy in 1994, 35,000 smoked crack, 757,000 drank alcohol, and 320,000 smoked tobacco. 15 Harvard Mental Health Letter, Cocaine Before Birth (Dec. 1, 1998). Debate continues about whether drug-using pregnant women should face criminal prosecution or be committed civilly for treatment. Many medical associations oppose prosecution of mothers who deliver babies harmed by substance abuse during pregnancy, concerned that the threat of prosecution would deter many expectant mothers from seeking drug treatment and general prenatal care. Some states have recently enacted statutes that would allow confinement of drug-using mothers to treatment centers. Wis. Stat. Ann. § 48.133 (alcohol and controlled substances, but not tobacco).

Nationwide, prosecutions under endanger-ment and abuse statutes have generally failed because courts have held that a fetus is not a "child" within the meaning of these statutes, or that prosecution for prenatal substance abuse was outside legislative intent. See, e.g., State ex rel. Angela M.W. v. Kruzicki (Wis.1997); but see Whitner v. State (S.C.1997) (criminal child neglect statute reached pregnant defendant's use of crack cocaine after the fetus was viable). Prosecutions have also failed under statutes proscribing distribution or delivery of drugs to a child. See, e.g., State v. Luster (Ga.Ct.App.1992). Courts have also rebuffed prosecutions grounded in the theory that the mother passed the drugs not to the fetus, but to the child during the brief moment when the child left the womb before severance of the umbilical cord. See, e.g., Johnson v. State (Fla. 1992).

Perhaps because of reliance on statutory interpretation, most courts have not wrestled with constitutional questions of whether prosecution of addicted mothers would violate their equal protection, procedural due process, or substantive due process privacy rights or whether prosecution would constitute cruel and unusual punishment. In Ferguson v. City of Charleston (S.Ct.2001), however, the Court held that the defendant state hospital violated the Fourth Amendment by performing diagnostic urine tests on pregnant women without their informed consent, and then providing positive test results to police for possible prosecution for cocaine use. The Court concluded that the interest in threatening criminal sanctions to deter pregnant women from using cocaine did not justify departure from the general rule that an official nonconsensual search violates the Amendment if not authorized by a valid warrant.

E. RESPONSIBILITIES OF CHILD PROTECTIVE SERVICES

1. NO DUTY TO INTERVENE

In DeShaney v. Winnebago County Department of Social Services (S.Ct.1989), the Supreme Court held that due process does not impose an affirmative obligation on states to protect persons, including children, from harm. The *DeShaney* plaintiffs were a mother and her son, Joshua, a four-year-old who had been beaten and permanently injured by his father, with whom he had lived. The defendants were social workers and local officials who had received reports that the boy was being abused and had reason to believe the reports were true, but did not remove him from his father's custody. In January 1982, the Department of Social Services (DSS) investigated the complaints Joshua's stepmother made to police and concluded that no action was needed. A year later, DSS obtained a court order placing Joshua in the temporary custody of a hospital that had reported the boy as abused. The case was dismissed and Joshua was returned to his father, who had agreed to certain DSS requirements. DSS assigned a caseworker to make monthly visits to Joshua's home and received two more hospital reports of abuse. The agency also received police reports of abuse from neighbors. The caseworker visited the home almost twenty times, recorded incidents of abuse, but did nothing more.

In affirming summary judgment for the defendants in the § 1983 action, the Court held that due process limits the state's power to act, but does not guarantee persons minimal levels of safety and security against the violence or other conduct of private actors. Nor does due process confer an affirmative right to governmental aid, even where such aid may be necessary to secure life, liberty or property interests.

The Court also rejected the plaintiffs' argument that a "special relationship" existed between the state and Joshua, because the state had undertaken to protect him from harm. The injuries inflicted upon Joshua occurred not while he was in state custody, but while he was in the custody of his father, who was not a state actor. According to the Court, by returning the child to his father's custody, the state placed him in a situation that was no worse than if the state had not acted at all.

After *DeShaney*, children harmed by state failures have only limited remedies. The Supreme

Court decision itself illustrates the limits on § 1983 claims for children who are not in state care. Chapter 4 discusses state liability for children harmed while in foster care, and efforts at systemic reform through class actions.

2. TORT LIABILITY

DeShaney itself did not foreclose state tort remedies, but barriers exist even in states that do not invoke sovereign immunity to preclude tort recovery. In Boland v. State (N.Y.App.Div.1996) for example, a child died from a beating before the agency received and investigated a misrouted hotline telephone report. The court held that the claimant father had demonstrated a special relationship between the child and the state because the "detailed and comprehensive statutory scheme at issue ... was designed to protect a discrete and limited class of individuals," namely abused children. The court also held that the father had demonstrated that the state officer negligently failed to perform a ministerial act— routing the hotline call to the correct child protective office.

The father lost, however, because he failed to establish proximate causation. The court required proof that "had the hotline report been correctly routed in the first instance, a timely investigation would have ensued, with the investigator assigned to the case interviewing the stepmother and the children prior to the infliction of [the victim's] fatal injuries and, based upon such interview, concluding that the stepmother posed such an imminent danger to the children's health that they would have been summarily removed from the home." Boland v. State (N.Y.App.Div. 1999).

3. SYSTEMIC PROBLEMS

Unfortunately the lack of intervention that resulted in Joshua DeShaney's injuries is all too likely to happen again. A 1997 U.S. General Accounting Office study of selected child protective services offices found that "[i]ncreases in the number of maltreatment cases, the changing nature of family problems, and long-standing systemic weaknesses have placed the CPS [Child Protective Services] system in a state of crisis and undermined its ability to fully carry out the responsibilities for abused and neglected children." The report pinpointed three chronic problems: "First, child maltreatment reports have risen steadily across the country. The caseloads of CPS units have grown correspondingly, and CPS units often cannot keep pace with this workload. Second, these caseloads are increasingly composed of families whose problems have grown more troubling and complicated, with substance abuse a common and pervasive condition. Finally, systemic weaknesses — such as difficulty maintaining a professional and skilled workforce, inconsistently implementing policies and procedures, a lack of automated case management in recordkeeping systems, and poor working relationships between CPS and the courts — have further weakened CPS units."

The GAO report concluded that "[t]he combined effect of difficult caseloads and systemic weaknesses (1) overburdens caseworkers and dilutes the quality of their response to families and (2) may further endanger the lives of children coming to the attention of CPS." United States General Accounting Office, Child Protective Services: Complex Challenges Require New Strategies __(1997).

4. WRONGFUL REMOVAL

DeShaney stemmed from failure to remove the child from the parent, but children can also suffer harm from unnecessary or improper removal. Nonetheless, it has been held that parents cannot maintain a § 1983 cause of action

against caseworkers or the department of social
services attorney for bringing a dependency action
that resulted in a wrongful removal. In Ernst v.
Child and Youth Services (3d Cir. 1997), for
example, the court conferred absolute immunity on
child welfare workers acting in a quasi-
prosecutorial capacity in dependency proceedings.
"Like a prosecutor, a child welfare worker must
exercise independent judgment in deciding
whether or not to bring a child dependency
proceeding, and such judgment would likely be
compromised if the worker faced the threat of
personal liability for every mistake in judgment.
Certainly, we want our child welfare workers to
exercise care in deciding to interfere in parent-
child relationships. But we do not want them to be
so overly cautious, out of fear of personal liability,
that they fail to intervene in situations in which
children are in danger."

When a caseworker removes a child from
his or her parents on an emergency basis without a
court order, the caseworker has qualified
immunity and is protected from liability, provided
an objectively reasonable basis existed for the
removal decision.

F. THE REASONABLE EFFORTS REQUIREMENT

During some periods of our history, removing abused or neglected children from their parents was considered the best approach to child protection. Placing the children in institutions or with other families was considered sounder policy than trying to rehabilitate the parents. In other periods, however, removal was considered less desirable because of concerns about family integrity and the harm caused to children by removal and extended foster care placement. After years of debate on these issues and documentation of children harmed by removal, Congress passed the Adoption Assistance and Child Welfare Act of 1980 (AACWA). The Act was intended to require states to keep abused or neglected children in their own homes when possible, and to require states to move aggressively to reunite the family when removal was necessary. If reunification was not possible within a reasonable time, the child would be placed for adoption. AACWA makes eligibility for specified federal funding contingent on a state's agreement, before placing a child in foster care, to make reasonable efforts "to prevent or eliminate the need for removal of the child from his home, and ... to make it possible for the child to return to his home." 42 U.S.C. § 671(a)(15).

By 1997, however, Congress had become concerned that the states were making too much, rather than too little, effort to reunite families of abused and neglected children. The Adoption and Safe Families Act of 1997 (ASFA) requires states to meet stringent time requirements for terminating parental rights when children cannot be returned home. The Act also specifies that in some cases, states are not required to make reasonable efforts to reunite families before moving to terminate parental rights. Reasonable efforts are not required when the parent has subjected the child to aggravated circumstances such as abandonment, torture, chronic abuse, or sexual abuse; when parental rights of the parent to a sibling have been terminated; or when the parent has: "(I) committed murder ... of another child of the parent; (II) committed voluntary manslaughter ... of another child of the parent; (III) aided or abetted, attempted, conspired, or solicited to commit such a murder or such a voluntary manslaughter; or (IV) committed a felony assault that results in serious bodily injury to the child or another child of the parent." 42 U.S.C. § 671(a)(15(D).

Some critics charge that despite the reasonable efforts requirement, states often do not provide adequate services to parents of abused or neglected children. Because of funding limitations, the services offered may not be appropriate to the parents' needs or may not continue for a sufficient time. Disagreement also persists concerning the proper division of responsibility between the child protective system and the welfare system; and between parents and the state. Homelessness, for example, is a significant factor in foster care placements. Some state courts have held that the social services agency can be ordered to provide housing as part of a reasonable efforts requirement when family reunification cannot otherwise be achieved because of the family's homelessness. In In re Nicole G. (R.I.1990), for example, the court rejected the agency's arguments that the "[l]egislature did not create or envision it as a housing or income-maintenance agency," and "that if the court may order it to make rental-subsidy payments, critical moneys and energies will be diverted from its primary mission of preserving and reunifying families."

But the reasonable efforts requirement has also been interpreted to allow removal of a child because the home was filthy, without requiring the state to provide a cleaning service that would be substantially less expensive than foster care. In In re N.M.W. (Iowa Ct.App.1990), for example, the court found that the chronic unsanitary conditions of the mother's apartment were sufficient basis for a neglect adjudication because they presented health hazards, especially animal feces scattered throughout the living area. Even in the absence of actual harm, the court permitted the agency to remove the child as a preventive measure. The mother was told she could regain custody of the child when she removed the pets and cleaned the apartment, but she did neither.

G. TERMINATION OF PARENTAL RIGHTS

When the state's efforts to keep a family together fail, the state may move to terminate parental rights, typically to free the child for permanent placement, with adoption usually preferred. Termination generally severs all parent-child ties permanently, particularly when the child is being freed for adoption by strangers. After termination, for example, the parent usually becomes a legal stranger to the child so the child has no right to support or inheritance from the parent, and the parent has no right to see the child or know where the child goes.

Because termination is such a drastic remedy (sometimes called the "death sentence" of abuse and neglect law), the Supreme Court has been sympathetic to parents' arguments that termination proceedings should carry greater due process protections than the usual civil case. Making termination of parental rights more difficult, however, is not necessarily in the best interests of abused and neglected children, who may end up consigned to a series of foster homes, unable to return to the abusive or neglectful home but also not free for adoption. This section concerns parents' due process protections and then examines some grounds for termination not seen in the decisions discussed earlier in this chapter. Chapters 4 and 6 will examine what happens to children in foster care and adoption, respectively, after removal from their parents.

1.   DUE PROCESS PROTECTIONS FOR PARENTS

In Lassiter v. Department of Social Services (S.Ct.1981), the Court held, in a 5-4 vote, that due process does not require appointment of counsel for indigent parents in all termination proceedings, but rather permits the trial court to determine the need for appointment on a case by case basis. *Lassiter* determined the due process claim by applying the three factors identified in Matthews v. Eldridge (S.Ct.1976): "the private interests at stake, the government's interest, and the risk that the procedures used will lead to erroneous decisions." "A parent's desire for and right to the 'companionship, care, custody and management of his or her children'," *Lassiter* began, "is an important interest that 'undeniably warrants deference and, absent a powerful countervailing interest, protection.'" The indigent parent's interest was not strong enough to prevail in all circumstances, however, against "the presumption that there is no right to appointed counsel in the absence of at least a potential deprivation of physical liberty." *Lassiter's* slim majority concluded that due process would require appointment of counsel when "the parent's interests were at their strongest, the State's interests were at their weakest, and the risks of error were at their peak," but not in all cases.

A year after *Lassiter,* Santosky v. Kramer (S.Ct.1982) held that due process permits a state to terminate parental rights only where a ground for termination is established by at least clear and convincing evidence, a standard of proof higher than the ordinary civil preponderance of the evidence standard. *Santosky* held that the clear-and-convincing standard is appropriate where the individual interests at stake are "particularly important" and "more substantial than mere loss of money." Applying the *Eldridge* factors in the context of termination dispositions, the Court found the parental interest commanding, the risk of error from using a preponderance standard substantial, and the countervailing governmental interest favoring that standard comparatively slight. (The Indian Child Welfare Act requires proof beyond a reasonable doubt; see chapter 4, section G.1.)

In M.L.B. v. S.L.J. (S.Ct.1996), the Court held that due process and equal protection prohibit a state from conditioning appeals from termination orders on the parent's ability to pay record preparation fees. *M.L.B.* stressed the importance of family life and the "unique kind of deprivation" worked by termination orders: "Choices about marriage, family life, and the upbringing of children are among associational rights this Court has ranked as 'of basic importance in our society,' rights sheltered by the Fourteenth Amendment against the State's unwarranted usurpation, disregard, or disrespect. ... In contrast to matters modifiable at the parties' will or based on changed circumstances, termination adjudications involve the awesome authority of the State 'to destroy permanently all legal recognition of the parental relationship.'"

2.   GROUNDS FOR TERMINATION

In a termination of parental rights proceeding, the state typically must establish (by at least the clear and convincing evidence mandated by *Santosky*) one or more statutory grounds for termination and that termination is in the child's best interests. Abuse and neglect were discussed earlier in this chapter. This section discusses additional grounds for termination.

a.   Out-of-Home Placement

Where (as in *Santosky*) a child has been in foster care for a period of time, the state may move to terminate on the ground that the parents have failed to take corrective actions necessary to allow the child to return home safely within a reasonable time. To overcome the parents' constitutional objections, the state must show that it clearly articulated to them the requirements for return of custody. In addition, the state may need to prove affirmatively that it made reasonable efforts to reunite the family by helping the parents meet the requirements. In termination proceedings asserting this ground, the underlying basis for the initial removal is not at issue. The dispositive

issues are the time in foster care and whether the
parents have complied with the state's
requirements.

b. Parental Absence

The court may terminate parental rights
when a parent totally abandons a child, or makes
only token efforts to visit and communicate with
the child while routinely failing to pay child
support. Parental absence constitutes abandonment only when the parent abandoned the child
intentionally and without just cause. The following
two decisions illustrate these distinctions. In In re
M.J.A.   (Mo.Ct.App.1992),   the   court   found
abandonment by the mother who, in difficult
financial straits, left the children with the
maternal grandmother, said the children would be
better off with the grandmother, did not indicate
whether or when she would return for them, and
did not say where she was going. The mother
signed a statement purporting to give the children
to the grandmother for adoption, and to leave her
with full responsibility for them. The mother did
not contact the children afterwards and failed to
provide them financial support while they were in
the grandmother's custody, even though the
mother was employed for part of the time in
question.

In In re Ayres (Mo.Ct.App.1974), however, the court reversed a neglect finding against a mother who fled the family home because her husband had savagely beaten her. A nine-month-old daughter was placed with friend of the family, with whom the girl remained for about eight years. During this period, the mother visited the child as often as she could. The court held that "when tragedy strikes and the parents are beleaguered by problems beyond their control ... a placement with a more fortunate relative or concerned friend would appear to be the best thing reasonable, concerned, caring parents could do for their children."

A parent's long-term incarceration may establish abandonment by leaving the parent unable to support or maintain contact with a child. Incarceration per se may not be a basis for termination, but imprisonment can be a factor the court considers. In Vance v. Lincoln County Department of Public Welfare (Miss.1991), for example, the court upheld termination of the parental rights of a mother who had concurrent sentences of fifty and thirty years for murder and armed robbery. Mississippi law permits termination of parental rights based on a "substantial erosion of the relationship between the parent and child which was caused at least in

part by the parent's ... prolonged imprisonment." If
the incarcerated parent can afford private care or
has relatives who can care for the child, however, a
state might have no interest in or grounds for
termination.

c. Abuse of a Sibling

As mentioned earlier, some parents abuse
the "target child," while leaving other children in
the household unharmed. Abuse of a sibling,
however, is considered probative of how the
parents might treat the other children in the
future. The abuse of one child is considered a high
risk factor, indicative of a dangerous environment
and likelihood of abuse of other children. In
extreme cases, the court may terminate parental
rights to a child based entirely on proof of abuse of
a sibling, even where no evidence is adduced
concerning injury to the child and where all
evidence concerns the sibling.

d. Mental Retardation, Mental Illness, or Immaturity

A parent's mental incapacity is not
typically a per se basis for termination, but also
does not justify a lesser level of care by the parent.
Courts focus on the child and on the parent's
ability to care for the child, rather than on the
parent's disability. The Americans With

Disabilities Act, 42 U.S.C. §§ 12131-12134, does not provide the parent a defense against conduct that would otherwise justify termination because termination proceedings are not "services, programs or activities" within the meaning of the Act. In In re B.S. (Vt.1997), for example, the court found the Act inapplicable, but held that even if the Act did apply, the mother had suffered no discrimination because state law did not make mental retardation, by itself, a ground for termination. A mentally retarded parent, the court continued, could meet the four criteria for determining the best interests of the child under the termination statute: "(1) the interaction and interrelationship of the child with the child's natural parents, foster parents, siblings, and others who may significantly affect the child's best interests, (2) the child's adjustment to home and community, (3) the likelihood the natural parent will be able to resume parental duties within a reasonable period of time, and (4) whether the natural parent has played and continues to play a constructive role in the child's welfare."

Because the touchstone is the best interests of the child, courts have similarly held that a parent cannot invoke his or her own adolescence to avoid a ground for termination otherwise established. In In re McCrary (Ohio

Ct.App.1991), for example, the court held that a maximum two-year time limit on reunification efforts did not violate the due process rights of the minor, who had given birth when she was fifteen. The mother urged that because minor parents often lack the social and emotional maturity necessary to rear a child, the limit should not begin to run until she turned eighteen and thus reached majority. The court of appeals concluded that allowing the child "at such a developmentally critical stage of its life to languish in a state of temporary custodianship ... is simply unacceptable."

e. Presumptive Grounds for Termination

ASFA requires states to initiate termination of parental rights proceedings and proceed to adoption in some cases marked by severe parental misconduct or the passage of time. The requirement applies "in the case of a child who has been in foster care under the responsibility of the State for fifteen of the most recent twenty-two months, or, if a court of competent jurisdiction has determined a child to be an abandoned infant (as defined under State law) or has made a determination that the parent has committed murder of another child of the parent, committed voluntary manslaughter of another child of the parent, aided or abetted, attempted, conspired, or solicited to commit such a murder or such a voluntary manslaughter, or committed a felony assault that has resulted in serious bodily injury to the child or to another child of the parent...."

The Act's requirements do not apply where the child is being cared for by a relative, where the state documents a compelling reason why termination would not be in the best interests of the child, or where the state has not yet provided the family reasonable services necessary for safe return of the child to the home.

Some state termination statutes create rebuttable presumptions that termination is in the child's best interests for serious parental misconduct that exceeds the ASFA requirements. Such misconduct includes causing the child to be conceived as a result of rape, incest, lewd conduct with a child under sixteen, or sexual abuse of a child under sixteen; murdering or intentionally killing the child's other parent, or being incarcerated with no possibility of parole. See, e.g., Idaho Code § 16-2005.

H. THE ROLE OF THE CHILD'S ATTORNEY

The Supreme Court has not extended the constitutional right to counsel to children in protection proceedings, and only a few states have conferred such a constitutional right. Virtually all states, however, have statutes requiring appointment of a representative for the child, who may be designated an attorney for the child, a guardian ad litem, a law guardian, or some other title. CAPTA conditioned eligibility for specified federal funding on a state's providing a guardian ad litem "in every case involving an abused or neglected child which results in a judicial proceeding." 42 U.S.C. § 5106a. CAPTA does not require that the guardian ad litem be an attorney and has been amended to specifically allow lay persons to be guardians ad litem. Some states use trained lay volunteers, rather than attorneys, to represent children in abuse and neglect cases. These volunteers are frequently called Court Appointed Special Advocates, or CASAs. CASA volunteers are used in a variety of models of representation; they may proceed independently, provide assistance to attorneys, or serve in addition to attorneys, sometimes with separate counsel to advocate their position in court.

In states that use attorneys as representatives, the role of the child's attorney is often ambiguous. Some lawyers pay little or no attention to their child client, believing they should advocate for what they believe is best for the child. Other attorneys believe they should advocate for what the child client wants and, as much as possible, try to advise and confer with the child as if he or she were an adult. Some jurisdictions expect the attorney to fulfill both roles. Underlying this ambiguity is concern about the child client's capacity, frequently coupled with a lack of clarity about the purpose of representation in a particular case.

This ambiguity is not resolved by the major model professional codes, the American Bar Association Model Rules of Professional Conduct and its predecessor, the Model Code of Professional Responsibility. The Model Rules, for example, provide that "when a client's ability to make adequately considered decisions in connection with the representation is impaired, whether because of minority, mental disability, or for some other reason, the lawyer shall, as far as reasonably possible, maintain a normal client-lawyer relationship with the client." Rule 1.14(a). The Rules are silent, however, about what standard should be used to judge the client's decision-making abilities.

Studies of representation of children in abuse and neglect cases have reported that the quality of representation is often low. In an effort to improve quality, in 1996 the ABA adopted Standards of Practice for Lawyers Who Represent Children in Abuse and Neglect Cases, which appear at http://www.abanet.org/child/childrep.html.

1. MALPRACTICE

If the child's representative assumes a traditional attorney's role, the usual malpractice standards should apply. See, e.g., Marquez v. Presbyterian Hospital (N.Y.1994). If the attorney assumes a guardian ad litem role, however, the attorney may qualify for the quasi-judicial immunity that most courts have conferred on these representatives: "A guardian ad litem serves to provide the court with independent information regarding the placement or disposition that is in the best interests of the child. This independent determination is crucial to the court's decision. The threat of civil liability would seriously impair the ability of the guardian ad litem to independently investigate the facts and to report his or her findings to the court. As a result, the ability of the judge to perform his or her judicial duties would be impaired and the ascertainment of truth obstructed." Ward v. San Diego County Department of Social Services (S.D.Cal.1988)

2.   ROLE AT TRIAL AND CONFIDENTIALITY

Because of ambiguity about the attorney's role, it may be unclear whether the child's attorney may or must testify, or whether attorney-child communications are confidential. In some jurisdictions, the child's representative can be cross-examined if his or her recommendations are based on an independent investigation that includes facts that have not been made part of the evidence. If the recommendations are based on evidence that has been presented to the court, however, cross-examination is not permitted because the recommendations are analogous to counsel's arguments on how the evidence should be viewed. See, e.g., In re J.E.B. (Colo.Ct.App.1993).

If the representative does testify, some courts protect the attorney-client privilege. See, e.g., Nicewicz v. Nicewicz (Ohio Ct.App.1995) (guardian ad litem, who was an attorney, allowed to testify about conclusions and recommendations, but asserted the privilege concerning confidential communications with the child); In re Order Compelling Production of Records of Maraziti (N.J.App.Div.1989)(communication between attorney and daughters of the defendant were protected by attorney-client privilege). Other courts, however, do not protect the privilege. See, e.g., Deasy-Leas v. Leas (Ind.Ct.App.1998) (no specific statutory privilege protects communications between a guardian ad litem and her client in a custody case, and the attorney-client privilege does not apply; a court may limit discovery in its discretion, however, based on the child's best interests); Ross v. Gadwah (N.H.1989) (privilege does not apply to guardian ad litem, even when the guardian is an attorney).

CHAPTER 4

FOSTER CARE

A. INTRODUCTION

When children who have been abused or neglected by their parents cannot remain at home safely, they may be placed in government sponsored foster care. The foster placement is intended to be temporary, with the children soon being returned to their parents or, if return is not possible, placed for adoption or in some other permanent arrangement. "Foster care" includes placement in private homes licensed and supervised by the state, group homes or institutions. If the child is placed with relatives rather than strangers, the foster care may be called kinship care, or kinship foster care.

Foster care remains a valuable resource for providing homes for children, but child welfare professionals generally agree that long-term foster care is not a good placement option because of its impermanence. Many children, however, suffer multiple placements over a lengthy period, sometimes characterized as foster care drift or limbo. The cost of foster care is also an incentive for reducing foster care stays. Federal foster care payments increased from $435.7 million in 1984 to $3.1 billion in 1996, with over $5 billion appropriated for 2001.

Successful family reunification is often difficult, because many foster children and the families that produced them suffer from complex and intractable problems. The children may have profound physical health, mental health, and educational needs. Their families may be debilitated by poverty, substance abuse, homelessness, incarceration, or physical or mental illness.

Major federal and state efforts to reduce the number of children in foster care and length of stays have met with only limited success. In September 2001, an estimated 542,000 children were in foster care nationwide. Twenty-four percent of these children were in kinship care and 48 percent were in foster care with non-relatives. Eighteen percent were in institutions or group homes. Only four percent were in pre-adoptive homes. Two percent were runaways. The remaining children were in a variety of other placements. The median age of the children in foster care was 10.6; four percent were under one year.

B. FOSTER CARE STRUCTURE

The rights and responsibilities of children, parents, foster parents and the government are complex. A child can enter care because parents have voluntarily relinquished custody to a state agency such as child protective services, or because a court has ordered the child's removal from the parents' care. In either event, the state agency then usually has custody, but parents generally retain the right to make significant decisions about the child such as major medical care or adoption decisions. The state agency typically delegates some of its custodial responsibilities to the foster care placement, thus splitting the responsibilities for the child three ways — with the agency, the parents, and the foster placement.

The foster placement–state relationship generally would be regulated by a combination of state law, agency rules, and contract. A contract with a foster parent might detail the foster parent's responsibilities and the decisions the foster parent can make, which usually would include day-to-day decisions about the child's food, clothing, homework and similar matters. The state is expected to monitor the placement to assure that the child is safe and receiving education and other services. Parents are responsible for complying with the state's plan for regaining custody of their children and usually would have visitation with the child. Once placed in state custody, the child may be moved through multiple foster placements or institutions or may stay with one set of foster parents for a substantial time. In some states, children may be provided with an attorney or guardian ad litem for court hearings regarding placement, but the ambiguity of the attorney's role (discussed in chapter 3) and counsel's inadequacies may leave the child's voice unheard.

C. PERMANENCY PLANNING

The Adoption Assistance and Child Welfare Act of 1980 (AACWA) requires states to make reasonable efforts to reunite foster children with their families, except where reasonable efforts are not required because of concerns about the child's safety. The exceptions are detailed in the Adoption and Safe Families Act (AFSA), which is discussed in chapter 3, Section F. If reunification is not possible, generally the state would decide to terminate parental rights and place the child for adoption, because long-term foster care and guardianship are considered less desirable placements.

To reduce the time children remain in foster care, ASFA imposes time limits on the states to expedite permanent placement decision-making. Within twelve months of when the child "is considered to have entered foster care," the court must hold a permanency hearing to determine the placement plan for the child, which may be family reunification, adoptive placement or some other goal. (The child is "considered to have entered foster care" on the earlier of the date of the first judicial finding of abuse or neglect or the date that is sixty days after the child was removed from home.) ASFA also permits states to use "concurrent planning," which allows the state agencies to work toward family reunification while simultaneously planning for adoption if reunification fails. Concurrent planning is intended to reduce the delay that would be caused by a failed family reunification effort. To further insure permanency, ASFA requires states to initiate termination of parental rights proceedings for a child who has been in foster care for fifteen of the most recent twenty-two months, with some exceptions. For example, a state may choose not to terminate parental rights when the child is in kinship foster care.

Courts are expected to take an active enforcement role in the permanency planning process. Even when there is no adjudication of neglect, abuse, or abandonment because a parent placed the child in foster care voluntarily, the court holds planning and review hearings. As noted above, permanency hearings and termination of parental rights proceedings are required within certain time limits. The court is expected to determine whether the state is making reasonable efforts to reunify the family, whether the family is complying with the state's requirements to allow the child to return home safely and other issues.

The federal permanency planning model has been criticized for exaggerating the harms caused by foster care and for other reasons as well. Successful reunification often requires extensive, long-term services and when these are not provided the child is at risk and may end up being harmed at home or returned to foster care. Critics also note that termination of parental rights may harm children by depriving them of contact with their parents, and that many children "freed" for adoption are never placed successfully in adoptive homes. See e.g., Marsha Garrison, Parents' Rights vs. Children's Interests: The Case of the Foster Child, 22 N. Y. Rev. L. & Soc. Change 371 (1996). Chapter 6 discusses the hurdles that impede efforts to place such "special needs" children for adoption and reasons why many remain in state care even after termination of parental rights.

Another concern, particularly directed at the ASFA time limits, is related to the disproportionate percentage of minority children in foster care, compared to their percentage of the general population. In 2001, the race/ethnicity of children in foster care was: Black Non-Hispanic, 38 percent; Hispanic, 17 percent; and White Non-Hispanic 37 percent. (The remaining percentages include unknown and other racial/ethnic groups.) Critics of ASFA policies have expressed concern that by moving black children into white homes through termination of parental rights and adoption, ASFA responds to two problems, namely the large number of children in foster care and the need of childless white couples for adoptive children. See Dorothy E. Roberts, Is There Justice in Children's Rights?: The Critique of Federal Family Preservation Policy, 2 U. Penn. J. Const. L. 112 (1999).

D. THE FOSTER CHILD'S RIGHT TO A "FAMILY"

As mentioned above, foster care is intended to be a temporary placement for children until they can be returned home safely or moved to a permanent placement such as an adoptive home. Unfortunately, a number of children remain in foster care so long that they develop emotional ties to their foster family. These ties may disserve the state's goals by making it difficult to return the child home or to place the child for adoption.

In Smith v. Organization of Foster Families for Equality and Reform [OFFER] (S. Ct.1977), foster parents and OFFER brought a § 1983 class action on their own behalf and on behalf of children for whom they had provided homes for a year or more. The suit alleged that the procedures governing removal of children from foster homes violated due process and equal protection. The District Court appointed independent counsel for the foster children, and permitted intervention by a group of mothers who had voluntarily placed their children in foster care.

OFFER considered the divergent views of the foster care system presented by the disputants – the state, parents, foster parents, and children. The state argued that because foster care was a temporary, short-term placement after which children are returned to their parents or freed for adoption, foster parents did not need extensive due process protections before the agency removed a foster child to another placement. The parents, however, characterized foster care as an intrusive intervention into the lives of poor parents who have no alternative to such care in a crisis and who may be coerced into placing their children "voluntarily" in state care. The parents were concerned that enhanced protections for foster parents might make it more difficult for them to regain custody of their children.

The foster parents viewed foster care as far from temporary, alleging that many children were placed in foster care for extended periods and developed close ties with their foster families. The foster parents argued that arbitrary state removal of children from one foster home to another did not respect these ties, particularly because, in their view, foster children were seldom removed for adoptive placement. The foster parents further argued that during a lengthy foster placement, the foster family becomes the child's "psychological family," with a due process liberty interest in remaining intact that guaranteed the foster parents a hearing before removal of the child.

OFFER provided limited recognition of the foster parents' claims, stating that the foster family could not be dismissed "as a mere collection of unrelated individuals." Any liberty interest held by the foster families, however, depended on state law because it arose only from the contract the foster parents signed with the state when they assumed temporary custody of the child. The Court found that "the limited recognition accorded to the

foster family by the New York statutes and the
contracts executed by the foster parents argue
against any but the most limited constitutional
'liberty' in the foster family," and that the state
and city procedures provided sufficient due process
protection. (Foster parents were provided a post-
removal hearing.)

The Court also noted that any liberty
interest held by the foster parents would be
entitled to significantly less weight when removal
was to return the child to the natural parents
rather than to place the child in another foster
home: "It is one thing to say that individuals may
acquire a liberty interest against arbitrary
governmental interference in the family-like
associations into which they have freely entered,
even in the absence of biological connection or
state-law recognition of the relationship. It is quite
another to say that one may acquire such an
interest in the face of another's constitutionally
recognized liberty interest that derives from blood
relationship, state-law sanction, and basic human
right an interest the foster parent has recognized
by contract from the outset."

Finally *OFFER* refused to recognize a
foster child's right to a hearing because the foster
parents could request one. The Court concluded
that if the foster parents did not request a hearing,

"it is difficult to see what right or interest of the foster child is protected by holding a hearing to determine whether removal would unduly impair his emotional attachments to a foster parent who does not care enough about the child to contest the removal." Ironically, the attorney appointed to represent the seven named children and the class (children who had lived continuously with the same foster parents for more than one year) never met with the named children, but rather advocated for what she determined was best for the class as a whole, based on her experience working with agencies. She took the position that the existing procedural protections were sufficient.

Post-*OFFER* efforts by foster parents and foster children to establish a due process liberty interest in their relationship have generally failed. Because the foster parent–foster child relationship is formed through a contract with the state, courts turn to state law to determine the parties' expectations and entitlements. Generally the state's contractual promises are not sufficiently explicit or binding to establish a liberty interest, even when foster parents had cared for a child for a number of years and expected to adopt the child. See, e.g., Procopio v. Johnson (7th Cir.1993) (foster parents nursed infant through drug withdrawal, cared for her for five years and had been assured by the state that she was adoptable, but foster parents had no § 1983 action when the child was returned to her biological parents).

Some states, however, have permitted foster parents to seek a custody award or guardianship under state law. In Division of Family Services v. Harrison (Del.1999), for example, the foster parents were granted standing to pursue a guardianship action because they had cared for the foster child for most of his life and thus enjoyed "a legally protected interest." The state failed to prove that the child could be safely reunited with his parents and the child was not a "dependent" child. The foster parents established that the guardianship was in the child's best interests.

E. THE FOSTER CHILD'S RIGHT TO SERVICES AND PROTECTION

As DeShaney v. Winnebago County Department of Social Services (S.Ct.1989) made clear, the state has no affirmative constitutional obligation to protect children from abuse by private actors, such as their parents. Through legislation, however, states have assumed affirmative obligations, particularly in response to federal requirements in the Child Abuse Prevention and

Treatment Act (CAPTA), AACWA, ASFA and other child welfare legislation. To receive federal funding, states were required to file plans with the Department of Health and Human Services that detailed how the state would meet federal requirements. To comply with AACWA, for example, the state plan must commit to the "reasonable efforts" requirement, that is, that "in each case, reasonable efforts will be made (A) prior to the placement of a child in foster care, to prevent or eliminate the need for removal of the child from his home, and (B) to make it possible for the child to return to his home."

Many states, however, did not fulfill their plan commitments. Further, the federal government did not actively enforce compliance, and even if it had, the enforcement mechanism was cumbersome and ineffective. Proving non-compliance was difficult because federal authorities determined compliance by relying primarily on the states' own reports. Federal funds to a non-complying state could be reduced or eliminated, but cutting funds was unlikely to improve the quality of services for families because noncompliance was often due to underfunding in the first place.

To secure compliance and improve the child welfare system, a number of class actions against the states have alleged violations of AACWA,

CAPTA and similar legislation. The plaintiffs sought injunctive or declaratory relief to force the states to comply with federal and state requirements. In 1992, however, the Supreme Court decided Suter v. Artist M., a class action based on Illinois' failure to meet AACWA's "reasonable efforts" requirements. The Court held that AACWA imposed only a generalized duty on the state, enforceable through federal action, without authorizing private enforcement.

Suter could have ended these lawsuits, but in 1994 Congress amended federal law to limit the decision to the reasonable efforts provision. See 42 U.S.C. §1302a-10. Under the amendment, whether a private right of action existed under other AACWA provisions or other child welfare legislation would be determined by a pre-*Suter* analysis. After *Suter*, some courts have found private rights of action in federal, as well as state, child welfare law, e.g. Marisol A. v. Giuliani (S.D.N.Y. 1996); other courts have not, e.g., Charlie H. v. Whitman (D.N.J.2000).

As of 1996, twenty-one states had been sued for inadequate child welfare programs. The level of state neglect alleged in these cases is typically horrendous. Consider, for example, the allegations of two of the eleven named plaintiffs in *Marisol A.*

Five-year old Marisol was born two days after her mother, Ms. A., was arrested for dealing drugs. Marisol was placed in foster care, but shortly returned to her mother, despite her mother's criminal history and reports that she was abusing Marisol during visitations. According to the court:

> CWA failed to assess properly the appropriateness of this placement and took no steps to supervise or monitor Ms. A.'s home. Upon regaining custody, Ms. A. confined Marisol to a closet for several months, deprived her of sustenance resulting in her eating her own feces and plastic garbage bags to survive, and both physically and sexually abused her to the point of injury. During this period, Ms. A.'s sister and Ms. C. filed multiple reports of abuse with CWA to no avail. A housing inspector familiar with the signs of abuse discovered Marisol during a chance visit and reported the situation to the police. Despite Ms. C.'s eagerness to adopt Marisol, CWA has not begun the process of terminating Ms. A.'s parental rights and has not provided Marisol with counseling or support services.

A second named plaintiff, fifteen-year-old Thomas C., had been in foster care since he was seven:

> In those eight years, Thomas endured numerous placements including a hospital, a diagnostic center, and a residential treatment center ("RTC"). In 1993, without adequate investigation, CWA approved Thomas' placement with Rev. D., a minister Thomas met at the RTC, who took him to South Carolina. There Rev. D. sexually abused Thomas who subsequently ran away. In 1994, Thomas was returned to the RTC where he now resides. He has since attempted suicide twice and has run away from the RTC only to return after facing hardship and abuse on the streets. CWA has failed to determine the appropriateness of the RTC placement, to pursue the possibility of adoption, or to provide Thomas with counseling.

The *Marisol* plaintiffs alleged that the agency failed to "(1) appropriately accept reports of abuse and neglect for investigation; (2) investigate those reports in the time and manner required by law; (3) provide mandated preplacement preventive services to enable children to remain at home whenever possible; (4) provide the least restrictive, most family-like placement to meet children's individual needs; (5) provide services to ensure that children do not deteriorate physically, psychologically, educationally, or otherwise while in CWA custody; (6) provide children with disabilities, including HIV/AIDS, with appropriate placements; (7) provide appropriate case management or plans that enable children to return home or be discharged to permanent placements as quickly as possible; (8) provide services to assist children who are appropriate for adoption in getting out of foster care; (9) provide teenagers adequate services to prepare them to live independently once they leave the system; (10) provide the administrative, judicial, or dispositional reviews to which children are entitled; (11) provide caseworkers with training, support, or supervision; and (12) maintain adequate systems to monitor, track, and plan for children."

Plaintiffs prevailed in *Marisol A.* and a number of similar lawsuits, securing injunctions or receiverships that required massive changes in program operations. See, e.g., LaShawn A. v. Kelly (D.D.C.1995). Unfortunately, winning did not necessarily result in major improvements in these cumbersome, underfunded systems. Even after extensive court oversight resulting from *LaShawn A.*, for example, the District of Columbia child welfare system showed little improvement. Systemic problems included lack of staff, untrained

and unsupervised staff, virtual cessation in all
adoptions, lack of a management information
system to keep track of where foster children were
located, lack of foster home placements, and lack
of a central source that listed potential placements,
so that children were placed in inappropriate,
successive emergency placements. Positive changes
have come about, however, when outside pressure
from litigation has coincided with administrative
and political commitments to improvement. See
Joel A. v. Giuliani (2d Cir.2000) (report of
settlement).

F. LIABILITY FOR HARM

1.   FEDERAL CIVIL RIGHTS ACTIONS

DeShaney establishes that a child living
with a parent has no due process right to
protection from parental abuse, but a different
situation arises once the state has taken the child
into custody. Courts have held that a child has a
constitutional right to a safe and secure foster
placement, and that a child harmed in a foster
placement may be able to successfully sue state
officials.

In Kara B. v. Dane County (Wis.1996), for
example, the two child plaintiffs were placed in the

temporary custody of the county department of
social services for foster placement. At different
times, the girls were placed in a foster home where
they were sexually abused. They sued county child
welfare officials under § 1983 and joined
negligence and professional malpractice claims.

As a threshold matter, the court rejected
the defendant officials' qualified immunity
defenses. The qualified immunity doctrine shields
public officials from civil liability unless their
conduct violates a person's clearly established
constitutional or statutory right. The court found a
clearly established constitutional right to a safe
and secure foster placement and held that a
reasonable public official would have been put on
notice that violation of the right could lead to
liability. But cf. Milburn v. Anne Arundel County
Dep't of Social Services (4th Cir.1989)
(distinguishing between voluntary foster care
placements and those in which the state had
ordered removal of the child).

Kara B. next applied a "professional
judgment" standard to determine the defendant
officials' constitutional duty to place foster children
in safe and secure environments. "[L]iability may
be imposed only when the decision by the
professional is such a substantial departure from
accepted professional judgment, practice or

standards as to demonstrate that the person responsible actually did not base the decision on such judgment."

The court rejected the "deliberate indifference" standard (which imposes liability only when "public officials exhibit deliberate indifference to a risk ... actually known to them") because this laxer standard would insufficiently protect foster children. Some courts, however, do apply a deliberate indifference standard to suits alleging harm in foster care. See, e.g., White v. Chambliss (4th Cir.1997). Even when a court applies a professional judgment standard, the standard may be more limited than *Kara B.'s* formulation. See, e.g., K.H. ex rel. Murphy v. Morgan (7th Cir.1990) ("[O]nly if without justification based either on financial constraints or on considerations of professional judgment they [agents of the state] place the children in hands they know to be dangerous or otherwise unfit do they expose themselves to liability.")

The federal circuit courts also disagree about state liability for returning a child to a parent who is known to be abusive and then harms or even kills the child. See, e.g. S.S. v. McMullen (8th Cir.2000)(no liability); Currier v. Doran, (10th Cir.2001)(liability).

2. TORT LIABILITY

In addition to § 1983 actions, children harmed in foster care might be able to sue state officials or foster parents for negligence. There are a number of barriers to successful suits, however, and the law is confusing because courts treat foster parents as private contractors in some contexts and as state employees in others.

Unless a statute imposes state responsibility, most courts hold that the state is not responsible for harm caused by foster parents, because no agency, respondeat superior, or vicarious liability arises from the state–foster parent relationship. See, e.g., Stanley v. State Industries, Inc. (N.J.1993). But see Miller v. Martin (La.2003) (vicarious liability found because the "the custodial duty of the Department of Social Services was so great it could not be delegated"). Unless barred by sovereign immunity, however, courts are willing to find negligence where the state placed the harmed child with foster parents who were known to be abusive.

Another possible avenue for recovery is suing foster parents. Foster parents, however, may not have sufficient assets to make a negligence suit worthwhile for the child. In addition, the parental immunity doctrine may bar recovery if foster parents are treated as "parents." As discussed in chapter 8, several states have abolished the doctrine; in some states where it survives, statutes provide foster parents immunity coextensive with parental immunity. See, e.g., Spikes v. Banks (Mich.Ct.App.1998).

If a state classifies foster parents as employees, the injured child may be able to recover from a foster parent with few assets if the state indemnifies employees or against the state itself if the "employee" foster parent is considered a state agent. See, e.g., Hunte v. Blumenthal (Conn.1996) (foster parents were "employees," not independent contractors, and thus were entitled to defense and indemnification in a wrongful death action brought against them by the estate of a foster child who died in their care).

G. TYPES OF PLACEMENTS

1. FOSTER PARENTS

a. Placement with Non-Relatives

In the typical foster placement, children are placed in private homes of foster parents licensed and supervised by the state under the foster care law. Because the foster care system is

designed to provide temporary care in a non-
institutional family setting, the act or its
regulations typically limit the number of children
who may be placed in a single home. The state
provides the foster parents a stipend for each child.

b. Kinship Care: Relatives as Foster Parents
          Federal law requires states to consider
"giving preference to an adult relative over a non-
related caregiver when determining a placement
for a child, provided that the relative caregiver
meets all relevant State child protection
standards." 42 U.S.C. § 671(a)(19). Kinship foster
care has increased until in some large cities almost
half the foster children are now in kinship care.
See General Accounting Office, Child Welfare:
Complex Needs Strain Capacity To Provide
Services (1995). Kinship care allows the child to
maintain family ties and may be more stable than
non-relative foster care. It has several
disadvantages, however, including a lack of
permanency and inadequate funding and
oversight.

          Some states provide no funding, or only
reduced-rate funding, for relative foster homes
compared to non-relative foster homes, a practice
that has survived constitutional challenge. See,
e.g., Lipscomb v. Simmons (9th Cir.1992). A lack of
funding may be particularly harmful to kinship

care because caretaker relatives may have a low income and be financially unable to meet the child's needs. When a foster home is funded with federal money, federal statutes require equal funding for kin and non-kin care. See Miller v. Youakim (S.Ct.1979).

An additional problem is that kinship care homes may be provided with less oversight or assistance than non-relative homes, which may leave the child at risk of abuse, especially because a kinship caretaker may find it difficult to keep the child separated from abusive parents who are related to the caregiver. A final concern is that state agencies may not feel as strong a need to work toward permanent placement when a child is in kinship care. For some children this may not be a disadvantage, but for others adoption or guardianship with kin or others might provide needed stability in their lives.

c. The Indian Child Welfare Act

As part of an assimilation policy, the U.S. Bureau of Indian Affairs historically facilitated removal of large numbers of Native American children from their homes and placed them with non-Indian parents. The Indian Child Welfare Act of 1978, 25 U.S.C. § 1901 et seq. (ICWA), limits removal of Native American children from their tribes. Section 1902 of the Act recites congressional policy to "protect the best interests of Indian children and to promote the stability and security of Indian tribes and families by the establishment of minimum Federal standards for the removal of Indian children from their families and the placement of such children in foster or adoptive homes which will reflect the unique values of Indian culture, and by providing for assistance to Indian tribes in the operation of child and family service programs."

As Congress considered enactment of ICWA in 1978, one tribal chief testified before a House subcommittee that "[c]ulturally, the chances of Indian survival are significantly reduced if our children, the only real means for the transmission of the tribal heritage, are to be raised in non-Indian homes and denied exposure to the ways of their People. Furthermore, these practices seriously undercut the tribes' ability to continue as self-governing communities." The chief continued that "[o]ne of the most serious failings of the present system is that Indian children are removed from the custody of their natural parents by nontribal government authorities who have no basis for intelligently evaluating the cultural and social premises underlying Indian home life and childrearing. Many of the individuals who decide the fate of our children are at best ignorant of our cultural values and at worst contemptful of the

Indian way and convinced that removal, usually to a non-Indian household or institution, can only benefit an Indian child." Mississippi Band of Choctaw Indians v. Holyfield (S.Ct.1989). ICWA establishes a federal policy that "where possible, an Indian child should remain in the Indian community," and ensures that Indian child welfare determinations are not made on "a white, middle-class standard which, in many cases, forecloses placement with [an] Indian family." H.R.Rep. No. 95-1386.

ICWA applies in state court "child custody proceedings" concerning an Indian child and, under the federal Constitution's Supremacy Clause, preempts state law inconsistent with it. These proceedings involve foster care placement, termination of parental rights, pre-adoptive placement, and adoptive placement; the Act expressly excludes delinquency placements, custody awards to a parent in divorce actions, and state intervention in Indian families that does not contemplate removing the child. 25 U.S.C. § 1903(1). An "Indian child" is any unmarried person under eighteen who (1) is either a member of an Indian tribe or is eligible for membership in an Indian tribe and (2) is the biological child of a member of an Indian tribe. Id. § 1903(4).

The Act provides that "[i]n any adoptive placement of an Indian child under State law, a preference shall be given, in the absence of good cause to the contrary, to a placement with (1) a member of the child's extended family; (2) other members of the Indian child's tribe; or (3) other Indian families." Id. § 1915(a). In the absence of good cause to the contrary, foster care placement of an Indian child must be made with (1) a member of the child's extended family, (2) a foster home licensed, approved or specified by the child's tribe, (3) an Indian foster home licensed or approved by a non-Indian licensing authority, or (4) an institution for children approved by an Indian tribe or operated by an Indian organization which has a program suitable to meet the child's needs. 25 U.S.C. § 1915(b). Placement agencies "must adhere to 'prevailing social and cultural standards of the Indian community in which the parent or extended family resides.'" Id. § 1915(b).

The ICWA includes stringent standards for removing children from the home and for terminating parental rights:

> (e) No foster care placement may be ordered ... in the absence of a determination, supported by clear and convincing evidence, including testimony of qualified expert witnesses, that the

continued custody of the child by the
parent or Indian custodian is likely to
result in serious emotional or physical
damage to the child.

(f) No termination of parental rights may
be ordered ... in the absence of a
determination, supported by evidence
beyond a reasonable doubt, including
testimony of qualified expert witnesses,
that the continued custody of the child by
the parent or Indian custodian is likely to
result in serious emotional or physical
damage to the child.

Id. § 1912. The Supreme Court has not addressed
ICWA's constitutionality, but lower courts have
found or assumed the Act is constitutional. For
example, in Angus v. Joseph (Or.Ct.App.1982), the
court found "protection of the integrity of Indian
families" a permissible goal rationally tied to the
fulfillment of Congress' unique guardianship
obligation toward Indians.

Courts remain split on whether to
recognize the judicially-created "existing Indian
family" doctrine, which precludes application of
ICWA when the Indian child's parent or parents
have not maintained a significant social, cultural
or political relationship with the tribe. Courts

applying the doctrine view it as effectuating ICWA's policy of maintaining tribal heritage; courts rejecting the doctrine view it as contrary to the Act's plain language. Further discussion of ICWA appears in chapter 6, Adoption.

d. Racial and Religious Matching

Requiring same-race foster placements would violate the Constitution (Drummond v. Fulton County Department of Family & Child Services (5th Cir.1977)), but race may be considered when determining the child's best interests. Much of the literature on racial matching deals with adoption and is discussed in chapter 6. The strong arguments that have been made for and against racial matching in adoption are also relevant in foster placements.

Most states consider the parents' religious preferences in making foster placements, but do not feel constrained to find foster homes that match the parents' preference. The free exercise rights of the parents and child are observed "[s]o long as the state makes reasonable efforts to assure that the religious needs of the children are met." Wilder v. Bernstein (2d Cir.1988). Religious matching is also discussed in chapter 6.

2. INSTITUTIONAL CARE

a. Placements and Poverty

Most children in the child welfare system come from families with incomes below the federal poverty threshold. The recent debate over welfare reform, which included proposals for orphanages and special group homes, brought new attention to the issue, but the question of what to do with the children of the poor has been debated for years. The welfare system has vacillated between providing help for poor children in their homes through assistance programs and removing them from their homes and placing them in foster care or institutions.

Historically institutions such as almshouses, asylums and orphanages have been extensively criticized for failing to provide adequate shelter, food, medical care, education or job training. Modern opposition to these institutions comes from the medical community as well as other sources. Infants and young children are especially susceptible to medical and psychosocial problems from institutionalization. Modern supporters of orphanages and other institutions, however, argue that they can provide for the needs of children, including the multi-problem children who emerge from seriously troubled families.

A significant risk with institutions is a heightened danger of abuse because institutional staff concerned about job loss may fear reporting abuse, and because institutionalized children are not seen by teachers, daycare workers, or other outsiders who might be more likely to report.

Present federal policy, embodied in AACWA and ASFA, supports keeping children at home, rather than in institutional or foster care, when the home can be made safe for the child. New federal welfare policies embodied in Temporary Assistance to Needy Families (TANF), however, provide less of a safety net for low-income families than did the Aid to Families with Dependent Children program. (See chapter 8.)

b. Types of Facilities

When a court has decided a child cannot return home safely, the court must decide whether the state's proposed placement is the least restrictive (most family like) and the most appropriate setting available in close proximity to the parents' home, consistent with the child's best interests and special needs. 42 U.S.C. § 675(5)(A). Foster and kinship care are considered less restrictive than institutional care.

"Institutional care" covers a range of placements, including residential treatment facilities, group homes, shelter facilities, or even hospitals. Usually group homes and shelter facilities are small, non-secure, and located in a community setting so residents can attend local schools and participate in community events. Distinctions among types of facilities are often blurred. A small facility that provides mental health treatment may be called a "group home" or a "residential treatment facility," for example. Or a "group home" may provide supervision, but no treatment. An institutional placement, such as a group home, also may be used for transitional care for older children to prepare them for independent living as adults, as well as for children who cannot function in a family setting.

Children may be placed in kinship care or other facilities outside the state, if their home state cannot provide necessary specialized care. Such placements implicate the Interstate Compact on the Placement of Children, which is discussed in chapter 6.

3.   AGING OUT OF FOSTER CARE

Of the children who exited foster care in 2000, an estimated 7 percent became emancipated prior to age eighteen. Children also "age-out" of foster care by by turning eighteen. Unfortunately many of these former foster children are not capable of taking charge of their lives. Studies of children leaving foster care have found that they often have not completed high school and many are unemployed. Homelessness and incarceration are substantial problems. The federal Foster Care Independence Act of 1999 was intended to aid this population, by encouraging states to find adoptive homes for older children, sponsoring independent living programs, and other initiatives.

Undocumented foster children may be eligible for Special Immigrant Juvenile Status, which allows them to become lawful permanent residents and to live and work in the United States (green card holders). They need to apply for this status while they are still in foster care, however.

H. GUARDIANSHIP

Generally the permanency plan for foster children who cannot be reunited with their parents is termination of parental rights followed by adoption. For some children, however, adoption is unlikely because of their special needs or a desire to continue contact with a biological parent. Children close to the age of majority may remain in foster care or move to independent living. For

children in kinship foster care, the foster parents
may not want to adopt because they do not want to
terminate the parental rights of the biological
parent, their relative. Guardianship may provide a
useful alternative to adoption and be more
permanent and family-like than long-term foster
care. ASFA permits "legal guardianship" as part of
a permanency plan. The Act does not provide
financial incentives for use of guardianships,
however, although it does provide adoption
incentives.

When a guardian is appointed for a foster
child, the child welfare system is relieved of
financial and oversight responsibility for the child.
Concomitantly, the guardian, who may have been
the foster parent, is relieved of the need to submit
to state rules, inspections and reports required by
the foster care system. As one scholar notes: "In
essence, guardians are substitute parents. They
have complete control over the care and custody of
their wards including responsibility for their
health, welfare and education. Unlike foster
parents, they need not ask an agency for
permission to vaccinate the child or to visit the zoo
in a nearby county. In contrast to long-term foster
care, guardianship cements the bond between the
child and the caregiver, localizes authority over the
child, and endows the relationship with an
expectation of continuity." Meryl Schwartz,

Reinventing Guardianship: Subsidized Guardianship, Foster Care, and Child Welfare, 22 N. Y. Rev. L. & Soc. Change 441 (1996).

A major disadvantage of a guardianship over foster care, however, is that the guardian may receive no state financial support or services for the child. A guardian is not obligated to support a ward, but generally for children coming out of foster care the parents would not provide any significant support because their rights have been terminated or they are low-income. Particularly for special needs children, even middle or upper-income families may fear that they could not provide their wards with necessary care and services without state aid. The child might be eligible for aid under some programs such as TANF, but the TANF amounts typically would be less than the foster care allotment. Few states provide subsidized guardianships and of these, some provide a lower level of support for kinship guardianships.

CHAPTER 5

CRIMINAL ABUSE AND NEGLECT

A.   THE NATURE OF CRIMINAL ENFORCEMENT

1.   THE ROLES OF CIVIL AND CRIMINAL ENFORCEMENT

This chapter is intimately related to chapters 3 and 4 because much conduct that would support a civil abuse or neglect petition and perhaps lead to foster placement would also support criminal prosecution. Each year the criminal justice system investigates and adjudicates a significant percentage of child abuse cases referred to law enforcement authorities by child protective agencies, families, victims, physicians, schools and others. Indeed, many state abuse and neglect reporting acts require child protective agencies to share reports with law enforcement.

Child abuse is a major responsibility of local law enforcement authorities. Data from twelve states for 1997 indicates that acts of child abuse committed by parents and other caretakers comprised about one-fifth (19%) of violent crimes against juveniles, and more than one-half of crimes against children aged two or younger, reported to the police. Thirteen percent of episodes of parental assault against children reported to the police were associated with an assault against a spouse or former spouse. See David Finkelhor and Richard Ormrod, Child Abuse Reported to the Police (OJJDP 2001).

The goals of civil and criminal intervention are related yet distinct. Civil intervention seeks to protect the child by treating the child and the family and, when necessary, removing the child from the home. Criminal enforcement seeks punishment and deterrence by arresting and prosecuting offenders. Civil proceedings focus primarily on the condition of the child and family; criminal prosecutions focus primarily on the defendant's guilt or innocence.

Ideally child protective agencies and law enforcement will cooperate to fashion a coordinated response to abuse and neglect. Inter-agency cooperation fosters reasoned decisionmaking about whether to move against a particular perpetrator civilly, criminally or both. In cases of neglect or physical, sexual or emotional abuse, several factors may affect the decision, including these:

The seriousness of the alleged conduct.
Serious injury to the child may be
prosecuted, but one slapping incident
might not be.

The perpetrator's evident state of mind.
Prosecution may be more likely if the
perpetrator acted wantonly, than if the
conduct smacked merely of immaturity or
frustration, or of not knowing how to raise
a child.

The perpetrator's amenability to treatment.
Prosecution may be more likely if the
perpetrator resists treatment or if civil
authorities have previously tried treatment
to no avail, but less likely if the perpetrator appears willing and perhaps able to
respond to treatment.

The strength of the proof. The criminal
burden of proof is beyond a reasonable
doubt; the civil burden is lower, either a
preponderance of the evidence or clear
and convincing evidence. The burden may
be particularly important in sexual abuse
cases, where the child victim (often the
only eyewitness other than the perpetrator) may be unwilling or unable to

testify, or may be ineffective on the stand.

Community outrage.   If the abuse or neglect is publicized and outrages the community, prosecution is more likely, perhaps partly for deterrent effect. Publicized acts are also likely to be serious, thus relating to the first factor listed above.

The remedy's likely effect on the child and family.   Will branding a parent with a criminal record hurt the family? If the parent has other children, should the parent be incarcerated? If authorities do not seek incarceration or termination of parental rights, would the child and family be better off if the parent is treated civilly? Would the child be better protected by civil removal from the home (for foster care or adoption) than by imprisoning the perpetrator for a short time?

Predictions of future abuse or neglect. Even if the abuse or neglect does not appear serious now, authorities may invoke the criminal process as a deterrent before the conduct escalates and causes death or serious harm to the child.

2. ISSUE PRECLUSION (COLLATERAL ESTOPPEL)

Child protective agencies and the prosecutor may employ both the civil system's protective function and the criminal justice system's punitive function in the same case. Ideally this dual approach would result from a cooperative decisionmaking process. Even where it does not, however, it has been held that issue preclusion (collateral estoppel) does not preclude criminal prosecution of the defendant for the same incident that resulted in an earlier civil neglect finding against him.

In People v. Roselle (N.Y.1994), for example, the family court found that the defendant had neglected his three-year-old daughter by placing her in a bathtub of scalding hot water, causing severe burns to her buttocks and right foot. The defendant was then indicted, among other things, for assault and endangering the welfare of a child in the scalding incident. The court of appeals held that collateral estoppel was inapplicable because the family court proceeding was not trial, no evidence was presented against the defendant in family court, and the family court act contemplated concurrent criminal and civil actions.

The criminal prosecution came first in In re Shulikov (Me. 2000), a proceeding to terminate the parental rights of a father convicted of sexually assaulting his daughter. The court held that relitigation of the facts resolved by the earlier conviction was precluded because the termination statute authorized a presumption of parental unfitness based on proof of such convictions.

B.   ABUSE, NEGLECT AND CHILD ENDANGERMENT

1.   OVERVIEW

A number of criminal statutes may be invoked against persons who inflict physical or emotional violence on children. Some of these statutes (such as ones proscribing murder, manslaughter or assault) apply when the victim is "any person" or "another person," and thus permit prosecution when the victim happens to be a child.

Complementing these general-application crimes are crimes applicable only when the victim is a child. These child-specific crimes carry a variety of names, such as endangering the welfare of a child, child abuse, criminal neglect, or cruelty to children. For example, Pennsylvania's child endangerment statute operates against "[a] parent, guardian, or other person supervising the welfare of a child" who "knowingly endangers the welfare of the child by violating a duty of care, protection or support." 18 Pa. Cons. Stat. § 4304. Florida's criminal child abuse statute operates against "[a] person who knowingly or willfully abuses a child without causing great bodily harm, permanent disability, or permanent disfigurement to the child." Fla. Stat. Ann. § 827.03.

As the Pennsylvania and Florida statutes indicate, the child-specific statutes typically extend beyond defendants having legal custody or control of the child. See, e.g., State v. Perruccio (Conn.1984) (teacher); City of Columbus v. Wolfinger (Ohio Ct.App.1996) (day care worker); State v. DeBoucher (Ariz.Ct.App.1982) (boarding school director). The defendant class may even include a child, including a child younger than the victim. See, e.g., K.B.S. v. State (Fla.Dist.Ct. App.1999) (affirming delinquency adjudication against 14-year-old for abusing a nine-year-old by burning him with a cigarette; court noted that the statute would also operate against a 9-year-old who abused a 14-year-old).

The typical endangerment statute, illustrated by the Pennsylvania statute quoted above, permits conviction for a wide range of conduct harmful to children. See, e.g., Hughes v. State (Nev.1996) (transporting a child in a stolen vehicle); People v. Suquisupa (N.Y.Sup.Ct.1996) (selling fireworks to unsupervised 13-year-old who suffered a serious hand injury from a premature explosion); State v. Marschat (Ohio Ct.App.1991) (leaving 6-year-old son in the car for approximately two hours in August with all the windows rolled up; son died from the heat).

2. CHILDREN WHO WITNESS DOMESTIC VIOLENCE

Many children who witness domestic violence inflicted on a parent suffer profound adverse effects, including post-traumatic stress disorder and other severe emotional and behavioral problems. Female child witnesses are more likely to be abused as adults, and male child witnesses are more likely to become abusers as adults. See, e.g., Lois A. Weithorn, Protecting Children from Exposure to Domestic Violence: The Use and Abuse of Child Maltreatment, 53 Hastings L.J. 1 (2001).

Some states specifically criminalize "domestic violence in the presence of a child." See, e.g., Idaho Code § 18-918(7)(b). In People v. Johnson (N.Y.2000), the court held that a defendant who committed vicious acts of domestic violence against his former girlfriend in her children's presence could be convicted under the state's endangerment statute, which criminalizes "knowingly act[ing] in a manner likely to be injurious to the physical, mental or moral welfare of a child less than seventeen years old."

3.   PARENTAL PRIVILEGE

As public debate continues concerning the efficacy and propriety of corporal punishment of children, the law continues to recognize a parental privilege for reasonable discipline. Section 3.08 of the Model Penal Code, for example, provides that "[t]he use of force upon or toward the person of another is justifiable if:

> (1) The actor is the parent or guardian or other person similarly responsible for the general care and supervision of a minor or a person acting at the request of such parent, guardian or other responsible person and:
>> (a) the force is used for the purpose

of safeguarding or promoting the welfare
of the minor, including the preventing or
punishment of his misconduct; and
        (b) the force used is not designed
to cause or known to create a substantial
risk of causing death, serious bodily
harm, disfigurement, extreme pain or
mental distress or gross degradation."

The privilege seeks to balance parents'
rights to direct their children's upbringing with
the state's parens patriae interest in preventing
child abuse. As the Model Penal Code formulation
indicates, the privilege extends beyond parents to
a wide range of other caretakers, though the
extension is not boundless. See, e.g, State v.
Dodd (Wis.Ct.App.1994) (live-in boyfriend of
child's mother not privileged).

4.   ABUSIVE DISCIPLINE

Abuse charges frequently arise from
serious physical or emotional injury inflicted by
parents or other caregivers on children they are
seeking to discipline. The precise number of
disciplinary abuse cases cannot be determined,
but the number is likely significant because
studies demonstrate that a majority of American
parents use physical force to punish their

children and that most abuse is perpetrated by caregivers. Whatever the relationship, reported decisions include children who are beaten with belts and bats, burned, locked in closets and deprived of food and force-fed. Abusive discipline leads to the child's death with disturbing frequency. See, e.g., Kandice K. Johnson, Crime or Punishment: The Parental Corporal Punishment Defense -- Reasonable and Neces-sary, or Excused Abuse?, 1998 U. Ill. L. Rev. 413.

In jurisdictions that have abrogated parental tort immunity, a child injured by unprivileged corporal punishment may maintain a damage action against the parent who inflicted the abusive discipline. See, e.g., Murray v. Murray (Ohio Ct.App.1993).

5. ABANDONMENT

Where child endangerment rises to the level of total neglect, a parent or guardian may face prosecution for abandonment. As discussed in chapter 9, more than a million children each year run away from home and live on the streets; many of these children are more aptly labeled "throwaways" because they are directly told to leave the household or because no one cares whether they return. At least with respect to older children, however, criminal abandonment statutes are rarely invoked against throwaways' parents.

6. CONTRIBUTING TO THE DELINQUENCY OF A MINOR

Most states have statutes criminalizing conduct that might lead a juvenile to commit delinquent acts. Massachusetts, for example, punishes "[a]ny person who shall be found to have caused, induced, abetted, or encouraged or contributed toward the delinquency of a child, or to have acted in any way tending to cause or induce such delinquency." Mass. Gen. Laws ch. 119, § 63.

As in Massachusetts, the defendant class typically includes "any person" who commits the proscribed conduct, a class considerably broader than the parents and other caregivers reached by the typical endangerment statute. See, e.g., State v. Barr (N.M.Ct.App. 1999) (affirming conviction of 31-year-old who left a party and drove juveniles to homes and burglarized them). These statutes may even reach juvenile defendants who contribute to the delinquency of other juveniles. See, e.g., In re Lomeli (Ohio Ct.App. 1995).

In most states, a defendant may be convicted of contributing to the delinquency of a minor even if the minor did not commit a delinquent act, or was never charged or adjudicated a delinquent. "The defendant is punished for his own acts, not those of the juvenile." State v. Trevino (N.M. 1993).

7. VOID-FOR-VAGUENESS CHALLENGES

Criminal endangerment statutes typically carry broad language designed to enable authorities to prosecute a wide range of physical and emotional mistreatment of children. Some questionable conduct, however, cannot fit under even broad statutory mandates. Where the fit seems difficult to make, constitutional challenge remains available under the void-for-vagueness doctrine.

Due process requires that a penal statute "define the criminal offense with sufficient definiteness that ordinary people can understand what conduct is prohibited and in a manner that does not encourage arbitrary and discriminatory enforcement." Kolender v. Lawson (S.Ct. 1983). Unless a vagueness challenge implicates what the Supreme Court has deemed "fundamental rights" in the Constitution, the challenger must establish that the assailed statute fails Kolender's test as applied to the facts of the particular case.

Where the conduct at issue appears particularly harmful to children and is arguably within the endangerment statute's proscriptions, courts normally reject vagueness challenges. See, e.g., State v. Mahurin (Mo.1990) (defendants nearly starved their child to death). Vagueness challenges to endangerment statutes sometimes succeed, however, where the seriousness of the defendant's conduct seems open to fair question. See, e.g., State v. Schriver (Conn.1988) (defendant grabbed fully clothed 13-year-old girl while making sexually suggestive comment). A defendant such as Schriver might be prosecuted for a crime with more definite elements such as assault, but not for endangerment.

8.   THE "CULTURAL DEFENSE"

Where a parent or other person commits acts or omissions that would support prosecution for endangering the welfare of a child or a similar offense involving abuse or neglect, should guilt be excused or punishment mitigated on the ground that the acts or omissions reflect the defendant's cultural background that differs from mainstream American culture? Similarly, should juvenile courts weigh cultural differences in determining whether to find a child abused or neglected in civil proceedings?

The "cultural defense" sometimes arises as the American population grows more diverse through immigration from nations with a variety of cultural traditions. The defense raises the question whether a pluralistic society tolerant of individual differences can (or should) have a culturally relative, rather than an absolute, child protective standard. Several cultural practices potentially clash with mainstream American views of child protection, including shaming, corporal punishment, parent/child co-sleeping arrangements, male facial scarification, female circumcision, arranged teenage marriage, and polygamy.

American criminal law has refused to recognize a formal cultural defense. Civil authorities are also wary of the defense, though a few states require child protective authorities to examine cultural differences when determining whether abuse or neglect has occurred.

9.   PARENTAL-LIABILITY STATUTES

In an effort to combat juvenile crime, several states and localities now authorize prosecution of parents following misconduct by their children. These parental liability statutes charge parents with omissions smacking of neglect, but they proceed a significant step further than endangerment and contributing-to-delinquency statutes. Some parental liability statutes criminalize particular parental acts or omissions. In Florida, for example, a parent or other adult can be prosecuted for allowing children to gain access to their firearms if the children kill or injure someone with them. See Fla. Stat. § 784.05. Other states have enacted broader legislation authorizing prosecution of parents for "failure to supervise" their children who commit a crime or other misconduct. See, e.g., Or. Rev. Stat. § 163.577. Courts generally reject challenges that the statutes are void-for-vagueness, overbroad, violate substantive due process, or constitute cruel and unusual punishment.

Even in the absence of parental liability legislation, parents can be prosecuted for acts related to their children's criminal conduct if the parents are accomplices or co-conspirators, or if they knowingly profit from the crime.

C.   SEXUAL ABUSE

1.   WHAT IS CHILD SEXUAL ABUSE?

According to the American Academy of Pediatrics, "[s]exual abuse occurs when a child is engaged in sexual activities that the child cannot comprehend, for which the child is developmentally unprepared and cannot give consent, and/or that violate the law or social taboos of society. The sexual activities may include all forms of oral-genital, genital, or anal contact by or to the child, or nontouching abuses, such as exhibitionism, voyeurism, or using the child in the production of pornography. Sexual abuse includes a spectrum of activities ranging from rape to physically less intrusive sexual abuse." Guidelines for the Evaluation of Sexual Abuse of Children: Subject Review, 103 Pediatrics 186 (1999).

Because of the attendant shame and embarrassment, sexual abuse is an under-reported crime among victims of all ages. Data from twelve states for 1991 to 1996 nonetheless indicates that 33% of all sexual assault victims reported to law enforcement were between twelve to seventeen, and that another 34% were under twelve. One of every seven sexual assault victims

(14%) was under six. In other words, more than two-thirds (67%) of sexual assault victims reported to police during this period were juveniles. Juveniles were the large majority of the victims of forcible fondling (84%), forcible sodomy (79%), sexual assault with an object (75%), and forcible rape (46%). Two-thirds of juvenile victims (67%) were sexually assaulted by adults. See Howard N. Snyder, Sexual Assault of Young Children as Reported to Law Enforcement: Victim, Incident, and Offender Characteristics (Bur. Just. Stats.2000).

2. REPRESENTATIVE STATUTES

Endangerment, criminal child abuse, and general criminal sexual abuse statutes reach much sexual exploitation of children. Child sexual abuse statutes, however, operate specifically against such exploitation and ordinarily carry greater penalties on conviction.

a. "Forcible" And "Statutory" Rape

"Forcible rape" statutes depend on proof that the victim submitted to sexual activity because of the defendant's physical force or threat of physical force. Forcible rape statutes generally criminalize conduct against "any person," and thus reach forcible conduct against children and adults alike.

To be distinguished from forcible rape is "statutory rape," an offense sometimes called by such names as indecent liberties with a child, lewd and lascivious activities with a child, or carnal knowledge of a child. Statutory rape does not include force as an element. The key element is the victim's age, and the prosecutor may prevail by proving that the proscribed sexual conduct took place between the defendant and the underage victim. The victim is deemed incapable of consent, as a matter of law, if he or she is below the statute's specified age (the so-called "age of consent"), or if more than the specified minimum age differential exists between the victim and the defendant. Purported consent would not be a defense, regardless of anything the young victim might have said or indicated to the perpetrator. Courts have rejected perpetrators' challenges to statutory rape statutes grounded in constitutional privacy rights. See, e.g., Ferris v. Santa Clara County (9th Cir. 1989).

The 1996 Welfare Reform Act urged states and local jurisdictions to "aggressively enforce statutory rape laws," 42 U.S.C. § 14016. Congress acted on the assumption that prosecution would create a climate of deterrence and help control the rate of teenage out-of-wedlock pregnancies, which has risen dramatically in the past two decades. In 2001, 33.4% of births were to single mothers, a substantial number of whom were teenagers. In 1995, a comprehensive nationwide study conducted by the Alan Guttmacher Institute reported that at least half of unwed teenage mothers are impregnated by men twenty or older. Some studies have placed the figure even higher, finding that almost two of every three births to unwed teenage mothers result from intercourse with men over twenty. By having sexual intercourse with girls below the age of consent, most of the adult men were committing statutory rape or another sex crime.

b.   Incest

Where a person engages in sexual activity with a family member such as a descendent or sibling, the person may face prosecution for incest. Incest statutes reach blood relationships, but are not uniform in their treatment of non-blood relationships (such as step or adoptive relationships). Section 230.2 of the Model Penal Code, for example, would criminalize sexual relations between adoptive parents and their adoptive children, but not between other family members related by adoption or between step relations. Where the step or adoptive relationship between defendant and victim is outside the incest statute, the defendant would remain subject to prosecution for other sex crimes if the victim is under the age of consent.

c.   Federal Legislation

Most prosecutions of sex crimes against children (like most prosecutions generally) occur in state courts, but Congress has also legislated in this area. See, e.g., 18 U.S.C. § 2422(b) (interstate coercion or enticement of a minor to engage in prostitution or criminal sexual activity); id. § 2241(c) (crossing state lines with intent to engage in a criminal sexual act with a child under twelve).

The Internet poses new challenges by enabling molesters to develop long-distance relationships with children in "chat rooms" and similar sites. A relationship may develop until the molester arranges a meeting with an unsuspecting child, frequently unbeknownst to the parents who may remain unsophisticated in Internet use.

In a nationally representative survey of regular 10-17-year-old Internet users in 2000, researchers found (1) that about one in five of the youths received a sexual solicitation or approach over the Internet in the past year, (2) that about one in thirty-three youths received an "aggressive" sexual solicitation (a solicitor who asked to meet them somewhere; called them on the telephone; or sent them regular mail, money or gifts), (3) that one in four youths had an unwanted exposure to pictures of naked people or people having sex in the past year, and (4) that one in seventeen youths was threatened or harassed. Less than 10% of sexual solicitations and only 3% of unwanted exposure episodes were reported to authorities such as a law enforcement agency or an Internet service provider. Only about a quarter of the youths who had a sexual solicitation (and about 40% of youths who reported unwanted exposure to sexual material) told a parent. See David Finkelhor et al., Online Victimization: A Report on the Nation's Youth (2000).

Law enforcement authorities have sometimes used undercover operations to catch and prosecute persons who use the Internet to seek to entice children into sexual encounters. Police officers often pose as children in communication with adults. Courts have upheld convictions for attempted child enticement and similar crimes, even where the defendant sought to entice a non-existent "child" because the target actually was a posing law enforcement officer. See, e.g.,

State v. Robins (Wis.2002). In Attorney Grievance
Comm'n v. Childress (Md.2001), the court upheld
the disciplinary committee's indefinite suspension
of a 32-year-old lawyer arrested by an undercover
officer. The committee found that the lawyer had
engaged in conduct prejudicial to the administration of justice by using the Internet to solicit
sex with young teenage girls.

Some state legislative efforts to control use
of the Internet by potential sex abusers have
encountered constitutional roadblocks. See, e.g.,
ACLU v. Miller (N.D. Ga.1997) (granting preliminary injunction against enforcement of state law
prohibiting Internet transmissions which falsely
identify sender); American Libraries Ass'n v.
Pataki (S.D.N.Y.1997) (granting preliminary injunction enjoining enforcement of state law that
made it a crime to use a computer to disseminate
obscene material to minors; plaintiffs demonstrated a likelihood of success on the merits of
their claim that the act violated the federal
Constitution's Commerce Clause).

In an effort to reach molesters who use the
Internet to converse with children and arrange
meetings, Congress in 1994 enacted 18 U.S.C. §
2423(b), which makes it a crime to travel in
interstate commerce to engage in any of a wide

range of criminal sexual acts with a person under eighteen. The section has been upheld against challenges that it exceeds Congress' commerce clause authority or impermissibly burdens the fundamental right of interstate travel. See, e.g., United States v. Brockdorff (D.D.C.1997).

3. THE CONTOURS OF CRIMINAL LIABILITY

a. Gender Neutrality

Statutory rape laws and other provisions criminalizing sexual activity with children formerly sought to "protect girls under the age of eighteen years from conscienceless men, as far as possible." State v. Henderson (Idaho 1911). Today statutes proscribing sexual activity with children carry gender-neutral language in virtually all states. The typical statutory rape prosecution still involves a male offender and an underage female victim, but prosecution of females for statutory rape of underage male victims remains possible. Prosecution is also possible where the perpetrator and the underage victim are of the same gender. See, e.g., State v. Buch (Haw.1996) (third-degree sexual assault).

In Michael M. v. Superior Court (S.Ct. 1981) (plurality opinion), the Court held that equal protection was not offended by California's statutory rape law, which operated only when the victim was female. (Even as the Court rendered its decision, the statute was an oddity because most states already had enacted gender-neutral statutory rape laws.) *Michael M.'s* plurality concluded that at least one purpose of California's law was to advance the state's strong interest in preventing teenage out-of-wedlock pregnancies.

In People v. Liberta (N.Y.1984), however, the court struck down a forcible rape statute that exempted females from criminal liability. *Liberta* distinguished *Michael M.* on the ground that the primary purpose of forcible rape statutes is not prevention of pregnancies, but rather prevention of the often violent assault on one's person that accompanies rape and may implicate the dignity of male and female victims alike.

b. Mistake of Age

In most states, statutory rape and other sex crimes are strict-liability offenses (that is, offenses not requiring proof of mens rea, or a culpable mental state), even though strict liability crimes are the exception in American jurisprudence. Mistake of age is no defense, regardless of the victim's appearance, sexual sophistication or verbal misrepresentations about age, and regardless of the defendant's efforts to learn the victim's age. Legislatures restrict or eliminate the mistake-of-age defense to protect victims and punish wrongdoers, and to limit or eliminate the need for testimony by or concerning the victim. Courts have rejected constitutional challenges to strict liability sex crimes. See, e.g., United States v. Brooks (9th Cir.1988).

Only about a third of the states have statutes permitting a mistake-of-age defense in some sex crime prosecutions. Some of these statutes provide the defense to crimes charging sexual relations with older underage victims but not with younger ones. See, e.g., Colo. Rev. Stat. § 18-3-406(2) (line of demarcation is fifteen). Other states make the defense available with respect to less serious sex crimes but not more serious ones. See, e.g., Minn. Stat. §§ 609.344-609.345 (defense available for some crimes below third-degree and fourth-degree criminal sexual conduct). In at least four states without sex crime statutes expressly creating the mistake-of-age defense, the highest courts have held that the statutes by implication require proof of a mens rea regarding the victim's age and thus make the mistake-of-age defense available. Where a mistake-of-age defense is available, the defendant has the burden of proving the reasonableness of his belief concerning the victim's age.

c.   Emancipation or Marriage

If the victim is below the age of consent, the sex crime defendant may not avoid liability by establishing that the victim was emancipated. Marriage, however, remains a defense for a husband to most statutory rape and other non-forcible sex crimes that impose liability based on the victim's age. The rationale is that because marriage emancipates a child, the law should not intrude on the marital relationship unless the defendant husband has resorted to force. The marital defense is unlikely to affect nonforcible sexual relations with particularly young minors because such minors normally do not marry, even under statutes permitting marriage with parental consent or court approval.

d.   Child Perpetrators

As many as one-third of sexual assaults against children are committed by perpetrators who are children themselves. Virtually all courts have upheld application of statutory rape laws against minor perpetrators, or against both minor participants on the ground that "each is the victim of the other." In re T.W. (Ill.App.Ct.1997). Evidently the only contrary state supreme court decision is In re G.T. (Vt.2000), which acknowledged that the holding rejected the statute's "apparent plain meaning."

In a particular case, coverage depends on the statutory language. Most statutes proscribing sexual conduct with an underage child operate broadly against "any person," or against "whoever" engaged in the conduct. A defendant of any age, including a minor, would be subject to prosecution. Some statutory rape laws, however, permit prosecution of a minor, but only where the difference in the ages of the perpetrator and the underage victim is at least a specified minimum. See, e.g., N.C. Gen. Stat. § 14-27.2(a)(1) (first-degree rape) (victim under thirteen and defendant at least twelve and at least four years older than the victim).

When the alleged perpetrator is a particularly young child, prosecutorial discretion may be a threshold issue. The National Task Force on Juvenile Sex Offending recommends that "[p]rosecution should be a component of most interventions in juvenile sex offenses," but recognizes that a court-imposed supervisory program without prosecution may be appropriate for prepubescent children who engage in sexual behavior.

The propriety of prosecution divided the

court in Scott E. v. State (Nev. 1997). The juvenile court adjudicated eleven-year-old Scott a delinquent and placed him on three years probation for "lewdness with a child under fourteen," a class A felony if committed by an adult. The charges were that Scott "touched" his eight-year-old step-cousin "on the top of her clothes" on her "personal spot," and twice exposed his penis and had her touch his penis. The state supreme court vacated the adjudication on procedural grounds.

One Justice in *Scott. E.* chided the prosecutor for "bring[ing] criminal charges against pre-adolescent children charged with engaging in consensual sex games" that may have amounted to nothing more than "playing doctor." The Chief Justice disagreed: "Juvenile court is supposed to teach juveniles the difference between appropriate and inappropriate behavior with the hope of preventing their getting into the adult criminal system. This purpose cannot be accomplished if all sexual activity between children is dismissed as mere games or a waste of time."

4.   PROVING THE CASE

a.   General Difficulties of Proof
Child sexual abuse is "one of the most

difficult crimes to detect and prosecute, in large part because there often are no witnesses except the victim." Pennsylvania v. Ritchie (S.Ct.1987) (plurality opinion). Detailed treatment of evidentiary issues is best reserved for evidence treatises, but this section highlights some major issues in child sexual abuse prosecutions.

Prosecutors may face a number of imposing obstacles in the effort to prove guilt beyond a reasonable doubt consistent with the presumption of innocence and other constitutional guarantees. Most sex crimes against children leave no physical or medical evidence to corroborate the charge. As *Ritchie* intimates, many sex crimes are committed in private, leaving the child victim the only eyewitness. The frightened or ashamed child may have delayed reporting the abuse, inviting suggestion that he fabricated the charge or that the child's memory has dimmed with the passage of time. The child may be an ineffective witness because she is scared, intimidated, less than fully communicative, or perhaps reluctant or unwilling to help convict a family member or other trusted person. The child may be unable to recall key events or may recant. The family may not want the child to suffer further trauma of public testimony.

In recent years, concern about child abuse has led states to relax rules concerning competency of child witnesses. Children under a particular age are generally competent unless they are shown to lack capacity to recall facts correctly or to testify truthfully. In many states, child abuse victims of any age are competent as a matter of law to testify about the abuse.

Despite this relaxation of competency rules, the obstacles discussed above frequently lead prosecutors to try to prove the case through expert testimony of physicians, psychiatrists, social workers or psychologists. The difficulties may also force prosecutors to forgo prosecution altogether, or to accept a plea bargain that sharply reduces the sentence imposed on a dangerous perpetrator.

In recent years, the law has fashioned a number of evidentiary and trial process devices in child sex abuse prosecutions. These innovations test the outer limits of the Sixth Amendment Confrontation Clause in an effort to facilitate admission of the victim's statements or testimony. The innovations stem largely from the sense that children's reports of sexual abuse are generally reliable because children would not persistently lie about sensitive sexual matters and would not know details necessary to sustain a lie. Some observers, however, maintain that an adult questioner (such as a physician, child welfare agency employee, or police officer) can sometimes lead a child to give answers the questioner wants to hear. Much scholarship and empirical research discuss the suggestibility of child interviewees and reveal sharp disagreements about the circumstances under which young sex abuse victims can or should be believed. See, e.g., Thomas D. Lyon, The New Wave in Children's Suggestibility Research: A Critique, 84 Cornell L. Rev. 1004 (1999), which cites and discusses much of the literature. The suggestibility issue is significant in light of legislation and decisions, discussed in the next several sections, which create a greater role for the child's hearsay testimony or limit the defendant's Sixth Amendment right to face-to-face confrontation.

b.   The "General Child Hearsay" Exception

Children's statements may be admissible under recognized hearsay exceptions such as the ones for excited utterances or statements for medical diagnosis or treatment, or under a residual exception. The Supreme Court has held that because a residual exception is not a "firmly rooted" exception within the meaning of the Confrontation Clause, a child's statement may be admitted under such an exception only on a finding that the statement is supported by "particularized guarantees of trustworthiness" drawn from the totality of the circumstances that surround the making of the statement and that "render the declarant particularly worthy of belief." Idaho v. Wright (S.Ct.1990). See also, e.g., White v. Illinois (S.Ct.1992) (Confrontation Clause does not require that before admission of a child victim's testimony under the spontaneous declaration or medical examination exceptions to the hearsay rule, the prosecution must produce the declarant at trial or the trial court must find the declarant unavailable).

About half the states have moved beyond these traditional exceptions and have enacted "general child hearsay" exceptions, which permit admission of a child sexual abuse victim's out-of-court statements that the court deems trust-worthy. In Missouri, for example, an otherwise inadmissible statement concerning a sex crime made by a victim under twelve is admissible in a criminal proceeding as substantive evidence to prove the truth of the matter asserted if: "(1) The court finds, in a hearing conducted outside the presence of the jury that the time, content and circumstances of the statement provide sufficient indicia of reliability; and (2)(a) The child testifies at the proceedings; or (b) The child is unavailable as a witness; or (c) The child is otherwise physically available as a witness but the court finds that the significant emotional or psychological trauma which would result from testifying in the personal presence of the defendant makes the child unavailable as a witness at the time of the criminal proceeding." Mo. Rev. Stat. § 491.075.

A "general child hearsay" exception statute may specify factors the court must consider in determining trustworthiness. In the absence of statutory specification, courts examine such factors as (1) the spontaneity and consistent repetition of the child's statement, (2) the child's mental state, (3) the child's motive to fabricate, and (4) the child's use of terminology or description not normally within the knowledge of a child of that age. See, e.g., State v. Redman (Mo. 1996). Where the child makes the statements in an interview, the court examines the interviewer's experience and looks at whether the interviewer used leading questions.

Normally a declarant's mere absence from the trial does not establish the declarant's unavailability. The party seeking to invoke a hearsay exception must also establish that the declarant could not be present or testify because of death or then-existing physical mental illness or infirmity, or that the party could not procure the declarant's attendance by process or other reasonable means. See, e.g., Fed. R. Evid. 804(a). The Missouri statute quoted above, however, illustrates the relaxed approach taken by the "general child hearsay" exception statutes. The child's significant emotional or psychological trauma can render the child "unavailable" even if the child is sitting at home a mile away. The child's trustworthy hearsay statement would be admissible, and the defendant would not have an opportunity to cross-examine the child who could otherwise be produced.

c.   The Victim's Ex Parte Videotaped Statement

A handful of states have enacted statutes permitting admission of a videotaped interview of particularly young child victims, without a showing that the child presently suffers from significant emotional trauma and without contemporaneous cross-examination. Kansas, for example, permits admission where the court finds that the interview offers sufficient indicia of reliability, the person conducting the interview is available to testify, the interview has not resulted from leading or suggestive questioning, the recording equip-

ment accurately recorded the interview, and the
videotape has not been altered or edited. Any
later testimony by the child may be in person, or
it may be by videotape or closed-circuit television
in accordance with the child witness protection
statute. See Kan. Stat. § 22-3433(a).

Courts have disagreed about whether
admission of ex parte videotaped interviews
comports with the Confrontation Clause. See,
e.g., State v. Schaal (Mo.1991) (yes); People v.
Bastien (Ill.1989) (no).

d.   Child Witness Protection Statutes

Most states have enacted statutes
designed to protect child sex abuse victims from
the trauma of testifying in the physical presence
of the defendant. Most of these states permit
introduction of video monitor testimony of
sexually abused children; about half of these
states authorize use of one-way closed-circuit
video monitor testimony. A few states authorize
use of a two-way system that permits the child
witness to see the courtroom and the defendant
on a video monitor and permits the jury and judge
to view the child during the testimony.

Maryland v. Craig (S.Ct.1990) concluded
that the Confrontation Clause normally requires

an actual face-to-face meeting between the defendant and the witness appearing before the trier of fact, but that the Clause's "strong preference" for face-to-face confrontation may yield where denial of such confrontation is necessary to further an important public policy and where the testimony's reliability is otherwise assured. One such policy, according to *Craig,* is the need to protect the physical and psychological well-being of child sex abuse victims from trauma that would be caused by testifying in the physical presence of the defendant. The Sixth Amendment thus does not bar child witness protection statutes that, like the Maryland statute under review, assure reliability by preserving three essential elements of confrontation: "The child witness must be competent to testify and must testify under oath; the defendant retains full opportunity for contemporaneous cross-examination; and the judge, jury, and defendant are able to view (albeit by video monitor) the demeanor (and body) of the witness as he or she testifies."

Craig held that even with these three essential elements preserved, the Sixth Amendment permits an exception to face-to-face confrontation only where the trial court also hears evidence and makes a case-specific finding (1) that the particular child witness "would be traumatized, not by the courtroom generally, but by the presence of the defendant," and (2) that "the emotional distress suffered by the child witness in the presence of the defendant is more than *de minimis, i.e.,* more than 'mere nervousness or excitement or some reluctance to testify.'"

Craig did not specify the standard of proof the trial court must apply to determine the requisite trauma to the child, and lower courts have disagreed about the answer. See, e.g., Felix v. State (Nev. 1993) (preponderance of the evidence); Reutter v. State (Alaska Ct. App. 1994) (clear and convincing evidence). *Craig* also does not expressly require the prosecutor to present expert testimony to establish the requisite trauma, though such evidence is frequently introduced. Lower courts have not viewed expert testimony as a constitutional requirement, but some state child witness protection statutes require it.

Most state child witness protection statutes apply not only to child victims who testify in criminal sexual abuse proceedings, but also to child victims who testify in civil abuse and neglect proceedings. In civil proceedings, the Sixth Amendment Confrontation Clause does not apply but procedure must satisfy due process.

The Confrontation Clause is applicable to the states through the Fourteenth Amendment, but *Craig's* Sixth Amendment holding does not foreclose challenges to child witness protection statutes under state constitutions whose confrontation clauses provide defendants greater protections.

e.   Federal Legislation

The Child Victims' and Child Witness' Protection Act of 1990, 18 U.S.C. § 3509, governs federal court testimony of children under eighteen who are victims of physical, emotional or sexual abuse; children who are victims of child exploitation (child pornography or child prostitution); or children who witness a crime against another person. The Act authorizes the court to permit these children to testify by two-way closed-circuit television where expert testimony provides basis for a case-specific determination that the prospective witness would suffer substantial fear or trauma and be unable to testify or communicate reasonably because of the defendant's physical presence, and not merely because of a general fear of the courtroom.

f.   The Oath

Craig holds that where a child testifies

under procedures established in a child witness
protection statute, the testimony must be under
oath. "No special litany is required in adminis-
tering the oath" under such a statute or
otherwise, however, provided the child understands the importance of telling the truth. State
v. Uelentrup (Mo.Ct.App.1995). Defendant Uelentrup sought reversal on the ground that the court
did not administer the oath in the traditional
fashion to the three-year-old and five-year-old he
was convicted of sodomizing and abusing. The
court of appeals rejected the contention because
each child "testified correctly as to her name, age,
birthday, grade in school, name of school, and
name of her teacher," and because each "stated
and demonstrated that she knew what a lie was
and that it was 'bad' to tell a lie."

g. Manner of Examination
      Trial courts have considerable discretion
to regulate the manner in which child witnesses
are examined. Courts ordinarily permit young sex
abuse victims to be accompanied during
testimony by parents, relatives, friends, guardians
ad litem, clergy or other adults. The child may
hold an absolute right to have a parent present
during testimony, even if the parent would
otherwise be subject to exclusion from the
courtroom as a potential future witness. See, e.g.,

State v. Uriarte (Ariz.Ct.App.1999).

In State v. Alidani (S.D.2000), the trial court permitted the victim-assistant to sit beside the eight-year-old victim and hold her hand during her testimony. The state supreme court affirmed the conviction because the record showed no indication that the assistant spoke or acted in any way to influence the child's testimony.

Leading questions on direct examination, normally inappropriate, may be permitted where the witness is a young, frightened child and such questioning does not prejudice the defendant. See, e.g., State v. Brown (R.I.1990).

The trial court's discretion is not unlimited. Where the court's behavior may amount to vouching for the child witness, the court commits reversible error. In People v. Rogers (Colo.Ct.App.1990), for example, the court of appeals held that the trial judge committed reversible error by personally escorting the six-year-old sexual abuse victim to and from the witness stand in front of the jury.

h.   Closing the Courtroom
The Sixth Amendment provides that a

criminal defendant "shall enjoy the right to a ... public trial." The right is not absolute, however, and courts have long held authority to exclude the public from sexual assault trials, particularly ones involving child victims. Nearly a century ago, for example, the Ninth Circuit upheld an order excluding spectators from the courtroom during a trial for rape of a child. The panel concluded that the "unfortunate girl who was called upon to testify to the story of the defendant's crime and her shame" should not be compelled to appear before a "crowd of idle, gaping loafers, whose morbid curiosity would lead them to attend such a trial." Reagan v. United States (9th Cir. 1913).

The public also holds a constitutional right to open criminal trials. Where the objection to a closure order comes from the media or other members of the public rather than from the defendant, however, the objection implicates the First Amendment rather than the Sixth Amendment.

In Globe Newspaper Co. v. Superior Court (S.Ct. 1982), the Court struck down a state statute that mandated exclusion of the press and the general public during testimony of minor victims of specified sexual offenses. *Globe Newspaper Co.*

found a compelling state interest in protecting child sex crime victims, but nonetheless held that mandatory exclusion violated the media plaintiffs' First Amendment rights. The Court held that "[i]n individual cases, and under appropriate circumstances, the First Amendment does not necessarily stand as a bar to the exclusion from the courtroom of the press and general public during the testimony of minor sex-offense victims." The trial court, however, must determine on a case-by-case basis whether closure is necessary to protect the victim. Among the factors to be weighed are the victim's age, psychological maturity and understanding, the nature of the crime, the victim's desires, and the interests of parents and relatives.

i.   The Child Sexual Abuse Accommodation Syndrome

Through shame or fear, children frequently delay reporting sexual abuse, even to members of their immediate family. Delay invites the defendant to claim that the child fabricated the story or suffers from memory lapse. The Child Abuse Accommodation Syndrome offers explanations about why a sexually abused child would accept the abuse or delay reporting it, behavior some adults might find unusual or even inconceivable. As formulated by Dr. Roland C. Summit in 1983, the Syndrome includes five behaviors most commonly observed in child sex abuse victims:

> *Secrecy.*   Because much sexual abuse happens only when the child is alone with the offending adult who often threatens her with injury to herself or her family if she discloses, the child gets the impression of danger and fearful outcome.

> *Helplessness.*   Because the child is in a subordinate role, totally dependent on the adult, her normal reaction is to "play possum."

> *Entrapment and accommodation.* Because of the child's helplessness, the only healthy option is to survive by accepting the situation.

> *Delayed, conflicted and unconvincing disclosure.* Most child victims never disclose the sexual abuse, at least not outside the immediate family. Disclosure may occur only after some years have passed and accommodation mechanisms break down.

Retraction. "Whatever a child says about sexual abuse, she is likely to reverse it."

When expert testimony is based on interviews with the child, most authorities consider the Syndrome's underlying theory and science valid as diagnostic tools to explain the child's seemingly unusual reactions to sexual abuse. But these authorities also recognize that behaviors characteristic of the Syndrome may also characterize children's reactions to disorders having nothing to do with sexual abuse, such as extreme poverty or psychological abuse.

Syndrome testimony has divided the courts that have ruled on its admissibility. Most decisions hold that the prosecutor may not use expert testimony concerning the Syndrome in the case-in-chief as substantive evidence that abuse occurred, and that the Syndrome may be introduced only to rehabilitate the child's credibility by explaining his or her coping mechanisms. A few decisions hold Syndrome testimony inadmissible either as substantive evidence or to rehabilitate.

5.   PROSPECTIVE RESTRAINTS ON THE
OFFENDER

a.   Civil Commitment

Prosecutors concerned with forcing the victim to relive the trauma at trial may decide not to charge the alleged perpetrator, or else may decide to accept a plea bargain. Following a plea bargain, a dangerous defendant may return to the streets considerably sooner than if sentencing had followed trial and conviction. On the other hand, many sex offenders are not recidivists. In an effort to protect future child victims while enabling offenders to reintegrate themselves peaceably into the community after serving their sentences, a number of states have enacted civil commitment statutes. These statutes authorize the court, after a hearing, to order commitment or other mandatory treatment of sexual offenders determined to be mentally abnormal and sexually dangerous when their criminal sentences expire.

In Kansas v. Hendricks (S.Ct.1997), the Supreme Court upheld that state's Sexually Violent Predator Act, which established procedures for civil commitment of persons who, due to a "mental abnormality" or a "personality disorder," the court finds likely to engage in future "predatory acts of sexual violence." The Act applied to persons presently confined and scheduled for release, persons charged with a "sexually violent offense" but found incompetent to stand trial, and persons found not guilty by reason of insanity or because of a mental disease or defect.

The initial version of the Kansas act required the custodial agency to notify the local prosecutor 60 days before the inmate's anticipated release date. The prosecutor was required to decide within 45 days whether to seek involuntary commitment. If the prosecutor sought commitment and the court found probable cause that the inmate was a "sexually violent predator," the court would order him transferred to a secure facility for professional evaluation. After evaluation, a trial would be held to determine beyond a reasonable doubt whether the inmate was a "sexually violent predator." If the finding were in the affirmative, the person would be transferred to state custody until his condition had so changed that he was "safe to be at large."

Hendricks upheld the Kansas act against substantive due process, ex post facto and double jeopardy challenges. "Hendricks' diagnosis as a pedophile, which qualifies as a 'mental abnormality' under the Act, ... plainly suffices for due process purposes." The Court rejected the ex post facto and double jeopardy challenges on the ground that the act does not establish criminal proceedings or impose punishment.

In Seling v. Young (S.Ct.2001), the Court held that where a commitment statute has been found to be civil rather than criminal in nature, a committed person seeking release may not challenge the statute as being punitive "as applied" to him in violation of the ex post facto and double jeopardy clauses. In Kansas v. Crane, (S.Ct.2002), the Court held that *Hendricks* did not require a showing that the offender totally and completely lacked ability to control his dangerous behavior, but that the Constitution does require the state to prove that the offender had serious difficulty controlling his behavior.

b. Registration and Community Notification
On July 29, 1994, seven-year-old Megan Kanka was abducted, raped and murdered by a neighbor who lived across the street from her family in suburban New Jersey. The confessed murderer enticed the child into his home with a promise to see his new puppy, then strangled her with a belt, covered her head with plastic bags, raped her as she lay unconscious, and left her body in a nearby park. Megan, her parents, local

police, and other members of the community were unaware that the murderer had twice been convicted of sex offenses against young girls, and that he shared his house with two other men also previously convicted of sex crimes.

New Jersey's governor and legislature responded swiftly to intense public reaction to Megan's murder by enacting the Registration and Community Notification Laws, collectively called "Megan's Law," within three months. The laws (1) required persons who had committed designated crimes involving sexual assault to register their addresses with local law enforcement authorities, and (2) provided for dissemination to the community of information about registrants deemed to pose a continuing danger to the public safety.

Most other states enacted their own versions of Megan's Law within a year. In 1994, Congress enacted the Jacob Wetterling Crimes Against Children and Sexually Violent Offender Registration Act, 42 U.S.C. § 14071, which conditioned the availability of a percentage of federal crime fighting funds on a state's creation of a sex offender registration program. The Act permitted, but did not mandate, community notification provisions. When it became apparent that only a few states would mandate notification, the lawmakers in 1996 enacted a federal version of Megan's Law, which requires states also to enact community notification provisions as a condition for receiving their full share of federal funds. Id. § 14071(d). Every state now has a registration statute, nearly all of which also mandate some form of community notification

Most courts have upheld the consti-tutionality of sex offender registration/notifi-cation acts. Courts have generally upheld community notification, however, only where the sex offender has opportunity for a pre-notification hearing, with judicial review, to determine whether he poses a continuing threat to children and other persons in the community. In Connecticut Dep't of Public Safety v. Doe (S.Ct.2003), however, the Court held that due process does not require a hearing into the offender's current dangerousness where the state act bases the registration requirement on the fact of a prior conviction, not on the fact of current dangerousness.

Most states require registration only by perpetrators convicted in criminal court, but other states also require registration by adjudicated delinquents. The affected juveniles range from ones who commit forcible rape to B.G., a twelve-year-old adjudicated delinquent for reportedly groping his eight-year-old stepbrother while they were in the bathtub. See In re B.G. (N.J.App.Div. 1996). Statutes applicable to juvenile offenders may mandate continuation of registration and notification requirements even after the delinquency adjudication's general effect terminates, usually at age eighteen. Courts have held that despite juvenile court confidentiality statutes, court records must be disclosed to the extent necessary to effectuate the registration requirement. See, e.g., Doe v. Attorney General (Mass. 1997).

Challenges to the general constitutionality of juvenile registration and notification statutes, pressed on a variety of grounds, have been unavailing. In Smith v. Doe (S.Ct.2003), the Court held that a statute requiring registration of offenders convicted before passage of the act does not impose retroactive punishment prohibited by the Ex Post Facto Clause. See also, e.g., In re C.D.N. (Minn.Ct.App.1997) (holding that mandatory registration did not violate delinquents' due process rights by imposing an "adult sanction" without granting them the right to a jury trial in juvenile court).

In In re Registrant J.G. (N.J. 2001), however, the court held that lifetime registration and notification requirements did not apply to a juvenile who, when he was ten years old, committed a sex crime against his eight-year-old female cousin. *J.G.* harmonized these requirements with provisions of the state juvenile court act that prohibit trying juveniles under fourteen as adults and that terminate all delinquency dispositions other than incarceration at age eighteen or within three years, whichever is later. The court held that with respect to juveniles adjudicated delinquent for sexual offenses committed when they were under fourteen, registration and notification orders terminate at eighteen if the court finds, by clear and convincing evidence, that the delinquent is not likely to pose a threat to the safety of others.

6.   CHILD PORNOGRAPHY

a.   **New York v. Ferber (1982)**

This chapter closes with New York v. Ferber (S.Ct.1982) because production and dissemination of child pornography -- "depictions of sexual activity involving children" -- is a form of sexual abuse. Defendant Ferber, owner of a bookstore specializing in sexually oriented products, sold an undercover police officer two films devoted almost exclusively to depicting young boys masturbating. The Supreme Court upheld his conviction under a New York statute that prohibited persons from knowingly promoting sexual performances of children under sixteen by distributing material that depicted such performances. The statute operated even where the sexual performance was not legally obscene.

Ferber held that child pornography, like obscenity, is unprotected by the First Amendment. The Court acknowledged that the Amendment protects depictions of sexual activity between adults unless obscene, but granted states "greater leeway" in regulating child pornography because of its effect on the child performers themselves, without regard for its effect on viewers.

Ferber concluded (1) that "the exploitive use of children in the production of pornography has become a serious national problem," (2) that states have a compelling interest in "safeguarding the physical and psychological well-being of a minor" and in "[t]he prevention of sexual exploitation and abuse of children," and (3) that "the use of children as subjects of pornographic materials is harmful to the physiological, emotional and mental health of the child" because "the materials produced are a permanent record of the children's participation." In dictum, the Court stated that "distribution of descriptions or other depictions of sexual conduct, not otherwise obscene, which do not involve live performance or photographic or other visual reproduction of live performances, retains First Amendment protecttion."

b.   *Ferber* In The Computer Age

Ferber, decided before the age of computer-generated images, defined child pornography to concern "the exploitive use of children." The decision removed child pornography from First Amendment protection because of its present and future harmful effects on actual child performers. *Ferber* stated in dictum that "the distribution of descriptions or other depictions of sexual conduct, not otherwise obscene, which do not involve live performance or photographic or other visual reproduction of live performances, retains First Amendment protection." The Court did not discuss any effect child pornography might have on viewers.

In the computer age, "virtual" child pornography has become a pressing issue. Computers can manipulate, or "morph," an innocent picture of an actual child to create a picture showing the child engaged in sexual activity. An obscene or nonobscene picture of an adult can be transformed into the image of a child. Computer graphics can even generate the realistic image of a nonexistent child.

The federal Child Pornography Prevention Act of 1996 legislated against non-obscene virtual child pornography. Congress based the act squarely on virtual child pornography's effect on viewers. The lawmakers found that pedophiles might use virtual images to encourage children to participate in sexual activity, and that pedophiles might also whet their own sexual appetites with the pornographic images. Congress also found that the existence of computer-generated images can complicate prosecutions of pornographers who do use real children by making it more difficult to prove that a particular picture was produced using actual children.

In Ashcroft v. Free Speech Coalition (S.Ct.2002), the Court struck down provisions of the 1996 act relating to materials that appear to depict minors but are produced without using real children. The plaintiffs did not challenge the provision criminalizing morphing, which (like the materials at issue in *Ferber*) implicates the interests of real children. *Ashcroft* also left undisturbed the provision criminalizing child pornography using actual children, *Ferber's* target. But *Ashcroft* held that the provisions relating to nonexistent children violated the First Amendment for prohibiting speech that "records no crime and creates no victims by its production." The Court found any causal link between virtual images and actual incidents of child abuse only "contingent and indirect."

c.   Child Nudity

Ferber concerned a statute that prohibited distribution of photographs and films depicting "sexual activity" by juveniles. In 1986, the Attorney General's Commission on Pornography stated that the distinguishing characteristic of child pornography is that "actual children are photographed while engaged in some form of sexual activity, either with adults or with other children." Atty. Gen. Comm'n on Pornography, Final Rep. 405 (1986). In recent years, however, a number of commercial photographers have used nude and partially nude children in photo essays displayed in public exhibitions or published in books.

The Supreme Court has not decided whether photographs and films of nude or partially nude children, without sexual activity, constitute punishable child pornography or First

Amendment-protected expression. In a footnote, *Ferber* stated that "nudity, without more is protected expression," but the statement was dictum because the Court was not reviewing a statute that presented the nudity issue. In the absence of Supreme Court resolution, most lower courts have regarded photographs and films of nude children, without more, as First Amendment-protected expression, but have upheld convictions under statutes that prohibit such depictions made for sexual gratification. As thus limited, the depictions become child pornography proscribable under *Ferber*.

d.   Private Possession and Viewing of Child Pornography

In Osborne v. Ohio (S.Ct.1990), the Court upheld a statute that prohibited private possession and viewing of non-obscene child pornography (including private possession and viewing in one's own home), even without proof that the possessor intended to distribute the material. The Court found that because "much of the child pornography market has been driven underground" since *Ferber*, "it is now difficult, if not impossible, to solve the child pornography problem by only attacking production and distribution."

e. Photo Processors

To help effectuate the proscriptive authority approved in *Ferber*, Congress and a number of states require photo processors to report customers' sexual depictions of children on film. These statutes typically extend beyond films made by commercial customers, and parents and guardians who do nothing more than film their toddlers on bear skin rugs and the like are sometimes reported. Processors are typically granted immunity from civil or criminal liability arising from filing a required report in good faith.

f. Federal Legislation

Neither Congress nor the states legislated against child pornography until the 1970s. Based on findings that the "highly organized, multi-million dollar" underground child pornography industry was interstate and international in scope, S. Rep. 95-438 (1977), the Protection of Children Against Sexual Exploitation Act of 1977 added two substantive sections to the federal criminal code. The first section, now 18 U.S.C. § 2251, prohibits the use of children in "sexually explicit" productions, and prohibits parents and guardians from allowing such use of their children. The second section, now 18 U.S.C. § 2252, makes it a federal crime to transport, ship or receive in interstate commerce for the purpose of selling, any "obscene visual or print medium" if its production involved the use of a minor engaging in sexually explicit conduct.

Because the 1977 Act required proof that the materials were obscene and that the defendant had a profit motive, the Act yielded only a handful of prosecutions in its first five years of operation. Relying on *Ferber*, the Child Protection Act of 1984 prohibited distribution of nonobscene material depicting sexual activity by children and eliminated the "pecuniary profit" element. The 1984 Act also legislated against possession by criminalizing the receipt in interstate or foreign commerce of materials showing minors engaged in sexually explicit conduct.

Congressional legislation has continued. In 1986, for example, the lawmakers prohibited production and use of advertisements for child pornography and created a private civil remedy in favor of persons who suffer personal injury resulting from the production of child pornography. 18 U.S.C. §§ 2251(c), 2255. The Child Pornography Prevention Act of 1996 is discussed above in section 6.B.

CHAPTER 6

ADOPTION

A.   INTRODUCTION

1.   HISTORICAL OVERVIEW AND THE PRESENT LANDSCAPE

Adoption was unknown at common law and did not become part of statutory law in the United States until the mid to late nineteenth century. The first modern adoption act was enacted in Massachusetts in 1851, oddly enough with little fanfare or public notice. Not only did the act depart from English law, which had long prohibited permanent transfer of parental rights and obligations to third persons; the act also specified that the child was the prime beneficiary of the adoption process. When considering whether to approve an adoption petition, the court would determine whether approval would serve the child's interests.

Today all states have statutes providing for adoption of children. The various acts are marked by both similarities and significant differences. Efforts at nationwide uniformity have largely failed. Only four states have enacted substantial portions of the 1969 Revised Uniform Adoption

Act, and only one state (Vermont) has enacted the Uniform Adoption Act (1994). Other states have maintained individual differences while enacting various provisions of these model acts wholly or in modified form.

Between 2% and 4% of American families have an adopted child. Courts grant at least 140,000 to 160,000 adoptions annually (that is, considerably more than a million each decade), though estimates remain inexact because the Census Bureau, other federal agencies, and most states do not systematically track the total number. Accurate records are maintained only of international adoptees who enter the United States with the cooperation of immigration authorities, and of "special needs" children who receive federal and state assistance.

Differences in statutory language from state to state may affect the outcome in adoption cases presenting apparently similar facts. Because of similarities among adoption acts, however, lawyers handling an adoption should remain alert to other jurisdictions' statutory and decisional law, which may provide persuasive authority. Where parties to an adoption proceeding reside in different states, conflict of laws rules may also require application of another jurisdiction's adoption law.

Reciting the historical pedigree of American adoption law, many decisions hold that adoption statutes are in derogation of the common law and thus are strictly construed. On the other hand, many adoption statutes mandate liberal construction to further the best interests of the child. Even where liberal construction controls interpretation of substantive adoption provisions, courts may strictly construe procedural provisions, which are designed to protect the child by enabling the court to decide based on the most complete information available. Much adoption procedure is set out in a state's adoption act itself. Because adoption is a civil proceeding, the state's general civil procedure code and general civil court rules normally govern procedural matters not explicitly addressed in the adoption code, including matters relating to service of process, pleadings, discovery, conduct of the proceeding, and post-proceeding matters.

2. THE EFFECT OF ADOPTION

Adoption is "the legal equivalent of biological parenthood." Smith v. OFFER (S.Ct. 1977). Except where the adoptive parent is a stepparent or other partner of the birth parent, a valid adoption permanently extinguishes the parent-child relationship between the child and the birth parents and creates in its place a new relationship between the child and the adoptive parents. Where the adoptive parent is a stepparent or partner, the adoptive parent replaces the birth parent whose rights have been terminated but the child's relationship with the other birth parent continues.

Adoptive parents thus assume the constitutional rights of parenthood discussed elsewhere in this book, including the substantive due process right to direct the child's upbringing free from unreasonable state interference. The adoptive parents and the adoptee also secure new rights and obligations under a variety of federal and state laws, including tax laws, workers' compensation laws, social security and other entitlement laws, welfare laws, inheritance laws, and family leave laws. See, e.g., Buchea v. United States (9th Cir.1998) (girl could not sue for her biological father's wrongful death because she had previously been adopted by her maternal grandparents and thus was no longer the biological father's "child").

Incest statutes are a major exception to the principle that a valid adoption extinguishes the child's relationship with the biological parents. Under statutes prohibiting marriage or sexual relations between parent and child, brothers and sisters, and other close relatives of the whole or half blood, proof that one of the parties had been validly adopted is not a defense to an incest prosecution.

B.   WHO MAY ADOPT A CHILD?

1. STATUTORY STANDING AND THE "BEST INTERESTS OF THE CHILD" STANDARD

A child is adopted only when the court enters a final decree approving the adoption. The court enters the decree only when it determines that adoption by a petitioner or petitioners with standing to adopt would be in the best interests of the child.

As a general matter, adoption acts confer standing on married couples petitioning jointly, stepparents wishing to adopt their stepchildren, and frequently on single persons. Courts determine the best interests of the child by examining the circumstances of the case, including the conditions of the prospective adoptive parents and the child.

"[C]ourts have not demanded perfection in adoptive parents." In re Michael JJ (N.Y App.Div. 1994). Adoption may be in the child's best interests, for example, even where the prospective adoptive parents have relatively modest means. Adoption seeks to "provide the *best* home that is available. By that is not meant the wealthiest home, but the home which ... the court deems will best promote the welfare of the particular child." State ex rel. St. Louis Children's Aid Society v. Hughes (Mo.1944).

An adoption petition is not necessarily defeated by the prospective adoptive parents' nondisclosure or misrepresentation in connection with the adoption. In In re Baby Girl W. (N.Y.App.Div.1989), for example, the court approved the adoption even though the petitioners misrepresented their educational backgrounds, employment histories and financial condition during the preadoption investigation, and equivocated when asked to explain discrepancies. The court concluded that adoption was in the best interests of the child because "the petitioners' character flaws are offset by their proven ability to care for the child."

Even a prospective adoptive parent's criminal record does not necessarily defeat the adoption petition. In In re Alison VV (N.Y.App.Div. 1995), for example, the court held that the 34-year-old petitioner's convictions for disorderly conduct and hindering prosecution when she was seventeen did not preclude her from being considered as an adoptive parent because she had engaged in no further criminal activity, had been steadily employed by the same employer for twelve years, and had been a foster parent. A more recent conviction, however, or one involving substance abuse or misconduct with children, might be a different matter.

The "best interests of the child" standard means that the ultimate question is whether the proposed adoption would serve the child's welfare, and not whether it would serve the welfare of the biological parents, the prospective adoptive parents or anyone else. For example, the court should not be moved by pleas that the infertile prospective adoptive parents need a child for their emotional well-being, or to help shore up their shaky marriage. Some critics charge that in recent years, however, adoption law has frequently focused not on the best interests of the child but on the interests of childless couples, assertedly sometimes at the child's expense.

2.   DETERMINING STANDING AND "BEST INTERESTS"

a.   Single Persons

Most states require married couples to petition jointly unless the petitioner is the child's stepparent. Some states permit single persons to petition to adopt a child. Two single persons, however, might not have standing to petition jointly. See, e.g., In re Jason C. (N.H. 1987).

b. Stepparents

Most stepparents do not adopt their stepchildren because they cannot unless the parental rights of the noncustodial biological parent are terminated by consent or court order. Nonetheless stepparent adoptions are the most common type of adoption today.

Most stepparent adoptions involve stepfathers adopting their wives' children born in or out of wedlock. Because an uncontested stepparent adoption generally gives the law's imprimatur to a family structure already in existence, adoption acts often exempt these adoptions from requirements relating to confidentiality, home studies, probationary periods and similar matters. Critics warn, however, that exemption and relaxation may prevent the court from discovering child abuse in the home.

Contested stepparent adoptions may be an entirely different matter. Where the stepparent and his or her spouse seek to establish abandonment or another ground for nonconsensual termination of the parental rights of the other biological parent, family disruption may ensue,

sometimes drawing in more distant family
members.

What if the surviving stepparent wishes to
adopt his deceased spouse's child? If no
competing petition is filed, the court would likely
approve the adoption unless the stepparent
appears unfit. If a close relative also petitions to
adopt the child, however, the stepparent may lose
because he (like the close relative) is a legal
stranger to the child. The stepparent's position
would appear most tenuous where the law grants
the relative a preference. On the other hand, the
stepparent's position would appear stronger if the
child has resided with him for a significant period
and if uprooting would likely cause the child
psychological harm. The "best interests of the
child" standard would determine the outcome.

c. Grandparents and Other Relatives

Grandparents or other relatives sometimes
seek to adopt a child whose birth parents have
died, have had their parental rights terminated, or
have become unable to care for the child because
of physical or mental disability, substance abuse
or other cause. A relative holds no substantive
due process right to adopt the child after the birth
parents' deaths or termination of their parental
rights. See, e.g., Mullins v. State (9th Cir.1995).
The relative's blood relation to the child, however,

is a factor to consider in determining the best interests of the child. See, e.g., Dunn v. Dunn (S.C. 1989).

Some decisions grant relatives a preference in adoption proceedings. In most states, however, a relative holds a preference only where a statute or rule grants one. See, e.g., In re Adoption of Hess (Pa. 1992). The preference usually depends on the relative's prior relationship with the child. See, e.g., Fla. Stat. § 63.0425 (where child has lived with the grandparent for at least six months, the grandparent has first priority to adopt the child unless the deceased parent has indicated a different preference by will or unless the stepparent wishes to adopt). Courts, however, show a marked inclination to honor the wishes of birth parents to place a child with a particular fit relative.

d. Foster Parents

A substantial number of adoptions each year are by the child's foster parents. At one time, public and private child placement agencies often required prospective foster parents, as a condition for receiving temporary custody of a child, to agree in writing not to seek to adopt the child. The purpose was to discourage emotional bonding while the agency sought to reunify the child with the biological family or to free the child for adoption.

The historical attitude has largely changed. Where foster parents petition to adopt, courts tend to refuse to enforce no-adoption agreements where adoption by the foster parents is in the best interests of the child. See, e.g., Knight v. Deavers (Ark.1976). Courts and child welfare professionals alike now recognize that arbitrary removal from the foster home for adoption by strangers may cause the child added hardship from severing a secure relationship. The hardship may be severe because many foster children already suffer from emotional or physical disability, frequently worsened by severed relationships before the adoption petition is filed.

Some statutes grant a preference to foster parents who have cared for the child for a specified period, though the court retains ultimate authority to grant or deny the adoption in the best interests of the child. See, e.g., N.Y. Social Servs. Law § 383(3) (more than two years). Where adoption by foster parents is in the best interests of the child, the court may grant the petition even where a blood relative of the child files a competing petition. See, e.g., Petition of Dep't of Social Servs. (Mass.Ct.App.1986) (three-year-old child's best interests served by adoption by foster parents with whom she had been placed when she was four days old rather than by the paternal aunt and uncle). Requirements for adoption agency consent are discussed above in section D.1.a.

Where the adoption agency's consent is necessary for adoption, the agency's refusal to consent to adoption by the foster parents may defeat the petition. In most states requiring such consent, however, agency refusal is persuasive only and the court may decide in the best interests of the child.

e. The Petitioners' Age

In most states, a person must be eighteen or older to adopt a child, at least unless he or she is the child's stepparent or is married to an adult petitioner. A few states establish a higher minimum age. See, e.g., Ga. Code § 19-8-3 (twenty-five). A few states prescribe no minimum age, leaving it to the courts to determine on a case-by-case basis whether adoption by a minor would be in the best interests of the prospective adoptee.

Where the adoption act precludes minors from adopting a child but does not specify that a married minor may not adopt, the act's silence does not necessarily disable married minors from adopting. Marriage emancipates a minor, and emancipation confers rights of adulthood.

When older persons petition to adopt children, courts decide in accordance with the best interests standard because adoption statutes do not establish a maximum permissible age. The court may be concerned that older petitioners might be physically incapable of raising a young child, or that their death or serious illness would leave the child an orphan.

Where the petitioners are the child's grandparents or other relatives, the factors discussed above come into play. In In re Adoption of Christian (Fla.Dist.Ct.App.1966), for example, the court approved a 68-year-old grandmother's petition to adopt her 13-year-old granddaughter. On the other hand, in Sonet v. Unknown Father (Tenn.Ct.App.1990), a woman approximately seventy years old petitioned to adopt a child who was nearly three; the court denied the petition based on the petitioner's age, her lack of parenting ability with no foreseeable improvement, and the child's failure to thrive in her care.

f.　Gays and Lesbians

One member of a gay or lesbian partnership may wish to adopt the other's child, who may have been conceived by reproductive technology or who may be the biological or adoptive child of the other's prior heterosexual marital or extramarital relationship. In In re Angel Lace M. (Wis.1994), the sharply divided court held that the adoption act granted the lesbian companion no standing to adopt, regardless of whether adoption might be in the best interests of the child. Other courts, however, have found standing under their state acts. See, e.g., In re Jacob (N.Y.1995); Adoption of Tammy (Mass. 1993).

As individuals or couples, gays or lesbians may also wish to adopt children of persons other than their partners. Two states expressly prohibit homosexuals or same-sex couples from adopting children. See Fla. Stat. § 63.042(3); Miss. Code Ann. § 93-17-3(2). Utah also evidently prohibits adoption of a child by homosexuals because the state permits adoption only by persons legally married to each other, or by single persons not living in a cohabitation relationship outside marriage. See Utah Code § 78-30-1(3). In other states, courts apply the best interests test to determine whether to grant adoption petitions filed by gays or lesbians with standing to adopt.

g. Disabled Petitioners

Several states prohibit discrimination against disabled adoption petitioners. Typical is Wis. Stat. § 48.82(5): "Although otherwise qualified, no person shall be denied [eligibility to adopt a child] because the person is deaf, blind or has other physical handicaps."

h. Adoption of Siblings

Neither the United States Supreme Court nor any state supreme court has articulated a constitutional right of a child not to be separated from his or her siblings in adoption. Nor does any statute prohibit, or create a presumption against, adoption of siblings into separate homes.

The rationale for avoiding separation of siblings is straightforward. "Young brothers and sisters need each other's strengths and association in their everyday and often common experiences, and to separate them, unnecessarily, is likely to be traumatic and harmful. The importance of rearing brothers and sisters together, and thereby nourishing their familial bonds, is also strengthened by the likelihood that the parents will pass away before their children." Obey v. Degling (N.Y. 1975).

Sometimes, however, courts and authorities are torn between the desire to keep siblings together and the difficulty of finding adoptive parents willing and able to adopt siblings. The children's longterm interest in sibling association may yield to their short-term interest in leaving foster care for permanent adoption into available homes. A child's special needs may also affect the outcome. See, e.g., Morgan v. Department of Social Servs. (S.C.Ct. App.1984) (ordering adoption by foster parents who had helped cure girl of severe emotional problems, though other parents had adopted her half-brothers).

The adoption touchstone remains the best interests of the child. "[A] sibling relationship is but one factor, albeit an important one, that a judge should consider in custody cases." Adoption of Hugo (Mass.1998). Courts hearing adoption petitions acknowledge that "[w]herever possible brothers and sisters should be kept together." In re L.B.T. (Iowa 1982). The principle also applies to half-siblings. See, e.g., Crouse v. Crouse (S.D.1996).

Courts, however, separate 35,000 children from their brothers and sisters in foster and adoptive homes each year. See William Wesley Patton and Sara Latz, Severing Hansel from Gretel: An Analysis of Siblings' Association Rights, 48 U. Miami L. Rev. 745 (1994). According to some estimates, 75% of sibling groups end up separated after they enter foster care, and more former foster children search for their siblings than for their birth parents. Courts have sometimes granted separated siblings visitation rights with each other, e.g., In re Adoption of Anthony (N.Y.Fam.Ct.1982), but post-adoption visitation orders opposed by the adoptive parents will face careful constitutional scrutiny after the parents' rights analysis in Troxel v. Granville (S.Ct.2000), which chapter 1 discusses.

3. "EQUITABLE ADOPTION"

Suppose an adult agrees to adopt a child but fails to complete the adoption process and secure an adoption decree. The child lives in the adult's household, and the adult raises and educates the child and holds him out as a family member. If the adult dies intestate, may the child inherit? Some states would refuse to recognize the adoption for failure to comply with statutory directives. Denying inheritance may produce a harsh result, however, perhaps leaving the child in economic distress while property passes to more distant relatives by operation of law.

More than half the states recognize the equitable adoption doctrine, sometimes also called adoption by estoppel, virtual adoption or de facto adoption. The doctrine enables courts to enforce agreements to adopt where the adult failed to complete the adoption process through negligence or design. The agreement may be with the child, the child's birth parents, or someone in loco parentis.

Most claimants invoking the equitable adoption doctrine seek to share in the intestate adult's estate, though courts have also applied the doctrine in suits to recover damages for the adult's wrongful death, recover support from the adult, establish adoptive status under inheritance tax laws, or recover life insurance, workers' compensation or other death benefits following the adult's death. The adult might also seek to invoke the doctrine, for example, in suits seeking damages for the child's wrongful death. In some jurisdictions recognizing the doctrine, however, courts hold that only the child may invoke it.

Equitable adoption does not confer adoptive status but, consistent with the maxim that equity regards as done that which ought to be done, merely confers the benefit the claimant seeks. Contract law has been the basis of most decisions recognizing equitable adoption. The claimant must prove (1) the adult's express or implied agreement to adopt the child, (2) the child's reliance on the agreement, (3) performance by the child's biological parents in relinquishing custody, (4) performance by the child in living in the adults' home and acting as their child, and (5) partial performance by the adults in taking the child into their home and treating the child as their own. See, e.g., Lankford v. Wright (N.C. 1997).

In jurisdictions that recognize equitable adoption based on contract law, the judicial embrace has been lukewarm and claimants are rarely successful in establishing the requisite agreement to adopt. Where the suit asserting equitable adoption is filed after the putative adoptive parent's death, courts are wary of fraudulent claims. Most jurisdictions require the claimant to prove the agreement by a heightened standard of proof, such as clear and convincing evidence. The heightened standard may be satisfied without particular difficulty where the agreement is in writing, but proof of oral agreements without witnesses remains difficult.

A handful of courts reject the contract basis for imposing a hurdle frequently harmful to the best interests of the child. Even without an express or implied agreement to adopt, these decisions find equitable adoption "when a close relationship, similar to parent-child, exists" and the parties have acted for years as if the child had been adopted. See, e.g., Atkinson v. Atkinson (Mich.Ct.App.1987).

C.   ADOPTION INTERMEDIARIES AND THEIR REGULATION

1. AGENCY ADOPTIONS AND PRIVATE PLACEMENTS

Particularly where the birth parents and the prospective adoptive parents are not related, intermediaries generally facilitate the adoption process. The intermediary may be a public or private adoption agency, or it may be a private person such as a lawyer, member of the clergy or physician.

a. Agency Adoptions

An adoption may be completed through a state agency, or through a private child placement agency (sectarian or non-sectarian) licensed and regulated by statute. In recent years, most agency adoptions have concerned children who have special needs under federal or state law or who are older or otherwise difficult to place.

In an agency adoption of a newborn, the birth mother typically consents to termination of her parental rights and relinquishes custody of the child to the agency for adoption after receiving counseling about her options and the conesquences of her decision, and after the agency secures information concerning the medical,

genetic and health history of the child and the
birth parents. If the mother consents before the
child's birth, the adoption act generally requires
that she reaffirm that consent within a short
period after birth. The child remains in the
agency's custody until placement with the
adoptive parents. The agency tries to locate the
father and secure his consent to termination of
his parental rights, but does not deny services to
birth mothers who refuse to name the father. If
efforts to locate the father prove fruitless, the
agency must move for involuntary termination.
The agency's counseling of the birth mother
should continue after placement. See generally
Jana B. Singer, The Privatization of Family Law,
1992 Wis.L.Rev. 1443.

During the adoption process and
afterwards, the agency should also counsel the
adoptive parents concerning the process and the
changes adoption will likely make in their lives.
The agency's eligibility standards for prospective
adoptive parents may exclude persons based on
such factors as age, marital status, race, religion,
financial stability and emotional health. At one
time, even discrimination based on outward
appearances was encouraged because adoption
was deemed an inferior way to constitute a family.
If parents and child looked sufficiently alike and
were within a particular age range, the family

could more easily hide the fact that an adoption had occurred.

Nowadays officially sanctioned discrimination is the exception rather than the rule throughout American life, and Congress has even mandated an end to race matching in adoption (see infra § F). Discrimination in adoption resists eradication, however, because it frequently results from exercise of agency discretion rather than from written rules and regulations. Because of the agencies' experience and expertise, courts may be reluctant to second guess their discretionary decisions.

Fees charged by adoption agencies have risen substantially in recent years and now can run as high as $7000 to $10,000 or more, with the highest fees being charged by private agencies. Joan Heifetz Hollinger, Introduction to Adoption Law and Practice § 1.05[3][a], at 1-67, in 1 Hollinger, supra.

b. Private Placements

A private placement adoption is arranged without an agency by the birth mother dealing with the prospective adoptive parents either directly or through a lawyer, member of the clergy, physician or other intermediary. Most states facilitate private placements by permitting advertising by persons wishing to adopt.

All states permit private placement adoptions by stepparents or other members of the child's family. All but a handful of states also permit private placements to adoptive parents unrelated to the child. Even in the few states that prohibit non-relative private placements, birth parents may sometimes reach agreement privately with the prospective adoptive parents, and then work with an agency to direct the child to the designated persons.

In recent years, most healthy infants have been adopted in private placements, which normally do not provide the counseling that agencies offer birth parents and adoptive parents. The steadily increasing volume of private adoptions is fueled in part by frustration with agencies' long waiting lists, restrictive guidelines, and sometimes intrusive investigations. A major reason for the increase is the contemporary shortage of adoptable children without special needs, and the resulting intense competition for these children among desirous adoptive parents.

The shortage of healthy infants available for adoption stems from several factors. Abortion and birth control are more widely available to unmarried women than in the past. Unmarried

birth mothers today are also much more likely to
keep their babies because the stigma of single
parenthood and out-of-wedlock births has mark-
edly diminished in the past generation. About
98% or more of unmarried women who deliver
babies now choose to keep the child. As a result,
prospective adoptive couples outnumber adoptable children by at least 20-1 and, according to
some estimates, ratios considerably higher. The
odds are particularly daunting for would-be
adoptive parents disfavored by agencies, such as
older couples and single persons.

In private placements, adoptive parents
may pay as much as $20,000, including their
legal fees, the birth mother's legal fees and
maternity-related expenses. Some observers
believe that in some private placements, "under
the table" payments may increase the amount
considerably.

2. BABY SELLING

Most states have enacted statutes
prohibiting baby selling and baby brokering. The
statutes regulate the money that can change
hands in an adoption, limiting payments by
prospective adoptive parents to reasonable
amounts for such items as agency or other
placement fees, counseling and attorneys' fees,

the medical expenses of the birth mother and the child, and the birth mother's living expenses during the pregnancy. Some statutes also permit the prospective adoptive parents to excuse child support arrearages owed by the birth parent who consents to termination of parental rights, at least where one petitioner is the child's stepparent. Some decisions permit the parties to excuse support arrearages even in the absence of statute.

The policy behind baby selling statutes is that adoption should be a donative transfer, and not a commercial transaction in which the birth mother or intermediary sells a product for profit. Some observers believe, however, that these statutes are ineffective in preventing an underground market in healthy babies. Because the demand for such babies far exceeds their numbers, would-be adoptive parents may be willing to pay considerable sums to birth mothers and intermediaries regardless of statutory proscription.

Baby selling prosecutions are few and far between, in part because there is usually no complainant unless the birth mother has second thoughts. Proof beyond a reasonable doubt is difficult to establish because the line between proper and improper payments can be hazy. Sanctions imposed on birth parents are both quite rare and quite minor. Courts normally do not withhold approval of the adoption because unlawful payments usually surface in private adoptions, if at all, only in an accounting after the child has been placed. By that time, courts are unlikely to upset the child's established relationship with loving adoptive parents.

Baby selling statutes apply to lawyers who act as intermediaries in private adoptions. In In re Thacker (Tex. 1994), for example, the court upheld disciplinary sanctions imposed on a lawyer convicted of purchasing five children from the same mother, including unborn twins. In affirming Thacker's conviction, the court of appeals found that the lawyer paid the birth mother about $12,000 for the five children. Thacker v. State (Tex.Ct.App. 1994, 1999). The state supreme court upheld the lawyer's disbarment on the ground that violation of the baby selling statute constitutes a crime involving moral turpitude.

3.　FEDERAL AND STATE SUBSIDIES

Psychologists recognize that children freed for adoption thrive best in permanent adoptive homes rather than in prolonged foster or institutional care. Growing numbers of special needs children, however, suffer through multiple foster placements deprived of permanency for lack

of available adoptive placements. (The definition
of "special needs" differs from state to state, but
the term generally includes older children,
children of racial or ethnic minority groups,
children with siblings who should be placed
together if possible, children who test positive for
HIV, children who suffered prenatal exposure to
drugs or alcohol, abused or neglected children,
and children with mental, emotional or physical
disabilities.) Agency eligibility standards for
prospective adoptive parents are frequently
relaxed when an applicant wishes to adopt a
special needs child, but adoption may nonetheless
remain difficult because parents willing to adopt
and nurture special needs children may face
imposing obstacles, including financial ones, not
faced by other adoptive parents.

        In an effort to facilitate adoption of special
needs children, federal and state law provide
financial assistance for parents willing to
shoulder the responsibility. The federal Adoption
Assistance and Child Welfare Act of 1980, 42
U.S.C. §§ 670-76, created an adoption assistance
program under the Title IV-E of the Social
Security Act. The program provides subsidies for
persons adopting children who have one or more
special needs according to the state's definition,
and who are SSI (Supplemental Security Income)
eligible or come from a family that meets the

eligibility requirements of the former Aid to
Families With Dependent Children program as of
July 16, 1996. (A child is "SSI eligible" usually
because he or she has a disability.) Eligibility for
Title IV-E adoption assistance does not depend on
the adoptive parents' financial circumstances.

The Adoption and Safe Families Act of
1997 encourages adoption of special needs
children by, among other things, (1) providing
incentive payments to states whose adoptions of
foster children exceed the previous year's number,
(2) requiring states to provide health insurance
coverage for any special needs child with an
adoption assistance agreement who the state
determines would not be adopted without medical
assistance, (3) guaranteeing that special needs
children will not lose eligibility for federal
adoption assistance if their adoption is dissolved
or their adoptive parents die, and (4) prohibiting
states from postponing or denying a suitable out-
of-state adoptive placement while seeking in-state
placement.

In 2001, Congress enacted the Hope For
Children Act, which increased to $10,000 a tax
credit for all adoptions other than adoptions of
children of the taxpayer's spouse. Taxpayers who
adopt a special needs child are entitled to the
credit regardless of their adoption costs.

Taxpayers who adopt a child without special needs are entitled to a credit only to the extent of their unreimbursed qualified adoption expenses. The amount of the credit begins to be reduced when the taxpayers' adjusted gross income exceeds $150,000, and is completely phased out when the taxpayers' adjusted gross income reaches $190,000.

Various states also allow tax credits for parents who adopt special needs children. States may also maintain adoption subsidy programs to assist parents of special needs adoptees ineligible for the federal IV-E program. The state subsidies generally cover medical, maintenance and special services costs. Eligibility for state assistance generally depends on the adoptive parents' financial circumstances and the child's special needs.

4. INVESTIGATIONS OR HOME STUDIES

In agency adoptions and private placements alike, adoption acts require at least one investigation or home study of the prospective adoptive parents. Some states permit courts to waive this requirement for good cause. Many states do not impose the requirement where the prospective adoptive parent is the child's stepparent or other close relative.

The investigation or home study enables the court to determine whether the prospective adoptive parents would be suitable for the child, helps the parents probe their capacity to be adoptive parents and the strength of their desire to adopt, and helps reveal factors about the parents or the child that might affect the adoption. The investigation or home study may protect the child from a placement undesirable because of the parents' circumstances, such as a history of abuse or neglect or the parents' likely inability to manage the child's special needs.

In agency adoptions, the agency must make an investigation or home study before placing the child with the prospective adoptive parents; the child may be placed in temporary foster care in the interim. The agency must follow up with a further inspection shortly after placement. In private placements, however, the investigation or home study might not be done until after the parent or an intermediary has transferred the child. Public concern about lax regulation of private placements has led some states to require that at least where the prospective adoptive parent is not the child's stepparent or other relative, a notice to adopt must be filed and an investigation or home study must be conducted before transfer. Transfer may not be made until the parents are certified as qualified. These requirements recognize that because of the child's need for stability, a meaningful post-transfer investigation or study may be impossible.

Except in stepparent adoptions and other unusual circumstances, the adoption does not become final until the child has been in the adoptive parents' custody for a probationary period which, depending on the state, may range from three months to a year. The court signs the final adoption order if circumstances warrant after a final home investigation.

5.   THE INTERSTATE COMPACT ON THE PLACEMENT OF CHILDREN

Children are frequently moved from one state to another for foster care or possible agency or private adoption. In light of the sometimes significant differences between state adoption laws, movement sometimes results from forum shopping by parties seeking states with comparatively favorable provisions.

To enhance protection for children moved interstate, all states have enacted the Interstate Compact on the Placement of Children, which was first proposed in 1960. An interstate compact is an agreement between two or more states which is both a binding contract between the states and a statute in each state. A compact takes precedence over the state's other statutory law. U.S. Const. art. I, § 10.

The Interstate Compact on the Placement of Children seeks to protect children transported interstate for foster care or possible adoption, and to maximize their opportunity for placement in a suitable environment with persons able to provide the necessary and desirable level of care. Compact, Art. I(a). Most decisions hold that the Compact applies to both agency adoptions and private placements.

The Compact provides that "[n]o sending agency shall send, bring or cause to be sent or brought into any other party state, any child for placement in foster care or as a preliminary to a possible adoption unless the sending agency shall comply with each and every requirement set forth in this article and with the applicable laws of the receiving state governing the placement of children therein." Id. Art. III(a). Sending agencies must notify the receiving state's compact administrator before placing a child. The receiving state's authorities must investigate and, if they are satisfied, must notify the sending state that the proposed placement does not appear contrary to the child's interests. The child may not be sent or brought into the receiving state until notification is given.

The "sending agency" may be either an entity or a natural person. Article VIII, however, excludes from the Compact's scope the sending of a child into the receiving state by "his parent, step-parent, grandparent, adult brother or sister, adult uncle or aunt or his guardian and leaving the child with any such relative or non-agency guardian in the receiving state."

The sending agency retains jurisdiction over the child in matters relating to custody, supervision, care and disposition until the child is adopted, reaches majority, becomes self-supporting or is discharged with the receiving state's concurrence. The sending agency also continues to have financial responsibility for support and maintenance of the child during the period of the placement. Id. Art. V(a).

Where a child is sent or brought across state lines in violation of the Compact, the violation is punishable under the child placement laws of either state and may be a ground for suspending or revoking the violator's license to place or care for children. Id. Art. IV. The Compact does not specify, however, whether violation may also be a ground for dismissing the adoption petition, a potent sanction indeed. Decisions tend to hold out the prospect of dismissal but ultimately refuse to make children pay the price of adult noncompliance. Courts decide in accordance with the best interests of the child, declining to upset the adoption and perhaps return the child to foster care.

A persistent barrier to the Compact's effectiveness is counsel's noncompliance, which may be unintentional due to lack of knowledge about interstate adoption requirements. Parties seeking redress for noncompliance with the Compact may file in the courts of the sending or the receiving state. Determining the jurisdictionally proper court may implicate the Uniform Child Custody Jurisdiction Act (which has been enacted in all states) and the federal Parental Kidnapping Prevention Act.

D.   THE CONSENT REQUIREMENT

1. THE REQUIREMENT OF INFORMED AND VOLUNTARY CONSENT

a. The Nature of Consent

The general rule is that on a petition by persons with standing to adopt, the court may not consider the best interests of the child unless consents to adoption have been secured from all persons with a right to give or withhold consent. Receipt of all required consents does not complete the adoption, but merely enables the court to order the adoption if it concludes all other requirements (including the best interests standard) have been satisfied.

Knowing and voluntary consent (or as some statutes call it, "release," "relinquishment" or "surrender") generally must be secured from both birth parents. A parent may execute a specific consent (authorizing adoption by particular named persons) or a general consent (authorizing adoption by persons chosen by the agency, an intermediary or the court). To preserve confidentiality, general consents are normally used in agency adoptions.

Consent is not required from a birth parent who is incompetent, whose parental rights have been terminated voluntarily or involuntarily, or who has abandoned or neglected the child for a period specified in the adoption act. If the birth parent is incompetent, the court may appoint a guardian of the child's person, with authority to consent in the parent's stead. In some states, the court in the adoption proceeding itself may determine whether to terminate parental rights; other states require that where termination is a predicate for adoption, the termination proceeding must take place before the adoption proceeding.

Because valid consent to adoption may terminate the parent-child relationship, adoption acts require formalities designed to bring home to the birth parent the gravity of consent. In almost all states, consent must be in writing. The act may specify that the consent be signed before a judge, notary or other designated officer. A particular number of witnesses may be required. The consent may have to be under oath.

Most states specify that parents may not execute consent until after the child is born. See, e.g., Ariz. Rev. Stat. § 8-107(B) (not before child is 72 hours old). In some states, this specification applies only to the birth mother; the birth father (who may disappear during the pregnancy) may consent either before or after the child's birth. See, e.g., 23 Pa. Cons. Stat. § 2711(c). In many states, consent may be revoked within the first few days after execution, or within the first few days or hours after the child's birth. The court then may determine whether revocation is in the best interests of the child. See, e.g., Ga. Code Ann. § 19-8-9 (ten days after signing).

Most states permit minor birth parents to execute out-of-court consents without the advice of their parents or guardians, other family members or counsel. To help reduce the adoption's vulnerability to later collateral attack, however, the adoptive parents' counsel may wish the minor to acknowledge her desires in open court.

In nearly all states, consent to the adoption must also be secured from the child where he or she is over a specified age. See, e.g., Cal. Fam. Code § 8602 (twelve or older). Some statutes authorize the court to dispense with the child's consent for good cause. See, e.g., N.M. Stat. § 32A-5-21 (ten or older, unless the court finds the child does not have mental capacity to make the judgment).

Where a child has been committed to the custody of a public or private child placement agency, the agency's consent may also be a factor. In a few states, agency refusal to consent divests the court of authority to grant the adoption. Many states make the agency's consent a prerequisite to adoption, but authorize judicial scrutiny by providing that the agency may not unreasonably withhold consent. See, e.g., Minn. Stat. § 259.24(1)(e), (7). Even where the adoption act seemingly makes agency consent mandatory without condition, many decisions hold that the agency's refusal to consent is nonetheless

persuasive only. The court may grant the
adoption if it finds agency's refusal to consent
contrary to the best interests of the child. See,
e.g., In re M.L.M. (Mont.1996). Under the familiar
judicial approach to review of agency decision-
making, however, the court will likely grant
deference to the agency determination because of
the agency's experience and expertise.

b. Notice
        A person's right to consent (or withhold
consent) to the adoption must be distinguished
from the right to notice of the adoption proceeding. A person with the right to consent, such as a
birth parent, is entitled to notice and may veto the
adoption by withholding consent.

        The adoption act, however, may also
require notice to other persons, who may hold the
limited right to address the court concerning the
best interests of the child, but without the right to
veto the adoption. To expedite the adoption
process, some states provide that notice need not
be given to a person who has executed a valid
consent to adoption. Not requiring notice may
make good sense because the person has no right
to veto the adoption and may be difficult to locate.
On the other hand, not requiring notice may
encourage persons to secure consents from
vulnerable birth parents under conditions

approaching fraud or duress.

c. Forcible or Statutory Rape

Several states authorize termination of the father's parental rights on the ground that the child was conceived as a result of a forcible rape or other nonconsensual sex crime committed by him. The father then may not veto adoption of the child. Courts hold or assume that the federal and state constitutions impose no barrier to such terminations.

Courts disagree about whether termination of parental rights may be ordered, as a matter of law, where the child was conceived as a result of a statutory rape in the absence of force. See, e.g., Pena v. Mattox (7th Cir. 1996) (yes); In re Craig "V" (N.Y.App.Div. 1986) (no).

2.   THE RIGHTS OF UNWED PARENTS

The birth mother has traditionally held the right to veto an adoption by withholding consent, unless consent was excused by operation of law. Because this right emanated from the mother's legal right to custody of the child, the right applied regardless of whether she was married to the father at conception and birth. The right was meaningful because the mother's identity is ordinarily ascertainable from the birth certificate, hospital records or witness' testimony.

Before Stanley v. Illinois (S.Ct.1972), the father's rights to notice of an adoption and to withhold consent was another matter. Where the child was conceived or born during marriage, the father's identity and whereabouts were ordinarily ascertainable and his consent to adoption was normally required, again unless excused by operation of law. See, e.g., Armstrong v. Manzo (S.Ct.1965) (absence of notice deprived divorced father of due process and invalidated purported adoption by mother's new husband). Unwed fathers, however, held no right to notice of the child's impending adoption and no right to veto the adoption under the federal constitution or under the constitutions or statutes of most states. An unwed father could not secure these rights by acknowledging the child as his own, supporting the child, or seeking to establish a relationship with the child or the mother. As a matter of law in most states, unwed fathers held no legal relationship to their children.

a. Stanley v. Illinois (1972)

Joan and Peter Stanley lived together "intermittently" for eighteen years. When Joan died, their three children became wards of the state by operation of law and were placed with court-appointed guardians. As an unwed father,

Peter was a non-parent -- a legal stranger to his children -- who held no statutory right to a fitness hearing before placement. In Stanley v. Illinois, however, the Supreme Court held that due process guaranteed the unwed father a fitness hearing before his children could be taken from him, and that the state violated equal protection by denying him a hearing while extending it to all other parents whose custody of their children was challenged.

Stanley was a dependency proceeding, but it immediately revolutionized adoption law. Previously a nonmarital child's adoption could be finalized on the mother's consent alone, regardless of whether the father appeared now or later to protest. By conferring due process and equal protection rights on the unwed father with respect to the child, however, *Stanley* and its progeny raised the specter that the father whose rights have not been terminated (including a father who cannot be located now) may appear sometime the future and contest the adoption.

Because *Stanley* concerned an unwed father who (as the majority read the record) had maintained a relationship with his children, the decision left open the question whether the decision conferred constitutional rights on all unwed fathers, or only on unwed fathers who had

maintained such a relationship. *Stanley* itself
sent conflicting signals. On the one hand, the
Court spoke about Mr. Stanley's interest in "the
children he has sired and raised"; on the other
hand, the Court suggested service by publication
on absent fathers.

The Court began answering this question a
few years later in two decisions concerning the
constitutional rights of unwed fathers to veto
adoptions. The first, Quilloin v. Walcott (S.Ct.
1978), concerned an unwed father who had never
sought custody or visitation of his 11-year-old
son, had supported the boy only irregularly, and
had had several contentious visits with him. The
Court held that *Stanley* did not entitle the father
to veto the adoption because he had "never
exercised actual or legal custody over the child,
and thus ha[d] never shouldered any significant
responsibility with respect to the daily supervision, education, protection, or care of the child."

In Caban v. Mohammed (S.Ct. 1979), a
year later, the unwed father had lived with his two
children and had supported and cared for them
for several years until he and the mother
separated. He continued to see the children often
after the separation and continued to raise them.
The Court held that *Stanley* granted Mr. Caban
an equal protection right to veto the children's

adoption because his "substantial relationship" with his children was different from Mr. Quilloin's "failure to act as a father."

b. Lehr v. Robertson (1983)

In Lehr v. Robertson (S.Ct.1983), the unwed father contended that due process and equal protection gave him an absolute right to notice and opportunity to be heard concerning the proposed adoption of his two-year-old daughter by the man who had married the girl's mother when the child was eight months old. In the two years between the girl's birth and the adoption proceeding, the unwed father had never supported the child, had rarely seen her, and never lived with her or the mother.

The Supreme Court rejected the unwed father's due process claim because he had not developed a relationship with the child. Nor had he entered his name in the state's putative father registry, which would have signaled his intent to claim paternity and would have conferred a right to notice of the adoption. The Court concluded that the registry "adequately protected his opportunity to form such a relationship" with the child. "The significance of the biological connection," Justice Stevens wrote for the Court, is that it offers the natural father an opportunity that no other male possesses to develop a relationship with his offspring. If he grasps that opportunity and accepts some measure of responsibility for the child's future, he may enjoy the blessings of the parent-child relationship and make uniquely valuable contributions to the child's development. If he fails to do so, the Federal Constitution will not automatically compel a State to listen to his opinion of where the child's best interests lie."

Lehr also rejected the unwed father's equal protection claim. Again the Court stressed that unlike the mother, he had never established any custodial, personal or financial relationship with his daughter. "If one parent has an established custodial relationship with the child and the other parent has either abandoned or never established a relationship, the Equal Protection Clause does not prevent a state from according the two parents different legal rights."

Lehr (like *Stanley, Quilloin* and *Caban*) concerned children who were at least a few years old when the adoption dispute arose, and children whose existence and whereabouts the fathers had known about since birth. The decisions do not explicitly speak to two recurrent questions:

> *Newborn adoptions.* Many transfers of children to nonrelative adoptive parents occur at birth or within days (but not

years) thereafter. Does due process or equal protection guarantee the unwed father a right to veto an adoption before he has had a meaningful opportunity to develop a relationship with the child?

The "thwarted" unwed father. Seeking to prevent the unwed father from developing the requisite relationship with the child, the mother may place the child for adoption at birth or shortly afterwards after hiding the child from him, after untruthfully asserting that she does not know the father's identity or whereabouts, after refusing to name the father, after forging his signature on consent documents, or after knowingly naming the wrong man. The unwed father may have a civil damage action against the mother, e.g., Kessel v. Leavitt (W.Va.1998) (fraud); Smith v. Malouf (Miss.1998) (intentional infliction of emotional distress and conspiracy), but damage recovery would not unravel the father's tangled rights with respect to the child.

The Court's next decision, *Michael H.*, may suggest a new approach to these and other constitutional questions raised by the *Stanley* line of decisions.

c. Michael H. v. Gerald D. (1989)

In Michael H. v. Gerald D. (S.Ct.1989)
(plurality opinion), the sharply divided Court
suggested that a state may constitutionally
protect a marital union by disregarding an unwed
father who had maintained a relationship with the
child. As noted in chapter 2, California law
presumed that a child born to a married woman
living with her husband was a child of the
marriage, provided the husband was not impotent
or sterile. The virtually conclusive presumption
was rebuttable only by the husband or the wife,
and only in limited circumstances. The Court
rejected Michael's contention that the statute
violated his due process liberty interest in his
relationship with his daughter without affording
him an opportunity to establish paternity.

The four-Justice plurality (Justice Scalia,
writing for himself, the Chief Justice and Justices
O'Connor and Kennedy) rejected Michael's
contention that the *Stanley* line of decisions
conferred a liberty interest "created by biological
fatherhood plus an established parental
relationship," two factors the Court recognized
were present in Michael's case. The plurality
concluded that under the *Stanley* line, a liberty
interest depends not on establishment of a

parental relationship, but on "the historic respect -- indeed, sanctity would not be too strong a term -- traditionally accorded to the relationships that develop within the unitary family."

As a matter of law, the plurality's rationale precluded Michael from establishing a liberty interest because Gerald, and not he, maintained the requisite relationship with Carole. Because no liberty interest meant no due process violation, California's statutory presumption survived. An unwed birth father seeking to veto an adoption based solely on his relationship with the child would similarly have no cognizable liberty interest if he had not established a legally recognized relationship with the mother.

Concurring Justice Stevens provided the fifth vote for the disposition, but did not embrace the plurality's reading of the *Stanley* line of decisions, which he concluded "demonstrate that enduring 'family' relationships may develop in unconventional settings."

Dissenting Justice Brennan (writing for himself and Justices Marshall and Blackmun) argued that the *Stanley* line had "produced a unifying theme: although an unwed father's biological link to his child does not, in and of itself, guarantee him a constitutional stake in his relationship with that child, such a link combined with a substantial parent-child relationship will do so. ... This commitment is why Mr. Stanley and Mr. Caban won; why Mr. Quilloin and Mr. Lehr lost ... ."

d. Putative Father Registries

Most states enacted putative father registries after *Lehr* upheld their general constitutionality. Where a man believes he is or may be a child's father, he must register (usually with the state department of health or similar agency) if he wishes to receive notice of a prospective adoption. Once the man receives notice, he may seek to establish paternity and assert his right to veto the adoption.

New York's registry statute at issue in *Lehr* established no time limit within which the putative father must register to preserve his claim of right. In some states, however, the statute requires registration before the child is born or within a specified short period after birth. See, e.g., Ariz. Rev. Stat. § 8-106.01B (before the child's birth or not later than 30 days after birth). Failure to register within the specified period may constitute waiver not only of the right of notice but also of the right to contest the adoption. Registry statutes with time limits are strictly construed against the putative father, both to avoid the lengthy custody battles the registries are designed to prevent, and to protect the birth mother. Courts have upheld the constitutionality of strict construction. See, e.g., In re Adoption of Reeves (Ark. 1992).

The wrinkle is that most men remain unaware of the registry's existence because they are not lawyers and most prospective parents do not consult with lawyers about childbirth. A few states seek to publicize the registry in places likely to be frequented by unwed fathers, such as hospitals, local health departments and other such health facilities, motor vehicle department offices, and schools and universities. Publicity or no, however, the putative father's lack of knowledge of the registry's existence, or of the pregnancy and birth, does not excuse non-registration. The rationale is that men "are aware that sexual intercourse may result in pregnancy, and of the potential opportunity to establish a family." In re Clausen (Mich. 1993).

Despite the statutory purpose to enable unwed fathers to protect their rights, registries are not foolproof. For one thing, each registry is a particular state's enactment, without reach or effect in other states. Assume two teenagers conceive a child while on summer vacation in state A, then return to their homes in states B and C respectively. With the help of her parents, the teenage mother in state C then places the child for adoption in state D, asserting that she does not know the father's identity or whereabouts. The father may have no idea that adoption proceedings are pending in state D, and registration in state A, the state of conception, would not protect him.

E.   OPEN ADOPTION

1. THE GROWTH OF OPEN ADOPTION

In an "open adoption," the child has continuing post-decree relations with the birth parents or perhaps other members of the immediate or extended birth family. The continuing relations may include contact through visitation, correspondence, telephone calls, or otherwise. Informal adoption, frequently with arrangements for openness, was the norm in the first decades after Massachusetts enacted the first modern adoption act in 1851. Only in the early twentieth century did states begin to mandate sealing of adoption records to insure confidentiality and sever the legal and social relationship between adoptees and their birth parents.

In recent years, the shortage of healthy adoptable children has helped increase the prevalence of open adoptions resulting from agreements between the birth parents and the adoptive parents. The shortage has provided leverage to birth mothers who seek a future right of contact with the child before consenting to a private placement adoption. Indeed, some adoption agencies facing loss of business now accommodate birth mothers who seek openness and might otherwise choose private placements. Unwed fathers holding a right to veto the adoption under the *Stanley* line of decisions may also insist on openness.

The growth of private open adoptions has also resulted from the changing demographics of adoption. In recent years, smaller percentages of adoptions have involved newborns and greater percentages have involved children over the age of two, including special needs children. More and more children have been adopted by their stepparents, relatives and foster parents. The result is that birth parents, adoptees and adoptive parents frequently know one another's identities and whereabouts before the petition is filed. For better or worse, the child may have had a relationship with the birth parents and other relatives that a stroke of the judge's pen cannot undo.

Where practical necessity or private

arrangement has not produced openness, however, confidentiality remains controversial as a policy matter. For some special needs and older foster children desperately needing adoptive homes, the openness option may help overcome judicial reluctance to order an adoption where complete severance of ties with birth parents or other close relatives may not be in the child's best interests. The option may also help overcome a birth parent's reluctance to consent to termination of parental rights, and thus may enable the child to secure an adoptive home without lengthy, and sometimes bitter, contested termination proceedings. Openness may also benefit an older child who has had a relationship with the birth parents or other close relatives. Finally, open adoption may enable disputing parties to settle contested proceedings without the trauma the child might otherwise suffer when birth parents and adoptive parents each hold out to the bitter end for an "all or nothing" outcome.

On the other hand, openness may deter many persons from adopting for fear they must "share" the child or might later lose the child. Openness also would sometimes produce continued relationships with abusive or neglectful parents, or leave the child confused by loyalties to more than one set of adults.

Disagreement remains concerning judicial authority to order open adoptions. Some adoption acts authorize courts to order visitation or other contact between an adopted child and persons other than the adoptive parents, including the natural parents, when visitation or contact would be in the best interests of the child. See, e.g., Wis. Stat. § 48.92(2). Other adoption acts, however, expressly preclude post-adoption visitation orders unless the adoptive parents agree to permit visitation. See, e.g., Tenn. Stat. § 36-1-121(f).

Where the adoption act is silent about post-adoption visitation, courts disagree about whether it may be ordered in the best interests of the child. In In re S.A.H. (S.D.1995), for example, the court held that visitation may be ordered when three factors indicate, by clear and convincing evidence, that visitation would serve the best interests of the child: (1) the child's psychological need to know his or her ancestral, ethnic and cultural background, (2) the effect of open adoption on the child's integration with the adoptive family, and (3) the effect of open adoption on the pool of prospective adoptive parents. Other decisions, however, have precluded courts from exercising inherent authority to enter post-adoption visitation orders on the ground that the adoption act, while silent about visitation itself, expressly terminates all rights and relationships between the adoptee and persons other than the adoptive parents. See, e.g., In re Adoption of C.H. (Minn.1996).

After Troxel v. Granville (S.Ct.2000), which is discussed in chapter 1, a court order granting birth parents or others visitation with an adopted child would raise serious constitutional questions if the order is opposed by the adoptive parents, who succeed to the birth parents' rights under the adoption act.

2.   ENFORCEABILITY OF PRIVATE AGREEMENTS FOR OPENNESS

As discussed above, prospective adoptive parents in private adoptions frequently agree to permit the birth mother or others to have visitation or other post-adoption relationships with the child. In a few states, the adoption code expressly authorizes courts to specifically enforce such private agreements found to be in the best interests of the child.

In the absence of express statutory authority, decisions disagree about the propriety of specific performance. See, e.g., Michaud v. Wawruck (Conn.1988) (written visitation agreement between birth parent and the adoptive parents may be specifically enforced where

enforcement is in the best interests of the child);
Hill v. Moorman (La.Ct.App.1988) (adoptive
parents' written agreement to allow the birth
mother reasonable visitation with the child was
unenforceable).

F.   CULTURAL AND RELIGIOUS IDENTITY

1. TRANSRACIAL ADOPTION

a. Overview of Domestic Transracial Adoption

The term "transracial adoption" would
describe any adoption in which the parents and
child are of different races. Nearly all transracial
adoptions in the United States, however, have
involved white parents and black or biracial
children. International adoption is discussed
below in section G.

The first recorded adoption in the United
States of a black child by white parents took place
in 1948. Transracial adoptions increased in the
1950s and 1960s. Then, in 1972, the National
Association of Black Social Workers condemned
transracial adoption as "cultural genocide" and
argued that "Black children should be placed only
with Black families whether in foster care or
adoption." National Ass'n of Black Social Workers,

Position Paper (Apr. 1972).

Transracial adoption continues to be relatively rare but still controversial. Professor Ruth-Arlene W. Howe, for example, has written that "[w]idespread, unregulated occurrences of private placements of infants of African-American descent with non-African-American adoptive parents place these children at risk of alienation from their natural reference group." Transracial Adoption (TRA): Old Prejudices and Discrimination Float Under a New Halo, 6 B.U. Pub. Int. L.J. 409 (1997). On the other hand, Professor Randall Kennedy argues that "[r]acial matching is a disastrous social policy both in how it affects children and in what it signals about our current attitudes about racial distinctions. ... What parentless children need are not 'white,' 'black,' 'yellow,' 'brown,' or 'red' parents but loving parents." The Orphans of Separatism: The Painful Politics of Transracial Adoption, 38 American Prospect 38 (Spring 1994).

b. Congressional Legislation

In 1996, Congress enacted the Small Business Jobs Protection Act of 1996 (SBJPA), which contained provisions seeking to end the practice of matching adoptive parents with children of the same race. The legislation prohibits private and public child placement agencies from denying any person the opportunity to become an adoptive or foster parent, or from delaying or denying placement of a child for adoption or into foster care, "on the basis of the race, color, or national origin of the adoptive or foster parent, or the child." Violations are actionable under title VI of the Civil Rights Act of 1964. 42 U.S.C. § 1996b(1),(2). The SBJPA, however, does not prohibit agencies from delaying or denying placement on the ground that the prospective adoptive or foster parents lack sensitivity needed to raise a child in a multiracial family.

The Supreme Court has not decided whether denial of an adoption on racial grounds would violate the Constitution. Some hints, however, may be provided in Palmore v. Sidoti (S.Ct.1984), an appeal by a white divorced wife who lost custody of her young child to her white former husband after she married a black man. The trial court found neither birth parent unfit but stated that placement with the birth father was in the best interests of the child because "it is inevitable that [the child] will, if allowed to remain in her present situation and attains school age and thus more vulnerable to peer pressures, suffer from the social stigmatization that is sure to come."

Palmore unanimously held that the order modifying custody violated equal protection. "The Constitution cannot control [racial and ethnic] prejudices but neither can it tolerate them. Private biases may be outside the reach of the law, but the law cannot, directly or indirectly, give them effect."

2. NATIVE AMERICAN ADOPTION

Congress' rejection of race-matching in the SBJPA stands in contrast to the lawmakers' recognition of tribal identity in the Indian Child Welfare Act of 1978, 25 U.S.C. § 1901 et seq. The Act provides that "[i]n any adoptive placement of an Indian child under State law, a preference shall be given, in the absence of good cause to the contrary, to a placement with (1) a member of the child's extended family; (2) other members of the Indian child's tribe; or (3) other Indian families." 25 U.S.C. § 1915(b). The SBJPA expressly exempts the ICWA from its provisions.

An estimated 1,000 to 2,500 Native American children are adopted each year. The ICWA seeks to protect the best interests of Indian children, and to promote the security, survival and stability of Indian families and tribes by recognizing Indian children as tribal resources. 25 U.S.C. § 1901(1), (3), 1902.

3. RELIGION

By statute or case law, courts deciding whether to approve an adoption are mandated or authorized to consider the religion of the prospective adoptive parents and of the child (or the child's birth parents). Wis. Stat. § 48.82(3) is typical: "When practicable and if requested by the birth parent, the adoptive parents shall be of the same religious faith as the birth parents of the person to be adopted."

Religious matching raises two fundamental questions. The first is whether the court may deny an adoption on the ground that the adoptive parents and the child (or the child's birth parents) are of different religions. Courts generally hold that where the statute requires religious matching when practicable or feasible without creating an inflexible rule of law, the First Amendment establishment and free exercise clauses are not offended when religious differences are considered as one factor in determining the best interests of the child. See, e.g., Petition of Gally (Mass. 1952) (religious matching was not practicable where the physically disabled two-year old would likely not be adopted by anyone other than the petitioners). Some courts have held, however, that the First Amendment is violated when religious matching is

the sole ground for denying an adoption by
otherwise fit petitioners. See, e.g., In re Adoption
of E (N.J.1971). Religious differences are less
significant where the birth parents consent to
adoption by a petitioner of a different faith. See,
e.g., In re Adoption of Anonymous (N.Y.Fam.Ct.
1965).

Should the child's age and maturity affect
the weight the court gives to the adoptive parents'
different religion? Where the child is a newborn
or an infant too young to express a religious
preference, courts may consider the birth parents'
preferences for the child, but these preferences
are not determinative. See, e.g., Cooper v.
Hinrichs (Ill.1957). Older children, however, may
have interests of their own that merit the court's
recognition.

The second fundamental question is
whether a court may deny an adoption on the
ground that a prospective adoptive parent does
not believe in a Supreme Being. Some decisions
have considered a parent's failure to believe in
God as indicating inability or unwillingness to
direct the child's religious and moral upbringing.
However, In re Adoption of E, supra, is typical of
decisions holding that without other facts, a court
may not find failure to believe in God controlling.
"Sincere belief in and adherence to the tenets of a

religion may be indicative of moral fitness to adopt in a particular case," but "we do not believe that any reasonable man no matter how devout in his own beliefs, would contend that morality lies in the exclusive province of one or of all religions or of religiosity in general."

G.   INTERNATIONAL ADOPTION

Adoption of foreign children by Americans, largely unknown before World War II, began in earnest with returning soldiers and media coverage of the plight of children and other refugees. The Korean and Vietnam wars produced heightened interest, which continues to this day. Proponents of international adoption have argued persuasively that international adoption offers a future to abandoned, homeless and sometimes starving children in many corners of the world while also serving the needs of loving parents in the United States who face a shortage of adoptable American children without special needs. On the other hand, many poorer nations remain wary of "child snatching" by citizens of the United States and other industrialized nations.

International adoption is no longer a product solely of war. In fiscal year 1999, United States citizens adopted 16,396 children from abroad, a number that exceeds the number of international adoptions completed by citizens of all other nations combined. Russia was the greatest source for intercountry adoptions, followed in descending order by China, South Korea, Guatemala. Romania, Vietnam, India, Ukraine and Cambodia. See National Adoption InformationClearinghouse, www.calib.com/naic/ pubs/f_inter.html. International adoption accounts for only about 5% to 6% of U.S. adoptions annually, but the numbers are increasing rapidly.

The Hague Convention on Protection of Children and Cooperation in Respect of Intercountry Adoption, presented in 1993 and ratified by the United States Senate in 2000, recognizes adoption as a positive alternative for children unable to remain with their birth families but unlikely to be adopted in their own nation. The Convention sets minimal international adoption standards and procedures to safeguard the interests of children, birth parents and adoptive parents. The Intercountry Adoption Act of 2000, Pub. L. No. 106-279, is implementing legislation that enables the United States to participate in the Convention and secures its benefits for U.S. adoptive parents and adoptees in international adoptions. The Child Citizenship Act of 2000, Pub. L. No. 106-395, confers U.S. citizenship automatically on certain foreign-born children who do not acquire citizenship at birth, including children adopted by U.S citizens.

H.   POST-ADOPTION DISPUTES

1. FRAUD OR NEGLIGENCE

A relatively small percentage of adoptions fail, frequently when the child manifests severe physical or emotional problems previously unknown to the adoptive parents, perhaps because the agency or other intermediary failed to provide them full and complete information at the time of adoption. Adoption's intended permanency faces a stern challenge when a party sues to recover damages or annul an adoption for negligence or fraudulent misrepresentation.

Burr v. Board of County Commissioners (Ohio 1986), was the first reported decision to impose liability on an adoption intermediary for nondisclosure of information about the adopted child's physical or mental condition. A number of jurisdictions now permit recovery for fraud or negligence, or both. See, e.g., Gibbs v. Ernst (Pa. 1994). Some states have also enacted statutes mandating disclosure of material information by adoption agencies.

Instances of fraudulent misrepresentation by adoption agencies and other intermediaries have evidently declined since *Burr*, but nondisclosure and inadequate disclosure smacking of negligence persist. Periodic damage actions are likely to continue because adoption dockets include greater numbers of emotionally and physically disabled foster children and of international adoptees. Complete information about foster children is sometimes unavailable because of poor recordkeeping, rapid turnover of social welfare agency personnel, and frequent movement of the child from home to home. Private adoption agencies frequently do not receive full information from foster care authorities. International adoptees may have been anonymously abandoned by their parents or may have come from poorly administered orphanages without adequate medical histories.

2. ANNULLING ADOPTIONS

Adoptive parents alleging fraud or negligence sometimes seek to annul the adoption rather than recover damages. A damage action leaves the adoptive family intact but awards compensatory or punitive damages, or both. Annulment, on the other hand, makes the adoption a nullity, and thus frees the adoptive parents of the rights and obligations that adoption creates.

Suits to annul adoptions tend to arise in three situations. The adoptive parents may find the child ungovernable and beyond their effective control; the child may manifest undisclosed severe emotional or physical disabilities unknown to the parents when they adopted; or an adoptive stepparent may seek annulment when he or she later divorces the birth parent.

Except where the adoptive parents appear defrauded or where other extreme circumstances appear, courts normally deny annulment as contrary to the best interests of the child. Annulment is particularly unlikely where the child has been in the adoptive home for a substantial period of time, or where the child's likely alternative is a return to state custody. "[P]ublic policy disfavors a revocation of an adoption because an adoption is intended to bring a parent and child together in a permanent relationship, to bring stability to the child's life, and to allow laws of intestate succession to apply with certainty to adopted children." In re Adoption of T.B. (Ind.1993). Because the law "abhors the idea of being able to 'send the child back'", only a strong showing of fraud will establish a ground for annulment. Many courts hold that a party may annul an adoption only where entitlement to annulment is established by clear and convincing evidence. See, e.g., In re Lisa Diane G. (R.I.1988).

Adoption codes normally establish a short period within which finalized adoptions may be challenged. The limitations statutes, however, frequently reach only challenges for procedural irregularities or defects in the adoption proceeding itself. See, e.g., Md. Code, Fam. Law § 5-325 (one year). The period is not tolled during the child's minority because tolling would defeat the purpose of the short period, which is to produce finality that protects children from the psychological trauma occasioned by disrupted lives.

A few states also create a limitations period for fraud challenges. See, e.g., Colo. Rev. Stat. § 19-5-214(1) (one year). Other states have enacted broad statutes of limitations that reach all challenges. See, e.g., 10 Okla. Stat. § 7505-7.2(A)(2) (three months).

Where the adoption code's statute of limitations reaches only procedural irregularities or defects, courts may permit challenges for fraud or other substantive irregularity under the state's civil procedure act or rules relating to vacatur of final judgments generally. The act or rules may be based on Fed. R. Civ. P. 60(b), which permits vacatur on a showing, among other things, of fraud, misrepresentation or other misconduct of an adverse party or voidness of the judgment.

Under general limitations doctrines, the limitations period for a fraud claim may be tolled until the allegedly defrauded party discovered or should reasonably have discovered the fraud. See, e.g., Mohr v. Commonwealth (Mass. 1995).

I.   ADOPTEES' RIGHTS TO "LEARN THEIR ROOTS"

1. INTRODUCTION

Entry of the adoption decree extinguishes the existing parent-child relationship, and creates a new parent-child relationship between adoptive parent and child. Statutes provide that when the court decrees an adoption, the state issues the child a new birth certificate naming the adoptive parents as the only parents, the child assumes their surname, and the original birth certificate and all other sealed court records ordinarily may be opened only on court order for good cause. In the absence of the severe necessity that establishes good cause, the birth parents may not learn the identity or whereabouts of the child or adoptive parents, and the adoptive parents and the child may not learn the identities or whereabouts of the birth parents.

Confidentiality legislation is grounded in the policy determination that closed records serve the interests of all parties to the adoption. The birth parents can put the past behind them, secure from embarrassment, and sometimes shame, arising from the adoption itself and perhaps the circumstances of the pregnancy and birth. The adoptive parents can raise the child as their own, free from outside interference and fear that the birth parent might try to "reclaim" the child. The adoptee avoids any shame from out-of-wedlock birth and can develop a relationship with the adoptive parents. By serving these interests of the members of the adoption triangle, confidentiality is also said to serve a state interest in encouraging persons to adoption children.

Confidentiality statutes lose their force when the court orders an open adoption, or specifically enforces a private agreement for such an arrangement. As a practical matter, confidentiality may also be impossible where the birth mother insists on maintaining contact with the child as a condition of her consent, where the adoption is otherwise concluded informally before the parties seek the decree, or where the child has had a pre-adoption relationship with the birth parents or other relatives.

In the absence of privately negotiated or court-mandated openness, however, a vast array of statutes and rules help assure confidentiality.

Adoption proceedings are not open to the public. Adoption records are exempt from state freedom of information acts and open records laws. The adoption agency, the attorneys and other participants face criminal or contempt sanction for making unauthorized disclosure.

Federal and state courts have upheld the constitutionality of confidentiality statutes. Even where the court acknowledges the adoptee's interest in disclosure, the state is found to have a rational basis for maintaining the birth parents' interest in privacy, the adoptive parents' interest in finality, and the state's interest in fostering adoption.

2. "GOOD CAUSE"

The good-cause exception permits disclosure of identifying information (that is, the birth parents' name, birth date, place of birth and last known address) only where the adoptee demonstrates urgent need for medical, genetic or other reasons. Even without such a showing, most states mandate or allow disclosure of an adopted child's health and genetic history, without revealing identifying information. Some states also grant adoptees, when they reach majority, the right to nonidentifying information concerning their birth parents (that is, information about the parents' physical description, age at the time of adoption, race, nationality, religious background, and talents and hobbies, without revealing the parents' identities).

Psychological need generally does not establish good cause for release of identifying information. In In re Linda F.M. v. Department of Health (N.Y.1981), for example, the adoptee unsuccessfully sought release of her forty-year-old adoption records. She alleged that her inability to discover her natural parents' identity had caused psychological problems because "I feel cut off from the rest of humanity. ... I want to know who I am. The only person in the world who looks like me is my son. I have no ancestry. Nothing." *Linda F.M.* acknowledged that "desire to learn about one's ancestry should not be belittled," but held that "mere desire to learn the identity of one's natural parents cannot alone constitute good cause, or the requirement ... would become a nullity." The court did state, however, that "concrete psychological problems, if found by the court to be specifically connected to the lack of knowledge about ancestry, might constitute good cause."

Medical problems may similarly not establish good cause, particularly where release of non-identifying information provides substantial information. In Golan v. Louise Wise Services (N.Y.1987), the 54-year-old movant had been adopted when he was less than fifteen months old. Suffering from a heart condition that produced a heart attack before the trial court heard the disclosure motion, he and his attending physicians asserted that genetic information would assist treatment and help enable the physicians to evaluate the severity of his condition.

The adoption agency supplied movant Golan with all medical and historical information it possessed concerning his birth parents, except his biological father's name and hometown and the name of the college the biological father allegedly attended. (Golan already knew his birth mother's name.) The court denied the disclosure motion, which sought to examine and reproduce any records or reports relating to his birth parents.

3. DISCLOSURE LEGISLATION

The efforts of many adoptees to locate their birth parents may be impeded not only by confidentiality statutes, but also by practical barriers. Poor recordkeeping at some adoption agencies may make any sustained search fruitless, particularly after the passage of decades.

Children adopted from orphanages overseas, sometimes after surreptitious abandonment by their birth parents, may have been subject to no recordkeeping in their native lands; the abandoned child might not even have a birth certificate or other proof of date of birth.

Neither statutory mandate nor practical barriers, however, extinguish the desire of many adoptees for disclosure. Recent years have witnessed the growth of advocacy and support groups to assist adoptees' efforts to locate their birth families, to challenge the constitutionality of sealed-records statutes, and to lobby for open-records legislation. Adoptees have sometimes hired private search consultants and have found new search avenues on the Internet.

Most states have enacted registry statutes, which permit release of identifying information where the birth parents, the adoptive parents and the adult adoptee all state their desire for release. Passive registry statutes allow parties to state their desires, and active registry statutes authorize state authorities to seek out parties' desires when one party expresses a desire for disclosure. In states without registry statutes, the parties' "unanimous" consent to disclosure may be insufficient to establish good cause and overcome the state's interest in secrecy.

A handful of states now grant adult adoptees an absolute right to their original birth certificates, or to the court records of their adoption proceeding. In Doe v. Sundquist (Tenn. 1999), the court upheld the constitutionality of legislation that allowed disclosure of sealed adoption records to adoptees twenty-one years of age or older. The court held that the legislation did not violate the state constitution by impairing the vested rights of birth parents who had surrendered children under the prior law, or by violating the rights to familial and procreational privacy and to nondisclosure of personal information.

CHAPTER 7

MEDICAL DECISION-MAKING

At common law, minors generally did not have capacity to consent to their own medical treatment. Instead their parents had the authority to consent (or withhold consent) on their behalf. Not surprisingly, the common law rule had a number of exceptions that authorized children to consent to medical care independent of their parents in some circumstances. In addition, parental authority could be transferred to the state when a court found that the child was a victim of neglect.

Today the common law rule requiring parental consent prevails except where statutes or case law vest authority in the child or the state. As applied to adults or children in the medical treatment context, the term "consent" means "informed consent"—a technical, context, and jurisdiction specific term that generally means that patients have been told their diagnosis, the recommended treatment and alternative treatments, the risks involved, the prognosis, and similar information. Conflict among the potential decision-makers – parent, child and state – raises the issues discussed in this chapter. To resolve these thorny medical decision-making cases, lawyers frequently need to elicit the expertise of professionals in medicine and other disciplines.

A. DECISION-MAKING AUTHORITY

1. CONSTITUTIONAL FRAMEWORK

Adults hold a substantive due process right to refuse medical treatment, even life-sustaining treatment, for themselves. See Cruzan v. Director, Missouri Department of Health (S.Ct.1990). Consistent with the fundamental due process right to direct their children's upbringing, parents also hold general authority to consent (or withhold consent) to medical care on their child's behalf, to approve withdrawal of medical care from the child, and to require the child to submit to medical care. Two important Supreme Court decisions refine the scope of the parents' constitutional authority and children's generally negligible role in determining the nature and course of their medical care.

The first decision, Parham v. J.R. (S.Ct.1979), was a § 1983 class action challenging Georgia procedures for committing children to state mental hospitals. The class plaintiffs included both children committed by their parents and children committed by the state who were already in state custody. Both types of commitments were considered "voluntary" because the children's custodians had consented to state care.

The plaintiffs alleged that the state's voluntary commitment procedures violated due process and sought to enjoin their future application. The named plaintiffs included J.R., who had been removed from his parents for neglect at age three months, and had been placed in seven different foster homes before his admission to a state hospital at age seven. The boy was diagnosed as "borderline retarded and suffered an 'unsocialized, aggressive reaction to childhood.'" Another plaintiff, J.L., was admitted to a state hospital at age six by his mother and stepfather. Attempts were made to return the boy home, but his parents were unable "to control [him] to their satisfaction, and this created family stress." Several hospital employees had recommended that J.L. be placed in a foster home with a supportive family, but the state had made no placement.

Parham assumed, without deciding, that children have "a protectible interest in not only being free of unnecessary bodily restraints, but also in not being labeled erroneously as 'mentally ill.'" The Court, however, required only minimal due process protections. The state must provide "some kind of inquiry" by a neutral factfinder to

determine whether the statutory requirements for
admission were satisfied. At the least, the inquiry
must include investigation of the child's
background and an interview with the child.
Provided the evaluation is independent and the
decision-maker can refuse to commit the child,
however, the hearing need not be a formal or
quasi-formal adversary hearing. Further, the
factfinder need not be legally trained or a court
employee, but can be a staff physician. After initial
admission, the state must conduct periodic reviews
to determine the continued need for commitment.
In addition, the lower court was to consider on
remand whether a different review process may be
needed for children already in state custody than
that required for children committed by their
parents. The Court suggested that state wards may
bear a greater risk of being "lost in the shuffle,"
resulting in unduly prolonged commitments.

Parham concluded that parents are the
prime decision-makers in the commitment process:
"The law's concept of family rests on a presumption
that parents possess what a child lacks in
maturity, experience, and capacity for judgment
required for making life's difficult decisions. More
important, historically it has recognized that
natural bonds of affection lead parents to act in the
best interests of their children. ... Most children,
even in adolescence, simply are not able to make

sound judgments concerning many decisions, including their need for medical care or treatment. Parents can and must make those judgments."

By characterizing commitment to a state mental hospital as voluntary and by assuming that custodians act in the child's best interests, *Parham* reached a stark conclusion about the custodial status of children: children's views play only a negligible role in the commitment process, at least as a constitutional matter.

Some states do provide greater procedural protections than *Parham's* due process minimum. New Jersey, for example, provides counsel for the child or the child's representative and requires a court hearing before a final commitment order can be issued. The court may order commitment only where it finds that the minor suffers from a mental illness that causes him to be dangerous to himself, others or property; and that the minor needs "intensive psychiatric treatment that can be provided at a psychiatric facility ... and which cannot be provided in the home, the community or on an outpatient basis ...." New Jersey Rules of Court Rule 4:74-7A.

Even where commitment to a state mental hospital is characterized as voluntary for admission purposes, lower courts have held that

children hold a substantive due process right to
safe conditions of confinement. See, e.g., Wyatt v.
Poundstone (M.D.Ala.1995) (detailing the gang
activity, physical and sexual abuse by staff and
other problems suffered by children while in an
Alabama mental health facility). The right is akin
to the substantive due process right to safe
conditions held by children in foster care (chapter
4) and in juvenile justice confinement (chapter 10).

In recent years, children have been
admitted to inpatient mental health facilities at
dramatically increasing rates. Critics charge that
many of these children are committed not for
severe mental disorders, but because they are
status offenders or other "troublesome" children
who exhibit behavior distressing to their families
or communities but who cannot be committed to
secure juvenile justice facilities because of the
deinstitutionalization mandate in the Juvenile
Justice and Delinquency Prevention Act of 1974.
According to one commentator, "[h]ospitals are
rapidly becoming the new jails for middle-class and
upper-middle-class kids ... usually committed for
medical problems that do not require
hospitalization and for which there is little
evidence that psychiatric intervention is
appropriate or effective." Ira M. Schwartz,
(In)justice for Children: Rethinking the Best
Interests of the Child (1989).

The second important Supreme Court decision is Bellotti v. Baird (S.Ct.1979), which introduced the mature minor doctrine into constitutional jurisprudence based on the right to privacy in a pregnant minor's abortion decision. (See chapter 1.) *Bellotti* held that where a state requires parental consent for a pregnant woman's abortion, the state must provide a minor the opportunity to demonstrate that she is "mature enough, and well enough informed to make her abortion decision, in consultation with her physician, independently of her parents' wishes." If a minor is not mature enough, she is entitled to judicial determination of whether the abortion would be in her best interests. *Bellotti* thus holds, as a constitutional matter, that parents' withholding of consent controls only where the abortion is not in the best interests of an immature pregnant minor.

The Supreme Court has not extended the mature minor doctrine to confer constitutional authority on children in medical decision-making outside abortion. Medical decision-making authority still generally resides in the parents unless their decision constitutes neglect or the decision fits within one of the exceptions discussed below.

2. COMMON LAW AND STATUTES

Where a minor lacks capacity to consent to
medical care, physicians commit a common law
battery when they treat the minor without
parental consent, just as they commit a battery
when they treat an adult without the adult's
consent. For children and adults alike, however,
one exception to the common law rule is that
physicians may provide treatment in an emergency
when the patient is unable to consent. Another
exception permits physicians to treat mature
minors in accordance with their wishes, even over
the parents' opposition.

a. The Mature Minor Doctrine

In medical decision-making cases, most
jurisdictions permit courts to consider a mature
minor's wishes without express statutory
authority, and may even find the minor's medical
care choice determinative. In In re E.G. (Ill.1989),
for example, a seventeen-year-old leukemia victim
and her mother refused on religious grounds to
consent to blood transfusions. The state filed a
neglect petition and sought appointment of a
guardian to consent to transfusions on the child's
behalf. The state adduced expert testimony that
without the transfusions, the child would die
within a month, but that transfusions and
chemotherapy achieve remission in about 80

percent of cases. The long-term prognosis, however, was not optimistic because the survival rate was only 20-25 percent. The patient testified that she fully understood the nature of her disease and the consequences of her decision. Several witnesses for the patient testified that she was a mature minor with sincere religious beliefs.

E.G. held that a mature minor may exercise a common law right to consent to or refuse medical care, but that this right must be balanced against the state's interest in preserving life, preventing suicide, maintaining the medical profession's ethical integrity, and protecting the interests of parents and other third parties. The court found the patient mature and allowed her decision to control her medical treatment. The court ordered that the neglect finding against the mother be expunged.

Some jurisdictions refuse to recognize a common law mature minor exception to the general parental consent requirement. In O.G. v. Baum (Tex.Ct.App.1990), for example, a sixteen`-year-old child severely injured in a train accident needed surgery to save his arm. The parents and child were Jehovah's Witnesses and refused to consent to a blood transfusion that might be needed during surgery. The court declined to determine the minor's maturity but appointed a temporary conservator with authority to consent to a transfusion.

b. The Child's Opinion

When a child is too young to be a "mature minor," but is old enough to have some understanding of the proposed medical treatment, a court hearing a medical neglect case may consider the child's views about the proposed treatment as one factor in determining which course of action is in the child's best interests. See, e.g., In re Green (Pa.1972).

Where the mature minor doctrine is not applied or where the court finds the child insufficiently mature concerning the issue at hand, parents may secure a court order compelling the child to submit to medical treatment. In In re Thomas B. (N.Y.Fam.Ct.1991), for example, a fifteen-year-old boy refused a biopsy because of his "phobia for needles." On the mother's status offense petition, the court ordered the child to cooperate with the hospital in obtaining treatment and directed the sheriff's department to take necessary steps to enforce the order.

An older child's persistent resistance to medical treatment, however, and the practical difficulties of requiring treatment may eventually convince the child's parents or other authorities to stop treatment. For example, sisteen-year-old Billy

Best ran away from home after 2½ months of
chemotherapy for Hodgkin's disease. He returned
home three months later in response to his family's
pleas and promises from his parents and
physicians that he would not be forced to receive
additional chemotherapy. See Jennifer L. Rosato,
The Ultimate Test of Autonomy: Should Minors
Have a Right to Make Decisions Regarding Life
Sustaining Treatment?, 49 Rutgers L. Rev. 1
(1996). Physicians also may play a key role when a
child objects to medical treatment by requiring the
child's consent as well as the parents' for elective
treatment for older children.

c. Statutory Exceptions

Statutes have carved out a number of
exceptions to the general rule that parental
consent is needed for a minor's medical care. Many
states have general medical emancipation statutes
that enable some minors to consent to their own
medical care, such as married minors, minors on
active military duty, and minors who otherwise
meet the common law or statutory definitions of
emancipation. Some states have also codified the
emergency exception and the common law mature
minor rule, sometimes in very broad language.
Nevada, for example, provides that a "minor who
understands the nature and purpose of the
proposed examination or treatment and its
probable outcome, and voluntarily requests it may

consent to medical care." Nev. Rev. Stat. Ann. §
129.030(2).

Most states also have statutory categories
of medical care minors can receive without
parental consent. Frequently these limited medical
emancipation statutes cover health problems that
minors might want to conceal from their parents
and hence might not seek to have treated if
parental consent were required, such as drug
abuse, alcohol abuse, pregnancy, or venereal
disease. These statutes generally do not relieve
the parent of the obligation to pay for the
treatment. See, e.g., Mich. Stat. Ann. §§ 333.5127
(venereal disease or HIV), 333.6121 (drug abuse),
333.9132 (prenatal and pregnancy care).

3. EXCESSIVE OR UNUSUAL TREATMENT

a. Munchausen Syndrome by Proxy

Munchausen syndrome by proxy, a rare
psychological disorder, is a form of child abuse that
causes a parent (usually the mother) to fabricate or
even induce medical problems in the child to gain
sympathy and attention for the parent from
medical personnel. Many children have undergone
unnecessary medical procedures and some children
have even died because of actions by parents
afflicted by this disorder. Munchausen cases can be
so extreme that they provide grounds for

terminating parental rights, e.g., In re S.R. (Vt.1991), or for convicting the parent of murder, e.g., People v. Phillips (Cal.Ct.App.1981).

b. Experimental Treatment

As a general rule, when parents request medical treatment for the child, the parents' informed consent is all that is needed to allow the procedure to be performed. Court approval usually is not required, even when the treatment is particularly risky or experimental. In 1984, for example, court approval was not obtained for using a baboon heart in an infant, Baby Fae, even though the procedure had not been tried on adults. The baby died shortly after the operation. See Children as Research Subjects: Science, Ethics and Law 127 (Michael A. Grodin and Leonard H. Glantz eds., 1994).

The Baby Fae treatment is a good illustration of the substantial discretion parents and their physicians have in deciding whether to provide, rather than withhold, treatment for a child. Because use of the baboon heart was considered beneficial treatment, it was treated like any other medical procedure.

It is possible to find situations in which court approval was required before a child received experimental treatment. In In re A.M.P.

(Ill.App.Ct.1999), for example, the court reviewed the parents' consent to electro-convulsive therapy (ECT) by providing the child an opportunity to be heard and receiving input from a health care professional. To determine whether the treatment was in the child's best interests and was the least intrusive treatment available, the court heard evidence about ECT's risks and the dearth of literature on its use on younger patients. The court authorized the treatment.

When a child is to be provided medical treatment as part of a research project, researchers must comply with U.S. Department of Health and Human Services regulations on research on human subjects, which contain special restrictions related to research on children. 45 C.F.R. § 46.408.

c. Organ and Bone Marrow Donation
Court authorization is frequently sought when a medical procedure on a child is solely for another's benefit, with no medical benefit to the child. Parents may want a child to donate organs or bone marrow, for example, to help save a sibling's life, but the hospital may be concerned about undertaking the procedure based on parental consent alone. The child's parents may also disagree with one another about whether the procedure is advisable. In Curran v. Bosze (Ill.1990), for example, a mother refused to allow

3½-year-old twins in her custody to be tested for bone marrow compatibility for possible donation to another child of their father. The court refused to authorize the procedure, holding that the father had failed to establish that the mother's withholding of consent was clearly contrary to the best interests of the twins.

Some states have enacted statutes permitting children to donate bone marrow in specified situations without court approval. Some of the statutes are very restrictive, allowing donations only for siblings and with a number of procedural protections, e.g., Wis. Stat. Ann. § 146.34; other statutes place the decision with parents, e.g., Ala. Code § 22-8-9.

B. MEDICAL NEGLECT

Where a parent fails to provide needed medical treatment for a child, the state can bring a medical neglect proceeding. The Illinois trial court in *E.G.*, for example, ruled that the child was medically neglected and appointed a guardian who had consented to blood transfusions. Courts have long recognized the state's parens patriae authority to take decision-making control from a parent when necessary to protect a child. See, e.g., Jehovah's Witnesses in State of Wash. v. King

County Hospital Unit No. 1 (Harborview) (W.D.Wash.1967; S.Ct.1968).

Broadly speaking, medical neglect mainly arises in two types of cases – those in which lack of necessary medical care is part of a pattern of neglect, and those in which the child is generally well-cared-for but the parents and state disagree about whether particular medical care must be provided. The first type of case involves parents, such as the *S.T* parents in chapter 3, section D.1.a., who fail to provide their children adequate food, shelter and other care, including medical care. The children may be deprived of routine medical care (such as immunizations or treatment for ear infections), or of special needs medical care. These parents are not necessarily opposed to the medical care, but they have not provided it. In these cases, medical neglect may be just one item on a lengthy list of parental failures.

This section focuses on the second type of medical neglect, which results from parental decisions, frequently religiously based, to forego medical care that the state views as necessary. These cases focus on the medical care issue because the parents generally do not neglect their children in other ways, and indeed may be very concerned about the children's health and well-

being. If the court finds neglect, the child may
remain with the parents but the state holds legal
custody for medical decision-making. The court
may appoint a guardian to make medical decisions
concerning the litigated issue. Unless a public
health issue is involved, courts in this type of case
usually do not authorize medical care over
parental objection unless the child's situation is
life-threatening or likely to result in serious,
permanent harm.

Even where the child's health is not in
immediate jeopardy, courts may order
immunization or screening based on public health
concerns and the relatively non-invasive nature of
the procedures. Mandatory immunizations (such as
ones for poliomyelitis, mumps, measles, and
diphtheria) require parental consent, but a court
may order immunization by issuing a medical
neglect order against a parent who withholds
consent. A number of states provide exemptions to
immunization requirements for parents whose
opposition is based on their religious beliefs,
although some state courts have struck down the
exemption. See, e.g., Brown v. Stone (Miss.1979)
(immunization exemption violated equal protection
rights of immunized children who would be at risk
of contracting communicable diseases from non-
immunized children). Screening for some diseases
such as phenylketonuria (PKU) in newborns is

required in many states and may be done without parental consent, although some states allow parents to object for religious reasons.

1.   DETERMINING MEDICAL NEGLECT

When the state seeks a medical neglect order, the state alleges that the parents' refusal to provide medical care, which a physician deems necessary, constitutes neglect. In their defense, the parents contend that their decision is a reasonable choice, made in the child's best interests.

In Newmark v. Williams/DCPS (Del.1991), for example, a court was asked to determine that a three-year-old boy with serious pediatric cancer was a neglected child and to order chemotherapy and other medical treatment over his parents' objections. The court balanced the competing interests of the parents, the state and the child. The boy's disease would be fatal if not treated, but the proposed medical treatment was highly invasive, painful, involved side effects, and had, at best, a 40 percent survival rate with a high risk that the treatment itself would cause his death. The court determined that the state's authority to intervene did not outweigh the parental prerogative to make medical care decisions and the child's inherent right to enjoy human dignity in the time left to him.

When a treatment is new and its long-term effects are unknown, the state may be unable to establish neglect by a parent refusing consent. See, e.g., In re Nikolas E. (Me.1998) (parent's refusal to allow HIV-positive child to be treated with drug therapy was not "serious abuse or neglect"). Parents who choose alternative treatment not accepted by the medical community may be found neglectful, however, unless they can convince the court that the alternative treatment is reasonable. See, e.g., Custody of a Minor (Mass.1979) (parents not allowed to use alternative treatment, laetrile metabolic therapy); In re Hofbauer (N.Y.1979) (parents allowed to use laetrile metabolic therapy as an alternative to chemotherapy).

2.   SPIRITUAL TREATMENT EXEMPTIONS

A court may find a child neglected when parents fail to provide medical care, even where the failure stemmed from the parents' religious objections to providing the care. First Amendment free exercise rights may be a factor in the parents' favor, but they do not prevent the state from intervening, or from prevailing on a contested neglect petition. Chapter 1, for example, discusses Prince v. Massachusetts, which upheld state authority to protect children and rejected a free exercise claim because "[t]he right to practice

religion freely does not include liberty to expose ...
the child... to ill health or death." *Prince* explained
that "[p]arents may be free to become martyrs
themselves. But it does not follow that they are
free ... to make martyrs of their children before
they have reached the age of full and legal
discretion where they can make that choice for
themselves." Medical neglect cases raising
religious liberty defenses challenge the courts,
which must apply not only the Free Exercise
Clause, but also the First Amendment's prohibition
on "law[s] respecting an establishment of religion."

After religious groups successfully lobbied
for spiritual treatment exemptions in the 1970s,
regulations under the Child Abuse Prevention and
Treatment Act (CAPTA) required states to include
such exemptions in their definitions of harm. A
majority of states passed religious exemption
statutes after CAPTA. In 1983, CAPTA regulations
were amended to permit, but not require, a
religious exemption, but few states have repealed
their exemptions.

The scope and location of religious
exemptions vary from state to state, but are
primarily grouped in three types of statutes: civil
neglect statutes, abuse and neglect reporting
statutes, and criminal statutes. Civil neglect
statutes typically provide that a child who "in good

faith is under treatment solely by spiritual means shall not, for that reason alone, be considered to have been neglected," or similar language. Courts have interpreted the phrase, "for that reason alone," to allow a neglect finding when the child's life is in imminent danger.

Spiritual treatment exemptions in civil neglect statutes can protect parents from criminal conviction when a child dies from a lack of medical care. In State v. McKown (Minn.1991), for example, eleven-year-old Ian Lundman died at his Minnesota home of diabetic ketoacidosis, a complication of diabetes mellitus. Ian had been occasionally ill in the weeks preceding his death and became seriously ill a few days before his death. Ian's mother and stepfather were Christian Scientists who treated the boy with spiritual healing methods in accordance with their religious beliefs, and without any conventional medical care.

The grand jury indicted the mother and stepfather for second degree manslaughter, but the state supreme court held that the indictments violated due process because the state sought to prosecute the parents for conduct permitted by the civil neglect statute's spiritual treatment exemption. The court reasoned that due process prohibited the state from enacting a statute clearly expressing intent to permit good faith reliance on spiritual treatment and prayer as an alternative to conventional medical care, and then prosecuting parents for their reliance.

In an effort to cure the due process barrier dispositive in *McKown*, some state statutes specify limits to the religious exemption. Oklahoma provides, for example, that "medical care shall be provided where permanent physical damage could result to such child." Okla. Stat. tit. 21, § 852. Some courts have allowed manslaughter prosecutions to proceed against parents whose religious beliefs led them to deny necessary medical care to their child who died. See, e.g., Walker v. Superior Ct. (Cal.1988). It has even been held that the spiritual treatment statutory exemption to a criminal abuse and neglect statute violates the Establishment Clause and equal protection. See State v. Miskimens (Ohio Ct.Com.Pl.1984).

Some prosecutors are sympathetic to the parents in these cases, feeling they are well-intentioned. In Commonwealth v. Nixon (Pa.Super.Ct.1998), however, the court sentenced the parents to 2½ to 5 years in prison and fined them $1000 for involuntary manslaughter and endangering the welfare of a child for the death of their daughter from diabetes. The sentences, which were above the aggravated range in the sentencing guidelines, were based partly on the repetitive nature of the parents' offenses and were upheld on appeal. Six years earlier, the parents had received two years' probation after pleading no contest to involuntary manslaughter and child endangerment for the death of their son from complications arising from an ear infection.

Where a parent withholds necessary medical care under a spiritual treatment exemption, the parent may face tort liability in addition to any prosecution that might occur. Ian McKown's father, for example, commenced a wrongful death action against the boy's mother and stepfather, Christian Science care-providers, and their church. The appellate court held that the jury's damage award unconstitutionally punished the church for a religious tenet supporting spiritual, rather than medical, treatment. The court also overturned the punitive damage award against the church because it had acted in good faith rather than with "deliberate disregard" for the boy, and because it owed Ian no duty of care.

The court, however, upheld the damage awards against Ian's mother, stepfather, and the care-providers, who all owed Ian a duty of care. The court determined it was required to consider the defendants' religious beliefs when applying the reasonable person standard. Even when the religious beliefs were considered, however, the court determined that reasonable Christian Science care is circumscribed by an obligation to favor the child's welfare, and thus that these defendants breached the standard of care of a reasonable Christian Scientist by not turning to conventional medicine when they knew the child was seriously ill.

C. WITHHOLDING OR TERMINATING MEDICAL CARE

1. WHEN PARENTS FAVOR WITHHOLDING TREATMENT

As an important corollary of the informed consent doctrine, a person with the right to consent to medical treatment generally also holds the right to withhold consent and thus refuse treatment. Because minors typically lack capacity to make decisions concerning their medical treatment, the parent usually holds the right to decline medical treatment on their behalf. Except where neglect is alleged, the decision-making process generally occurs in the clinical setting without resort to the courts. When parents decide to withdraw or withhold lifesaving or life prolonging measures, however, their decisions may be challenged, either because state law is unclear about whether court approval is required or because the hospital or other medical provider is concerned that withholding care would constitute neglect, perhaps with serious criminal or civil consequences.

Courts have found a right to forego life-sustaining medical treatment in three sources: (1) the common law right to freedom from unwanted interference with bodily integrity, (2) the constitutional right to privacy or liberty, and (3) statutory law. As *Cruzan* and *E.G.* demonstrate, adults and mature minors, with some limitations, may refuse treatment for themselves. When adults or mature minors are incapacitated or otherwise unable to communicate at the time of the decision, the alternative decision-makers may take direction from the patient's prior oral or written declarations about medical care; or (in some jurisdictions) they may decide based on what they believe the patient would have decided if competent (a substituted judgment standard). In a jurisdiction that does not recognize a mature minor exception to the parental consent requirement, and in cases involving immature minors, however, the consent decision should be based on the patient's best interests and be made by the parents or a surrogate decision-maker, if parents are unavailable or unsuitable for some reason.

a. Older Children

In Rosebush v. Oakland County Prosecutor (Mich.Ct.App.1992), the court authorized parents of eleven-year-old Joelle Rosebush to make medical decisions for their child, including the decision about whether to remove her life-support systems. Joelle was in a car accident that left her in a persistent vegetative state, but not "brain dead" as defined by Michigan law. The court held that judicial involvement was not required when parents were deciding whether to withhold or withdraw life-sustaining treatment for their child, but that the courts should be available to resolve disputes between parents and medical personnel or for other appropriate reasons.

Except when a mature minor is involved, parental consent is sufficient and the minor's consent is not also required. In Belcher v. Charleston Area Medical Center (W.Va.1992), for example, the parents of a seventeen-year-old child who was suffering from muscular dystrophy and related serious illness executed a "do not resuscitate" order. After the child died, the parents sued the hospital, alleging that the child's consent to the order was required. The court recognized the common law mature minor exception to parental consent and remanded the case for a determination of whether the child was mature. If the child was mature, the child's consent was needed, but otherwise the parents' consent was sufficient.

b. Special Rules for Newborns

Special rules have evolved concerning medical treatment of newborns, mainly in response to federal regulations. After the highly publicized 1982 case of parents who refused consent to medical care for their disabled newborn, "Baby Doe," before the infant died, the federal government sought to insure that medical care would be provided for newborns with any chance of survival. After a misguided effort to regulate the care of newborns through Section 504 of the Rehabilitation Act of 1973, the federal government added rules to the Child Abuse Prevention and Treatment Act that substantially limit when medical care can be withheld from newborns.

These rules require that state child protective legislation address the withholding of "medically indicated treatment from a disabled infant with a life-threatening condition." 45 C.F.R. § 1340.15(b). This administrative mandate permits such treatment to be withheld only in narrow circumstances: (1) When the infant is chronically and irreversibly comatose; (2) When provision of such treatment would merely prolong dying, would not be effective in ameliorating or correcting all the infant's life-threatening conditions, or would otherwise be futile in terms of the survival of the

infant; or (3) When provision of such treatment
would be virtually futile in terms of the survival of
the infant and the treatment itself under such
circumstances would be inhumane.

The Baby Doe rules make it more difficult
to withhold medical care from newborns than from
older children. On *Newmark's* facts, for example, a
court following these rules should have ordered
treatment had the child been a newborn instead of
three years old.

2.   WHEN PARENTS OPPOSE TERMINATION

Just   as   physicians   and   parents   may
disagree about whether medical care should be
withheld, they may also disagree about whether it
should be provided. As noted above, sometimes the
parents' desire to have the child treated is a form
of abuse, involving parents who trick physicians
into performing unnecessary medical procedures
(Munchausen syndrome by proxy). Parents with
good intentions, however, may also want their
child   to   receive   medical   treatment   when   the
treating   physicians   believe   that   continuing
treatment and life support systems would be futile
and cruel. Generally the parents' decision to
continue treatment controls. See, e.g., In re Jane
Doe (Ga.1992). Physicians who remove life
supports from a child without parental consent

may be liable for wrongful death, even if the child
was terminally ill and in the process of dying. See,
e.g., Velez v. Bethune (Ga.Ct.App.1995).

An extreme example of continuing care
over the objections of treating physicians is the
case of Baby K., who was born with anencephaly, a
congenital malformation in which a major portion
of the brain, skull, and scalp are missing. The
presence of a brain stem supported Baby K.'s
autonomic functions and reflex actions, but she
was permanently unconscious because she lacked a
cerebrum. Thus, she had no cognitive abilities or
awareness, and could not see, hear, or otherwise
interact with her environment. Her father
consented to cessation of treatment, but her
mother did not, and the child was kept alive for
over two years. See In re Baby K. (4th Cir. 1994).

Is a court order to terminate life-support
over the parents' objections equivalent to a
termination of parental rights? In In re Tabatha R.
(Neb.1997), an infant was placed in the custody of
the state Department of Health and Human
Services (DHHS) after suffering severe brain
injury from a vigorous shaking while with her
parents. DHHS was authorized to consent to
medical care. The court decided that the DHHS
decision to withdraw life support and not
resuscitate Tabatha was likely to result in her

death, "essentially severing the relationship
between the infant and the parents." In re Tabatha
R. (Neb.1998). Hence the trial court needed to find
by clear and convincing evidence that the parents'
rights should be terminated.

D. PAYMENT FOR THE CHILD'S MEDICAL CARE

Parents' responsibility to care for their
children includes the obligation to provide them
needed medical care. Because the law requires
parental consent to treatment, the medical care
provider often contracts with the parent for
payment before treating the child. The provider
could also invoke the parents' general support
obligation, or the necessaries doctrine, to require
an unwilling parent to pay for treatment provided
without the parent's consent, for example in an
emergency. Because parents are responsible for the
child's medical expenses, at common law parents
could sue a tortfeasor for medical expenses but the
child could not. Cf. Boley v. Knowles (Mo.1995)
(abrogating the common law rule and allowing the
child's suit even though the parent's claim was
time-barred).

As noted earlier, most states allow minors
to consent to specified types of medical care. The

minor's agreement may also serve as a contract to pay for the medical services, which binds the minor. Parents might also be obligated to pay for the treatment, but some medical consent statutes obligate parents or guardians to pay only if they consented to the treatment. See, e.g., Mo. Rev. Stat. § 431.062.

Unfortunately, large numbers of children go without medical care because their parents are uninsured or otherwise cannot pay for it. Some children are eligible for Medicaid, 42 U.S.C. § 1396a et seq., a cooperative federal-state public assistance program that pays for "necessary medical services" for eligible children of low-income families, described as "categorically needy." 42 U.S.C. § 1396(a). Parents of Medicaid-eligible children often are employed, but their wages are low. Unfortunately, an estimated 4.7 million Medicaid-eligible children are not enrolled in the program.

Congress created the Children's Health Insurance Program (CHIP), 42 U.S.C.A. § 1397aa, to provide insurance to children whose parents earn too little to afford private health insurance but too much to qualify for Medicaid. CHIP provides states with federal money to expand their medicaid coverage, to expand or develop a new program, or to use a combination of these approaches. States have responded by developing a wide variety of programs. Some states have been very successful in increasing the number of children included in a health program, but other states have actually seen a decrease in enrolled children because their outreach and enrollment programs have failed.

CHAPTER 8

FINANCIAL RESPONSIBILITY AND CONTROL

A. THE CHILD SUPPORT OBLIGATION

1. HISTORICAL BACKGROUND

America has long recognized parents' common law obligation to support their children. In the nation's early years, the primary support obligation resided in the father, with mothers responsible only when the father was unable to fulfill the obligation. Today, however, each parent must provide support within his or her respective means. Child support claims can arise in a variety of contexts, for example in a divorce action, a paternity action, a neglect action, a criminal proceeding, or a state's suit for reimbursement for welfare expenditures. In addition, claims arise when a third party sues under a family expense statute or the common law necessaries doctrine seeking payment for goods or services furnished a child.

In addition to the private parental support obligation, child support also has a public aspect. A few state constitutions obligate states to support the needy (including children), although the federal

Constitution imposes no such obligation. Statutes, however, may require the federal or state governments to provide support to eligible children under social security, workers' compensation, and various welfare programs.

As noted in chapter 2, concern about rising welfare costs has produced extensive federal involvement in paternity determination and child support, beginning in 1975 with establishment of the Office of Child Support Enforcement in Title IV-D of the Social Security Act. Congress conditioned state receipt of related federal funds on compliance with federal law and passed new legislation requiring states to amend their child support laws extensively. Before these federal initiatives, state child support systems were in dire need of repair. Child support awards were frequently inadequate and erratic, varying from case to case for no clear reason. Noncustodial parents frequently failed to make child support payments, and no effective mechanism existed to compel and collect payment, particularly when the parents lived in different states.

a.   Inadequate and Inconsistent Awards

Federal law now requires states to adopt child support guidelines that standardize support awards and control the broad, essentially

standardless discretion judges formerly exercised to
determine awards on a case by case basis. The
guidelines create a rebuttable presumption; if the
court's award deviates from the guideline amount,
the record must provide reasons for the departure.
42 U.S.C. § 667(b)(2). Congress did not impose
uniform national guidelines but rather allowed the
states to design and implement their own. A state's
guidelines, however, must be a numerical formula
that considers all the noncustodial parent's income
and provides for the child's health care needs. See
45 C.F.R. § 302.56.

States use three different guideline models:
the income-shares model, the percentage-of-income
model, and the Delaware Melson formula. More
than thirty states use the income-shares model,
which is based on empirical studies of the amounts
families spend to rear their children. The goal is to
insure that children in single-parent families
receive the same basic measure of support they
would receive if their parents lived together. The
model produces a presumptive support amount,
which is then prorated between the parents, based
on each one's proportion of total parental income.

Fewer than fifteen states use the
percentage-of-income model, which considers only
the noncustodial obligor parent's income and

presumes that the custodial parent contributes an
appropriate amount in money and in-kind services.
The award is a set percentage of the obligor parent's
income. In Wisconsin, for example, the
noncustodial, obligor parent must pay seventeen
percent of adjusted gross income for one child,
twenty-five percent for two children, twenty-nine
percent for three children, thirty-one percent for
four children, and thirty-four percent for five or
more children. Wis. Admin. Code § DWD 40.03.

The Delaware Melson formula, developed in
that state, with similar versions used in about four
other states, is based on the income of both parents
and considers the amounts needed to support the
parent, the amount needed for the child, and any
remaining income.

b.   Child Support Enforcement
Child support obligations once were easy to
avoid and collection was burdensome. The obligor
might disappear or hide assets and income. A court
proceeding was necessary to secure a judgment for
child support arrears, which might be difficult to
enforce, particularly if the obligor had moved to
another state. Judges might reduce the amount of
arrears, making already low support orders even
less adequate. The modern child support system is
vastly different, thanks to automated collection,

major advances in locating delinquent parents, and
more effective interstate collection and enforcement
tools. See, e.g., Paul K. Legler, The Coming
Revolution In Child Support Policy: Implications of
The 1996 Welfare Act, 30 Fam. L.Q. 519 (1996).

To assist in locating delinquent parents,
child support enforcement agencies now have access
to an extensive network of locator services and
records, including federal military, tax, and social
security records; state and local government records
such as income and property tax records, motor
vehicle records, and occupational and professional
license records; and records of private entities such
as utilities, cable companies and financial
institutions. Further, enforcement is now a
proactive process that does not rely on the custodial
parent to enforce orders. In addition, much
collection and enforcement is an automated,
administrative process without the need for court
involvement. For example, states must allow wages
to be attached for child support and a majority of
child support now is collected through wage-
withholding. Switching jobs is no longer an effective
method of avoiding child support obligations
because employers must report all new hires to a
designated state agency and the new wages are
attached as part of an administrative process.

To improve interstate enforcement, Congress has required states to enact the Uniform Interstate Family Support Act (UIFSA), which replaced the Uniform Reciprocal Enforcement of Support Act. Under UIFSA, states agree that only one order in a support case will be in force at one time, and the state that issued the order will have continuing, exclusive jurisdiction over the case. Hence, if state A orders a parent to pay child support and the parent moves to state B, state B does not issue a new order, but rather enforces state A's existing order. States also agree to a number of procedures designed to simplify and expedite enforcement. For example, UIFSA contains a broad long-arm statute designed to secure jurisdiction over non-resident parents, including jurisdiction where "the individual engaged in sexual intercourse in this State and the child may have been conceived by that act of intercourse; the individual asserted parentage in the [putative father registry] maintained in this State by the [appropriate agency]; or there is any other basis consistent with the constitutions of this State and the United States for the exercise of personal jurisdiction." UIFSA § 201.

Another important aid to interstate enforcement is the Federal Full Faith and Credit for Child Support Orders Act, 28 U.S.C. § 1738B, which

requires states to give full faith and credit to other
states' child support orders and to enforce them
without modification in most cases. The Act also
contains jurisdictional rules intended to be
consistent with those in UIFSA.

Enforcement techniques that existed before
federal involvement in child support collection are
still available to the states. Courts may use their
contempt power, for example, to jail a parent who is
in arrears on child support and willfully fails to pay.
Contempt has even been used for arrearages that
have been reduced to a money judgment. See, e.g.,
Pettit v. Pettit (Ind.1993). In Hicks v. Feiock
(S.Ct.1988), the Supreme Court held that in civil
contempt proceedings, states may presume the
obligor parent is able to pay, thus shifting onto the
parent the burden to rebut the presumption.
Congressional mandates also require states to add
some new payment incentives to the child support
collection arsenal, such as suspending or revoking
the motor vehicle, professional, occupational and
recreational licenses of willful nonpayors. Removing
licenses is a particularly effective remedy against
self-employed parents who might otherwise evade
wage attachment procedures.

Failure to pay court ordered support may
also violate a professional ethics code and be a

predicate for disciplinary sanction. Attorneys, for example, have been suspended from the practice of law for willful failure to pay. See, e.g., In re Petition for Disciplinary Action Against Giberson (Minn.1998) (the attorney's willful failure to obey court rules was "prejudicial to the administration of justice and caused substantial injury to [his] wife and children"; the court suspended the attorney indefinitely and required him to demonstrate compliance with the court's support order as a condition of reinstatement).

In addition to civil proceedings, states may prosecute parents for non-support of their children. If more than one state is involved and the amount owed under court or administrative order is greater than $5000 or has been owed for more than one year, failure to provide support is now also a federal crime under the Deadbeat Parents Punishment Act of 1998 (previously the Child Support Recovery Act of 1992), 18 U.S.C. § 228. Courts disagree about whether the Act is a proper exercise of Congress' commerce clause authority. See, e.g., U.S. v. Faasse (6th Cir. 2000) (striking down Act); United States v. Crawford (8th Cir. 1997) (upholding Act's constitutionality).

2. THE SCOPE OF THE PARENTAL OBLIGATION

a. The Intact Family

When a child is living with both parents, the parents determine the level of support the child should receive, a function both of their substantive due process right to direct the child's upbringing and of the law's distaste for intervening in the domestic affairs of intact families. The law does not require billionaire parents to provide their child with an affluent lifestyle or a college education. Parents must provide only a minimally adequate level of care (including support) that avoids a neglect finding, and children have little ability or authority to force their parents to provide more. The common law necessaries doctrine allows a merchant or other third party to compel parents to pay for basic goods or services, such as food or medical care, the third party provides to the child; practical obstacles prevent most children from actually acquiring assistance in this manner, however, because most persons expect payment before delivery.

The parental support obligation continues at least until the child reaches the age of majority, which is eighteen in nearly all states. Because a child may turn eighteen even before graduating from high school, however, some states continue the child support obligation for a longer period. See, e.g., N.Y. Fam. Ct. Act § 413 (until twenty-one). States may also require parents to support disabled children as long as they are unable to support themselves, even well after reaching majority. See, e.g., Haxton v. Haxton (Or.1985). As discussed below, the parental support obligation may end before the age of majority if the child becomes emancipated by court order or operation of law.

b. When Parents Live Apart

When parents are not living together, parental discretion about support levels may be replaced with a child support order as part of a paternity action, a divorce or a similar proceeding. The order typically would follow the state's guidelines and would be for a set amount calculated according to the parents' income. The duration of the child support obligation may also be different than for intact-family parents. A number of states authorize courts to require divorced or separated parents to pay for a child's post-secondary education if they can financially do so, for example. Generally equal protection challenges have been unsuccessful. See, e.g., In re Marriage of Kohring, (Mo.1999). But see Curtis v. Kline (Pa.1995).

c.   No Excuses

Because the state has a strong interest in assuring children support, the support obligation generally prevails even when the parent is a minor, was deceived about the other parent's nonuse of contraceptives, or lacked knowledge of paternity. In State ex rel. Hermesmann v. Seyer (Kan.1993), for example, a thirteen-year-old boy and his seventeen-year-old babysitter conceived a child. The boy sought to avoid the support obligation on the grounds that he was a minor legally incapable of consenting to sexual intercourse and was a statutory rape victim. The court ordered him to pay support because the newborn infant was the truly innocent party, and the state's interest in her support outweighed the father's objections.

Being tricked into unprotected sexual intercourse by the other parent generally does not absolve a parent of the support obligation either. See, e.g., Pamela P. v. Frank S. (N.Y.1983). Nor is lack of knowledge of paternity generally an excuse. In Brad Michael L. v. Lee D. (Wis.Ct.App.1997), for example, a father was ordered to pay child support arrearages even though he maintained he was unaware of the child's existence before the paternity action was filed when the child was fifteen. Equitable doctrines such as laches, however, may sometimes bar delayed paternity actions.

d. The Obligor's Death

Interestingly enough, at common law, dying
was a way to escape paying child support because
the ongoing child support obligation was not
charged against the parent's estate. Some states
have abrogated the common law rule, however, and
continue the support obligation after death,
allowing a lump sum payment by the estate to settle
the charge. Other states have granted courts
authority to order the obligor parent to purchase life
insurance to secure payment. When parents are
divorcing, the possibility that the obligor parent
might die before the child reaches majority may be
dealt with by private agreement, for example by
including a life insurance requirement in the
parents' separation agreement.

Minor children are not guaranteed a share
of their parents' estates. Parents may disinherit
their minor children in all states but Louisiana,
which follows the civil law tradition of allowing
disinheritance only for cause. Children sometimes
gain a measure of protection because a disinherited
surviving spouse in a common law state is entitled
to a forced share of the estate; in these days of
multiple marriages and single parenthood, however,
the surviving spouse might not be the parent of all

the testator's children and usually would have no
obligation to support stepchildren.

When a parent dies intestate, a surviving
spouse and the decedent's children typically receive
the estate under intestate succession laws, which
provide that children take equally, without regard
to age or relative need. This "sibling parity" rule
may be harsh on younger children or children with
special needs, for whom the parent might have
made special provisions in a will.

e.   Stepparents

Most states follow the common law rule that
stepparents are legal strangers to their stepchildren
with no direct obligation to support them. In the few
states with statutes imposing a stepparent support
obligation, the obligation usually is more limited
than the support obligation imposed on biological
parents. The stepparents' obligation may be
secondary to that of the biological parents, the
obligation may be imposed only if the stepchild
would otherwise be a public charge, and the
stepparent may be able to secure reimbursement
from the noncustodial natural parent. In any event,
a stepparent support obligation does not excuse the
obligation of either biological parent but is designed
to provide the child a "safety net" against
nonpayment by a biological parent.

The "safety net" varies from state to state. North Dakota, for example, continues a stepparent support obligation after the end of the marriage of the biological parent and stepparent, but only where the stepparent has received the stepchild into the stepparent's family and the stepchild continues to reside there. N.D. Stat. Ann. § 14-09-09. Regardless of the stepparent's legal obligation, most wage-earning stepparents probably do contribute to their stepchildren's support while they are married to the custodial parent.

The in loco parentis doctrine (chapter 2) can also be a basis for a stepparent support obligation. The doctrine tends to affect only prior support obligations, however, because the in loco parentis relationship can be terminated at will and the stepparent can avoid continued financial responsibility by simply declaring that the relationship no longer exists.

Courts may also require stepparents to support stepchildren where the facts present a particularly compelling case for ordering support. Thus, stepparents who promised support, treated the child as their own, and discouraged biological parent-child contact could be required to pay support based on equitable doctrines such as

estoppel. A support obligation does not arise,
however, simply because the stepparent had an in
loco parentis relationship during the marriage and a
continuing, caring relationship with the stepchild
after the end of the marriage.

Even where stepparents are not legally
obligated to support children directly, they may be
obligated indirectly. Major welfare programs, such
as TANF, infra, may their income into account in
deciding on a child's welfare eligibility and grant
amount. The income of a wage-earner who marries
a welfare recipient with children, for example, may
be deemed available to support the children,
resulting in reduction or loss of the welfare grant.
Stepparents can also be indirectly responsible for
supporting stepchildren when their income is taken
into account in determining the financial resources
of their spouses (the biological parents) in child
support determinations.

3.   CHILD POVERTY

The United States has an appallingly high
number of children living in households below the
federal poverty threshold. In 2001, sixteen percent
of America's children lived below the threshold, a
child poverty rate among the highest in the
developed world.

The sixteen percent child poverty rate
underestimates the percentage of children in
difficult financial straits because the federal poverty
threshold is unrealistically low. "Since 1946, in
Gallup and Roper polls Americans have been asked
what they consider the smallest amount of money a
family of four in their community needs to get
along, the figure below which a family could be
considered 'poor.' Year after year their answer has
been not the poverty line but rather a figure
approximating half the median income for such a
family." Kenneth Keniston and the Carnegie
Council on Children, All Our Children: The
American Family Under Pressure (1977). In 2003,
a family of four with an annual income below
$18,400 fell below the federal poverty guideline,
while the median income for a family of four was
$62,228.

Despite the lack of a federal constitutional
imperative to support needy children, a number of
government programs – generally described as
"welfare" programs – assist low-income families
with children. The largest cash benefits program is
Temporary Assistance to Needy Families (TANF),
which was established by the Personal
Responsibility and Work Opportunity Reconciliation
Act of 1996 (PRWORA). TANF replaced the Aid to

Families with Dependent Children (AFDC) program, a cash benefits program that began in 1935 as part of the Social Security Act. Like AFDC, TANF is a cooperative federal-state program, a mix of federal and state regulations and funding. Unlike AFDC, however, TANF is not an entitlement program with open-ended funding. Instead, TANF funds are limited so eligible families might be denied aid if the funds have been exhausted. In addition, families are eligible for TANF funds for not more than five years, a time limit that states may reduce. Also, TANF grants states more discretion than AFDC to limit eligibility requirements.

In addition to cash programs, several in-kind programs provide children services or goods. Some programs are aimed specifically at children, such as the Special Supplemental Food Program for Women, Infants, and Children (WIC), school nutrition programs (breakfast and lunch), child health insurance programs, and Head Start. Other programs – such as Food Stamps, Medicaid, and housing assistance programs – assist low-income persons generally and thus reach children in low-income households.

Another approach to the problem of poor children, with foundations in the Elizabethan Poor

Laws, is to find private individuals who can be
made to support the child. Federal attention to
collecting child support from absent parents
illustrates this approach. In addition, embedded in
the eligibility requirements for public assistance are
relative responsibility requirements. The income of
stepparents and grandparents can often be taken
into account when determining eligibility and grant
amounts, for example, even though the relative may
not be required to support the child under state law.
A state may even use the child support paid for one
child to reduce the amount of a welfare grant to
other children in the same household. See Bowen v.
Gilliard (S.Ct.1987).

4. THE CHILD'S OBLIGATIONS

Children, as well as parents, have
responsibilities attending the parent-child
relationship. Children are required to obey their
parents' reasonable commands, and a parent may
be justified in eliminating certain kinds of support
when the child refuses to obey. In Oeler v. Oeler
(Pa.1991), for example, seventeen-year-old Paula
had lived with each of her separated parents, but
was with her mother when the court issued the
disputed support order. On the day of the order, the
mother relocated to Connecticut and left the girl
behind. Paula's father told her that she could live

with him and finish school. Instead, Paula and her
mother unilaterally, without discussion with the
father, rented a one-bedroom apartment for Paula.

   Oeler upheld the father's refusal to
reimburse the mother for a portion of the child's
expenses. The court held that the duty to support a
minor child is absolute, but that the purpose is to
promote the best interests of the child. The father
was willing to provide Paula housing, food, clothing
and an education, but was not willing to allow her
to live in her own apartment and dictate the proper
allocation of support monies. The court concluded
that because Paula's best interests would not be
served by permitting her to reside alone, her father
could not be compelled to support her.

   Oeler is typical of decisions that allow a
parent to terminate support for a disobedient child
who is nearing the age of majority and is employed
or employable. Courts also have permitted
termination of a noncustodial parent's future
support obligations where the child unreasonably
refuses all contact and visitation with the parent.
See Comm'r of Social Services v. Jones-Gamble
(N.Y.App.Div.1996). Disobedience cases sometimes
lead courts to speak of a constructive emancipation
doctrine. Where a minor of employable age in full
possession of his or her faculties voluntarily and

without cause abandons the parental home to evade parental control, the child may lose the right to receive further parental support. The doctrine terminates the support obligation only where the court finds termination appropriate in the light of the child's age and ability. Parents sometimes seek to emancipate an ungovernable child they cannot control, but courts may deny emancipation where the child is not capable of self-support.

5. EMANCIPATION

Emancipation is the process by which a child under the age of majority gains many adult rights and responsibilities by operation of law or by court order. Emancipation typically ends the obligations stemming from the parent-child relationship. For example, parents no longer are required to support the child and have no further right to obedience or to the child's wages; the child has capacity to establish a domicile rather than being assigned the parents' domicile. Emancipation may also affect the child's relationship with third parties, allowing the emancipated minor to enter into binding contracts, sue and be sued in his or her own name and consent to medical care, for example. The emancipated child gains more autonomy but loses some legal protections, such as the right to support and coverage under child protective statutes. Emancipation may be reversible if the child again becomes financially dependent before reaching majority. See, e.g., Wulff v. Wulff (Neb.1993).

Children typically become emancipated by operation of law when they marry or go on active military duty. Courts may order emancipation when the child lives apart from his or her parents and is capable of managing his or her own financial affairs. Statutes may also recite a broad, discretionary basis for emancipation. See, e.g., Conn. Gen. Stat. § 46b-150b (court may order emancipation if "for good cause shown, it is in the best interest of the minor, any child of the minor, or the parents or guardian of the minor").

About twenty states have emancipation statutes that list grounds for emancipation and define its effects. In Connecticut, for example, emancipated minors may consent to medical care, may enter into binding contracts; may sue and be sued in their own name; are entitled to their own earnings and are free of parental control; may establish their own residence; may buy and sell real and personal property; and may obtain adult status in a number of other areas.

In states without emancipation statutes, the propriety of judicial emancipation and its effects depend on the attendant circumstances. The child or parent often seeks an emancipation order only when the need arises, such as when a victim seeks to hold a parent liable in tort for damages caused by the child or when the parent is worried about liability for the child's debts or misconduct. A child may also seek an emancipation order to avoid the need for parental consent for medical care and to be able to contract for housing.

B. CAPACITY TO CONTRACT

At common law, persons achieved general contractual capacity at twenty-one, the age of majority. In the early 1970s, virtually all states lowered the general age of majority, and with it the age of general contractual capacity, to eighteen. In the absence of a contrary statutory directive, a minor's contract is voidable by the minor, provided the minor "disaffirms" the contract during minority or within a reasonable time after reaching majority. Disaffirmance occurs where the minor expresses any desire to void the contract, whether by a lawsuit, by interposing minority as a defense to an enforcement action, or by stating orally or in writing a desire to void the contract. The minor must disaffirm either the entire contract or none of it.

Once the minor disaffirms the contract, the action is irrevocable.

Because the operative policy is to protect children from overreaching by adult parties, the power to disaffirm is usually held only by the minor or, in the event of his death, by his heirs or personal representatives. Occasional decisions also permit parents to disaffirm a contract on behalf of their unemancipated child, but an adult party may not disaffirm the contract on the ground of the other party's minority.

Mitchell v. Mizerski (Neb.Ct.App.1995) demonstrates the effect of a minor's disaffirming a contract. Sixteen-year-old Travis Mitchell brought a car into Mizerski's auto shop for repairs. Shortly after Mizerski finished the repairs, the parties disagreed about their quality and costs and Travis sought to disaffirm the repair contract. Because the repairs were not necessaries, the court held that Travis could disaffirm the contract during minority and regain all amounts he paid under it.

The common law rule is that when the minor disaffirms, the minor must return any property he received under the contract and still possesses or controls. If the minor has dissipated or negligently destroyed the property in the interim,

however, he may disaffirm without returning the
property. The common law concludes that to
condition disaffirmance on return of the property as
received would penalize the minor for the very
improvidence that underlies the capacity doctrine.
By statute or judicial decision, some states have
tempered the harshness of disaffirmance by
requiring the minor to pay the fair value the minor
received from use of the property, or to pay
depreciation on the property returned.

1.   THE NECESSARIES DOCTRINE

The necessaries doctrine limits the minor's
right to disaffirm. When a person provides a minor
with a necessity of life under circumstances
indicating that the person expected payment
pursuant to an agreement with the minor, the
minor is liable for the reasonable value of the goods
or services provided under the agreement. The
common law permits a party to invoke the doctrine
only where the unemancipated child's parents or
guardians have refused to provide the goods or
services in question.

No bright line rule determines what is a
necessity. "What constitutes a necessary is not
fixed, but depends upon such factors as the minor's
standard of living and particular circumstances, as

well as the ability and willingness of the minor's
parent or guardian, if one exists, to supply the
needed services or articles." Rodriquez v. Reading
Housing Authority (3rd Cir.1993) (public housing
authority was justified in refusing to lease to the
plaintiff, who was a minor single parent, because
housing might not be a necessary and the minor
could disaffirm the lease).

2.   LIMITS ON DISAFFIRMANCE

In addition to the necessaries doctrine, the
common law deprives minors of the power to
disaffirm in other, limited circumstances. Statutory
restrictions may also operate. For example, minors
may not disaffirm agreements to perform
obligations the law otherwise commands that they
perform, such as agreements to support their
children born in or out of wedlock. A number of
states have enacted statutes codifying this rule. See,
e.g., Idaho Code § 32-105 ("A minor can not
disaffirm an obligation otherwise valid, entered into
by him under the express authority or direction of a
statute."). Insurance and banking laws also
frequently deprive children of the power to
disaffirm. Some statutes prohibit disaffirmance
when the minor has misrepresented his or her age
or conducts business as an adult. Several states
have statutes prohibiting disaffirmance of contracts

for particularly important items, such as student
loans and some types of medical care to which the
minor may consent.

The effect of statutory change was central to
the decision in Shields v. Gross (N.Y.1983). In 1975,
ten-year-old Brooke Shields posed nude in a bathtub
in a series of photographs financed by Playboy
Press. On the child's behalf, her mother executed
two unrestricted consents in the defendant
photographer's favor. In the next few years, the
photographs were used, with the knowledge of
Brooke and her mother, in various publications and
in a display of larger-than-life photo enlargements
in the windows of a store on Fifth Avenue in New
York City. In 1980, the child actress became
concerned that the defendant planned further
publications of the photos. After failing in her
attempt to purchase the negatives, she sued for
compensatory and punitive damages and an
injunction permanently enjoining the defendant
from any further use of the photographs. The court
held, however, that the minor could not disaffirm
where the legislature had expressly permitted
minors to enter into this type of agreement and
provided a means for obtaining minors' consent,
which in this instance was the written consent of
parents or guardians.

3.   RATIFICATION

Minors lose the right to disaffirm a contract when, after reaching majority, they "ratify" it before disaffirming. The minor may ratify only after reaching majority because any purported ratification during minority would be the product of the same incapacity that attended the contract. Ratification occurs when the minor agrees, after reaching majority, to perform all or part of the minor's obligations under the contract. See Restatement (Second) of Contracts § 85. The minor may ratify by express statement (which may be oral unless a statute requires a writing), or by conduct (such as by using property received under the contract without disaffirming within a reasonable time). Statutes frequently prescribe acts that constitute ratification as a matter of law. Mo. Rev. Stat. § 431.060, for example, prescribes these acts: "(1) An acknowledgement of, or promise to pay such debt, made in writing; (2) A partial payment upon such debt; (3) A disposal of part or all of the property for which such debt was contracted; (4) A refusal to deliver property in his possession or under his control, for which such debt was contracted, to the person to whom the debt is due, on demand therefore made in writing."

4.   MARRIAGE

Marriage, like other civil contracts, requires capacity and consent to entering into the relationship. In virtually all states, eighteen is the age of consent to marry (that is, the age at which a person may marry on his or her own consent, without the need for parental or judicial consent). Where a party seeking to marry is under this age of individual consent, states typically require older minors to secure the consent of a parent or guardian, and younger minors to secure both parental consent and judicial approval. States do not clearly articulate a minimum age of capacity, the lowest age at which a person may marry under any circumstances, though marriage of particularly young children is virtually unknown in contemporary America.

C.   THE CHILD'S PROPERTY

Minors may own real and personal property, but they generally cannot manage property effectively because their power to disaffirm contracts, deeds, agreements to purchase, leases and other arrangements leaves parties reluctant to deal with them. Minors thus need a guardian or conservator who can make binding arrangements and otherwise manage their property.

In the absence of a contrary determination,
parents are naturally the guardians of the person of
the child, and thus are also a logical choice to
manage the child's property. Guardianships can be
cumbersome, however, particularly if court approval
is needed for property transfers. To permit
management of the minor's property without court
supervision, persons transferring property to a
minor frequently use trusts or the Uniform
Transfers to Minors Act (or its predecessor, the
Uniform Gifts to Minors Act).

1. TRUSTS

Trusts are useful mechanisms for managing
gifts to minors because the donor transfers the
property to a trustee who manages it for the benefit
of the minor, the trust beneficiary. The trustee is
directed by the donor's instructions expressed in the
trust instrument and does not need prior court
approval to buy, sell, or distribute the property.
Trusts have some advantages over custodianships
created under the Uniform Transfers to Minors Act
(UTMA), particularly for large amounts of property,
because the donor can tailor the trust to fit a variety
of circumstances. A trust can have all the donor's
children or grandchildren as beneficiaries, for
example, with the trustee authorized to postpone

distribution until all the children reach the age of
majority, or to make unequal distributions among
the children according to their respective needs. The
UTMA custodianship ends when the child reaches
twenty-one, but a trust can postpone distribution
until the child is older. In addition, a trust that
accumulates income can be taxed separately,
whereas the custodianship is not a separate tax
entity.

2.   UNIFORM TRANSFERS TO MINORS ACT

The National Conference of Commissioners
on Uniform State Laws promulgated the Uniform
Gifts to Minors Act (UGMA) in 1956. The Act went
through several revisions and is now called the
Uniform Transfer to Minors Act (UTMA). Every
state has some version of the UGMA or the UTMA.
Under the UTMA, the broad definition of "custodial
property" is intended to include legal and equitable
interests in all types of property, including real
property. A "minor" is a person under twenty-one.

The procedure for transferring property
under the UTMA is very simple. A grandmother
wishing to give stocks to a granddaughter with her
daughter as custodian, for example, usually may
simply transfer the stocks to the daughter "as
custodian for [name of granddaughter] under the

[name of state] UTMA." The transfer is irrevocable, and the property is indefeasibly vested in the minor. The custodian manages the property without prior court approval or oversight, although a family member or a minor fourteen or older may petition the court for an accounting by the custodian. The Act enumerates the custodian's responsibilities. The custodian must adhere to the standard of care that "would be observed by a prudent person dealing with property of another." When dealing with custodial property, the custodian must keep the minor's property separate from other property so it can be clearly identified. When the minor turns twenty-one, the custodian must transfer the property and accumulated proceeds and profits to the minor. A major advantage of the UTMA is that it permits transfer of property to the child without requiring the donor to spend time and money preparing a trust instrument.

3. USE OF THE CHILD'S ASSETS

As a general rule, the child's property should not be used to help fulfill the parents' support obligation, unless the parent is destitute and cannot otherwise support the child. The parent may control the child's property as a guardian, but has a fiduciary obligation to manage the property for the child's benefit, not for the parent's. At

common law, and by statute in some states, parents
are entitled to their children's wages and can use
them to support the child or for any other purpose,
but the child's property belongs to the child. (See
chapter 9, Child Labor).

The UTMA and UGMA are confusing on
this issue because they suggest that custodial
property can be used for the child's support. The
acts' language has been interpreted to mean,
however, that the custodian may not use custodial
property for expenditures a parent is legally
obligated to make for care of the child. In Sutliff v.
Sutliff (Pa.1987), for example, the court held that
where a father and his parents gave his children
cash, stocks and bonds under the UGMA, the
custodian could not use that property to fulfill the
father's child support obligation under an interim
support order connected to the parents' separation.

When the child receives money intended to
substitute for loss of a parent's wages, however, the
money may be used for the child's support. Children
may be eligible for social security survivor benefits
due to a parent's death, for example. As the child's
guardian and representative payee under the Social
Security Act, the surviving parent may use the
benefits to pay for necessities for the child, such as
food and shelter, even though the surviving parent

also has an obligation to support his or her own child, apart from the benefit money. Because the payments are intended to replace the deceased parent's wages, they should be used for the child's current maintenance, not saved for the child's future use. 20 C.F.R. § 404.2040; In re Guardianship of Nelson (Minn.Ct.App.1996). Social Security benefits may also be used to reimburse the state for foster care expenditures. Washington State Dep't of Soc. and Health Ser. v. Guardianship Estate of Keffeler (S.Ct. 2003).

4. WILLS

States typically require that testators be eighteen or older to write a valid will, although emancipated minors may be excepted from this rule. Without a will the minor's estate would pass by intestate succession laws, which generally provide that the child's parents would inherit the child's estate. This distribution might not be in accord with the child's wishes and could be manifestly unfair. A stepparent who had served as the child's "parent," providing emotional and financial support, for example, would receive nothing while an absent biological parent would receive half. A particularly egregious case was that of James Brindamour, whose fifteen-year-old biological daughter Colleen was killed in a car accident. Brindamour had

deserted Colleen and her mother over ten years
earlier, owed thousands of dollars in back child
support, and did not attend her funeral. He
nonetheless claimed his right to one-half her estate,
which was valued at $350,000 due to an insurance
settlement. The case inspired the state legislature
to amend its wrongful death statute to deny
payment to anyone who was more than six months
in arrears on child support. R.I. Gen. Laws § 10-7-2.

D. TORTS AND FAMILY RELATIONS

In strong contrast to contract law, minors
have significant rights and responsibilities in tort
law. Some special rules apply, however. Although
children can sue and be sued for their torts, they
usually cannot bring or defend a legal action in their
own name, but must have a court-appointed
representative. In addition, the child's age may be
relevant to the issue of intent in suits alleging
intentional torts and capacity for negligence. Some
jurisdictions conclusively presume that a child
under age seven is incapable of negligence.

The parent-child relationship also may
create special tort rules concerning liability and
compensable interests. In many jurisdictions,
parents may be held partially responsible for some

of their children's torts. Immunity doctrines may bar intrafamily tort suits. Wrongful death and loss of consortium actions may depend on family relationships.

1.   THE CHILD'S LIABILITY

Generally minors are liable for their intentional and negligent torts. Qualifications to this rule, however, frequently enable children to avoid tort liability in circumstances that would leave adults subject to liability.

a. The Standard of Care for Children

Generally children are held to an individualized, subjective standard of care, rather than to the more objective reasonable person standard, or even to a reasonable child standard. See Dan B. Dobbs, The Law of Torts § 124 (2000). Children are expected to conduct themselves only with the care of a child of the same age, intelligence, and experience. The Restatement (Second) of Torts explains that "a child is a person of such immature years as to be incapable of exercising the judgment, intelligence, knowledge, experience, and prudence demanded by" the adult standard. §283 A, cmt a. "The special standard to be applied in the case of children arises out of the public interest in their welfare and protection, together with the fact that

there is a wide basis of community experience upon
which it is possible, as a practical matter, to
determine what is to be expected of them." Id. cmt.
b.

b. Mental Capacity

In addition to using a subjective standard,
some jurisdictions may apply different rules for
assessing a child's mental capacity than the rules
applied to adults. Where a particularly young child
is charged with negligence or an intentional tort,
the child may be effectively immune from common
law liability because of a presumed lack of capacity
or ability to hold the requisite intent. A four-year-
old child, for example, may by law lack capacity to
be negligent or reckless, being unable to
comprehend a duty to exercise care. Price v. Kipsap
Transit (Wash. 1994) (child under age six who
reached into bus driver's area and engaged an
emergency stop switch, resulting in injury to a
fellow passenger, was incapable of fault). A similar
result may be reached with intentional torts. See,
e.g., DeLuca v. Bowden (Ohio 1975) (as a matter of
law, child under seven incapable of committing
intentional tort). A child's violation of a safety
statute, such as a jaywalking statute, may be
excused because of the child's minority, so that the
child is not negligent per se for running into the
street. See Dobbs, supra at § 140.

In negligence claims, ten to twelve states follow a "rule of sevens" with children under seven incapable of negligence as a matter of law, children between seven and fourteen presumptively incapable, and children over fourteen presumptively capable. Dobbs, supra at § 126. Whether a presumption has been rebutted is normally a fact question for the jury. See, e.g., Cates v. Kinnard (Ill.1994). The question of the child's capacity has arisen most frequently on affirmative defenses that the child plaintiff bears responsibility for contributory or comparative negligence. Courts might be more sympathetic to child plaintiffs (and thus unwilling to let adults profit by these defenses) than they would be to child defendants.

A majority of jurisdictions, however, do not use a fixed-age cutoff, but rather consider the child's individual ability. The child must have some awareness of the natural consequences of intentional acts. In Seaburg v. Williams (Ill.App.Ct.1959), for example, a child who was five years and eleven months old set fire to some papers in a neighbor's garage, resulting in a blaze that destroyed the garage and its contents. The court held that a child of that age may be liable for an intentional tort, but that whether the child was capable of intent was a question of fact. *Seaburg* held that "[b]ased upon the evidence of defendant's age, capacity, intelligence and experience, ... he lacked the mental and moral capacity to possess the intent to do the act complained of."

Some states have expanded or limited the common law rules. Children thirteen and younger are immune from tort liability in Georgia, for example. See, e.g., Horten v. Hinely, (Ga.1992) (interpreting Georgia statute that provides that "infancy is no defense to a tort action so long as the defendant has reached the age of discretion and accountability prescribed by [the statute] for criminal offenses," and determining that the minimum age of criminal responsibility is thirteen). Some states, however, have broadened the minor's liability. See, e.g., Mont. Code Ann. 41 1 201. ("A minor is civilly liable for a wrong done by him but is not liable in exemplary damages unless at the time of the act he was capable of knowing that it was wrongful.")

c.   Adult Activities

The law generally recognizes a limited exception to the doctrines stated above. The adult reasonable person standard applies when the negligence suit arises from a child's engagement in an activity normally undertaken only by adults, and for which adult qualifications are required.   The adult-activity exception applies even if at the time of the incident, it was obvious to the other party that he or she was involved with a child

What constitutes an "adult activity" is not always clear. Should golf, for example, be considered an "adult activity"? See, e.g., Restatement (Second) of Torts 283A, cmt. c. Most cases holding children to an adult standard of care involve operating a motorized vehicle such as a car, boat, airplane or snowmobile. See Dobbs, supra at § 127. Riding a bicycle is generally held not to be an adult activity. See, e.g., Chu v. Bowers (Ill.App.Ct.1995) (citing decisions.).

d. Interaction between Contract and Tort Laws

In some circumstances children might avoid contract-based tort liability. A contract might create a duty of care, for example, making a negligent failure to perform the contract or omission of a duty actionable in tort. Allowing a tort action, however, may undermine the protection of disaffirmance by allowing indirect enforcement of the contract. Most courts do not permit tort recovery unless the child breached an obligation imposed by law independent of the contractual obligations, except when the child has committed fraud by misrepresenting his age or some other action. See W. Page Keeton et al.,

Prosser and Keeton on the Law of Torts § 134 (5th
ed. 1984). Courts have held minors liable in tort for
conversion, for example, when minors rightfully
came into possession of an automobile under a
contract, but then misappropriated it for their own
use. See, e.g., Vermont Acceptance Corp. v.
Wiltshire (Vt.1931) (unauthorized use of auto
terminated bailment and amounted to conversion).

2. PARENTS' LIABILITY

In the absence of a statute, parents are not
vicariously liable for their children's torts merely
because of the parent-child relationship. Because
the common law does not impose general vicarious
liability on parents, many tort judgments against
children go unrecovered unless insurance covers the
child.

Parents may be held liable for their
children's torts, however, if the facts fit specific tort
principles related to vicarious liability. A parent
might incur respondeat superior liability, for
example, if the child was acting in the parent's
employ. Liability also could attach if the parent
aided and abetted the child's commission of a tort or
if the parent and child acted in concert. Negligent
entrustment might also be a basis for liability if
parents unreasonably allow the child to use a

dangerous instrument such as a firearm or an automobile, or if they carelessly leave such an instrument in a place where the child may gain access to it. Finally, where the parent has notice of the child's propensity for dangerous or violent conduct that might injure third parties, the parent may have a duty to warn others of the potential danger or otherwise take reasonable measures to protect their safety.

A better approach than vicarious liability may be to sue the parents for negligently failing to supervise or control their child. Suppose, for example, that parents are told that their six-year-old child has a rifle and is shooting at a target on a public street. The target shooting endangers other users of the street. The parents fail to take the rifle away from the child or to take any other action. The child unintentionally shoots a pedestrian in the leg. Section 316 of the Restatement (Second) of Torts is worthy of the pedestrian's attention:

A parent is under a duty to exercise reasonable care so to control his minor child as to prevent it from intentionally harming others or from so conducting itself as to create an unreasonable risk of bodily harm to them, if the parent

(a) knows or has reason to know that he has the ability to control his child, and

(b) knows or should know of the necessity and opportunity for exercising such control.

   In addition to these common law remedies, most states now have statutes imposing parental liability for some intentional, and generally malicious, conduct by their children. The evident aim is to give parents a financial incentive to control their children. These statutes normally cap parental liability at an amount between a few hundred and a few thousand dollars, although some are more generous. See, e.g., Ga.Code.Ann. § 51-2-3 ($10,000 cap). A tort lawyer working on a contingency fee probably would not be interested in a case with such limited recovery. Florida is typical of states that have repealed their caps. See Fla. Stat. Ann. § 741.24.

3.   LOSS OF CHILD OR PARENT

a.   Loss of Consortium
   When a child has been severely injured, parents may want to sue for loss of the child's companionship in addition to other damages such as

medical expenses. Most states, however, do not
allow a loss of consortium action by a parent
because of the difficulty of measuring damages, and
the resulting increase in litigation, multiple claims,
and the rise in insurance costs. States disagree
about whether to permit children to recover for
injury to a parent that causes a loss of parental care
and society.

b. Wrongful Death

Parents can sue for their child's wrongful
death, a statutory remedy based on the deceased's
economic value to the plaintiff. Nineteenth century
courts priced a child by estimating the value of the
child's services from the time of death to the age of
majority, less the expense of maintaining the child.
As the economic value of children decreased,
however, this formula resulted in some nominal
awards. Gradually courts began to consider
noneconomic factors to establish the child's
emotional value, such as the quality of the parent-
child relationship, the extent of the parent's grief,
and the child's characteristics. Ironically, the value
of contemporary children in wrongful death actions
has increased, even though most children today are
major financial liabilities to their parents rather
than sources of additional family income. Some
wrongful death awards for a child's death have
exceeded two million dollars.

Wrongful death statutes generally entitle children to compensation for a parent's wrongful death, but the statutes may define "child" and "parent" narrowly to exclude some children who were dependent on the decedent. For example, a dependent stepchild often is not considered a "child" under the statutes. The Social Security Act and workers' compensations statutes typically are less restrictive and allow actually dependent children, such as stepchildren and grandchildren, to receive benefits for the death or injury of the wage-earner who had supported them.

c.   Wrongful Birth and Wrongful Life

Parents may also want to recover expenses of caring for a "defective" child (wrongful birth) or an unwanted child (sometimes called wrongful conception). A "defective" child, or the child's guardian, may want to recover general damages for having been permitted to be born (wrongful life). A number of courts have allowed actions for wrongful birth, although fewer have allowed actions for birth of an unwanted, but healthy child. Very few courts have allowed recovery for wrongful life, and some states have even gone so far as to prohibit such claims by statute. Wrongful life recovery, when allowed, may be very limited.

4. IMMUNITY

At common law, the parental immunity doctrine prohibited unemancipated children from suing their parents for intentional or negligent torts. The doctrine sought to preserve family harmony, prevent fraud and collusion between parent and child, encourage support for parental authority and protect family assets. In the 1930s, however, courts began to limit parental immunity, recognizing that the doctrine generally protected insurance companies and not parents' purses. A few states have abolished the doctrine entirely. In Hartman v. Hartman (Mo.1991), for example, the court found that the interest in allowing injured children to recover damages outweighed the interest in family harmony, which would likely already be weakened by contemplation of a lawsuit anyway. *Hartman* adopted a "reasonable parent" standard, which the court determined would limit recovery to clearly unacceptable parental acts, not ordinary parental acts of discipline or supervision.

A number of states, however, continue to recognize the parental immunity doctrine. For instance, in 1995 the Connecticut Supreme Court applied the doctrine to bar the strict liability action by a four-year-old child who was attacked and bitten by the dog his father owned. See Squeglia v.

Squeglia (Conn.1995). In 1994, a Texas court held
that that the doctrine precluded suit on behalf of a
sixteen-year-old son whose friend fatally shot him in
the head after the defendant father left the loaded
gun with the son and the friend, failed to tell them
it was loaded, and failed to supervise them. See
Hoffmeyer v. Hoffmeyer (Tex.Ct.App.1994).

5.   EXCULPATORY CLAUSES AND
SETTLEMENT

a.   Releases and Waivers

As a condition of participation, schools,
athletic leagues and other youth activities
frequently require parents to sign releases waiving
not only their own right to sue, but also the child's
right. These releases are also frequently required by
private businesses such as ski slopes. The releases
are not nearly as ironclad as they may appear.
Consistent with the doctrine that competent adults
generally may execute binding contracts, parents
may waive their future right to sue on claims they
themselves might have arising from their child's
injury, such as claims for medical expenses and loss
of the child's services and companionship. The
general common law rule, however, is that a parent,
guardian ad litem or next friend may not waive the
child's future right to sue. See, e.g., UAW v.
Johnson Controls, Inc. (S.Ct.1991) (White, J.,

concurring in part and concurring in the judgment)
("parents cannot waive causes of action on behalf of
their children").

The common law prevails except in the
relatively rare circumstances in which a statute
speaks to the question. Having a child sign the
release does not produce a different result because
the release is a contract which the child may
disaffirm during minority or within a reasonable
time after reaching majority.

Where the activity involves volunteers and
non-profit sponsors, however, courts sometimes
uphold parents' releases concerning their claims
and those of their children. See, e.g., Zivich v.
Mentor Soccer Club, Inc. (Ohio 1998) ("parents have
the authority to bind their minor children to
exculpatory agreements in favor of volunteers and
sponsors of nonprofit sports activities where the
cause of actions sounds in negligence"). The Federal
Volunteer Protection Act of 1997, 42 U.S.C. §14503,
protects volunteers of nonprofit organizations or
governmental entities against liability for harm "not
caused by willful or criminal misconduct, gross
negligence, reckless misconduct, or a conscious,
flagrant indifference to the rights or safety of the
individual harmed by the volunteer." The liability
limitations explicitly do not apply to specified

misconduct, including violations of civil rights laws, sexual offenses, hate crimes and acts "where the defendant was under the influence ... of intoxicating alcohol or any drug at the time of the misconduct."

b. Settlement

Consistent with the doctrine that competent adults generally may settle their existing civil claims, parents may settle their own claims arising from the child's injury. But they may not settle the child's existing claims without court approval on a finding that the settlement is in the child's best interests. Where a parent's effort to settle the child's claim precedes the filing of a lawsuit, an action may be filed to secure judicial approval. Some states permit court approval of a parent's settlement of the child's claim only after the court has appointed the parent as guardian ad litem or next friend. Where parents reject a settlement offer that the court thinks is fair, or where a conflict of interest exists between the child and the parent, the court may appoint a guardian ad litem other than the parent to determine whether the settlement offer is in the child's best interests.

Because waivers and unapproved settlements of the child's claims are void agreements contrary to public policy, they do not preclude the child from suing during minority or

within the applicable limitations period after
reaching majority. See, e.g., Scott by Scott v. Pacific
West Mountain Resort (Wash.1992).

c. Indemnification Agreements

Another approach some businesses have
tried is to have parents sign an agreement to
indemnify the business against any litigation
expenses and damages the business might have to
pay in a damage suit by their child. These
agreements have not been looked upon favorably by
the courts. See, e.g., Valdimer v. Mount Vernon
Hebrew Camps, Inc. (N.Y.1961) (indemnity
agreement unenforceable because it would motivate
the parent to discourage the child's claim and would
disturb family harmony if the child ignored the
settlement and sued).

6. STATUTES OF LIMITATION

Once a civil cause of action accrues, the
statute of limitations defines the time within which
suit may be filed. If the person fails to sue within
the limitations period, the person loses the right to
sue on the claim. In the absence of legislation
relating to children's claims, statutes of limitations
apply to adult and child claimants alike.

Children, however, generally receive special

protection. The general approach is to enact tolling statutes, which provide that where a civil cause of action accrues to a child, the limitations period begins to run only when the child reaches majority. The child then has the full limitations period within which to sue. Some statutes operate differently, providing that the limitations period on the child's claim begins to run as it would if the claimant were an adult. If the period expires before the child reaches majority, the child upon reaching majority may sue within a specified period, which may be shorter than the ordinary limitations period. Some statutes also have repose provisions stating that regardless of the child's age when the cause of action accrued, suit may not be maintained more than a specified number of years after accrual.

Affording minors special protection may seem unfair to potential defendants because statutes of limitations are intended in part to protect against open-ended exposure to litigation and liability. On the other hand, absence of these protections may disadvantage children. See e.g., Gasparro v. Horner (Fla.Dist.Ct.App.1971) (tort claim of four-year-old who was orphaned and severely injured in a car crash was barred by four-year statute of limitations). In this area, the law generally opts for child protection.

Chapter 4 discusses special limitations that arise in civil suits by adults alleging childhood sexual abuse by the defendant.

CHAPTER 9

REGULATION OF CHILDREN'S CONDUCT

The modern parens patriae doctrine is grounded in the proposition that children need the law's protection from their improvidence or immaturity, and sometimes even from the conduct of their parents. One result has been protective legislation that began in earnest with enactment of child labor laws during the latter part of the nineteenth century and has spread to other areas of our national life. Juvenile protective legislation generally operates until the age of majority, though some statutes end protection earlier or extend it longer.

Challengers sometimes mount age discrimination challenges to a juvenile protective statute, contending that the line drawn creates unlawful age discrimination. These challenges regularly fail because age classifications are not suspect and need satisfy only rational basis scrutiny. See Massachusetts Board of Retirement v. Murgia (S.Ct.1976).

A. CHILD LABOR LAWS

1. INTRODUCTION

a.   The Sources of Regulation

Child labor is regulated by federal, state and municipal legislation, each typically refined by administrative rules and regulations. The Fair Labor Standards Act of 1938 (FLSA), 29 U.S.C. § 201 et seq., is the major federal regulation. Every state also has a child labor law, and many municipal ordinances regulate work by children. State laws tend to follow a common pattern because many are modeled on the Uniform Child Labor Law, which the Uniform Law Commissioners first proposed in 1911. A covered person is subject to the strictest standard -- federal, state or municipal -- in a particular case.

Child labor laws can be confusing because the meaning of broad statutory and administrative provisions may be unclear when applied to particular facts. Also some state restrictions are also found outside the child labor act. Alcohol control laws, for example, may prohibit or regulate employment of children in establishments where beer or liquor is sold or consumed. Other statutes may restrict or prohibit employers from hiring children to work in such places as gambling establishments or pool halls, or to manufacture or sell such products as explosives, fireworks or firearms.

The constitutionality of federal and state child labor legislation was assured when the Supreme Court unanimously upheld the FLSA in United States v. Darby (S.Ct.1941). Three years later, Prince v. Massachusetts, discussed in chapter 1, upheld general state authority to enact child labor legislation under the police power.

b.   Agricultural Employment
        Child labor legislation sought initially to protect children from work in the factories, sweatshops and mills that began dotting the landscape with the advent of industrialism. Today, however, children are more likely to be harmed by work on commercial farms.

The Fair Labor Standards Act and typical state child labor legislation nonetheless provide broad exemptions allowing employment of particularly young children in agriculture. Federal and state agricultural exemptions, perhaps the product of strong farm lobbies and idyllic visions of the family farm, persist even as family farms yield to mechanized conglomerates whose pesticides and heavy machinery invite serious injury to child workers.

Agricultural employment is particularly harsh on young children of migrant workers. The United States has about six million migrant farmworkers, most of whom are young married Hispanic men with families who travel to find seasonal farm work and who take up temporary residence at the work sites. The migrants are generally among the working poor, with average annual earnings below the poverty level, even with two-wage-earner families. Most migrant families qualify for public assistance, but less than a quarter receive it.

Because most migrant farm workers are paid by the bucket, bushel or basket, young children frequently supplement the family income, often working long hours beside their parents in hot fields exposed to pesticides from direct spray or working with recently sprayed crops. Without access to day care, migrant workers may have little alternative but to bring their children into the fields to work or play amid the pesticides and dangerous farm machinery. The parents may not know the identities and dangers of the specific chemicals to which they are exposed, the children's access to quality health care may be limited or nonexistent, and the children may be encouraged or permitted to operate the machinery and perform other hazardous farm work without adequate training. Because migrants are always on the move, their children are typically also deprived of appropriate formal education, which Americans correctly perceive as key to escape from poverty.

c. Parents Rights to a Child's Earnings

The common law gave parents the right to their unemancipated children's wages, which demonstrated the law's willingness to permit parents to put their children to work at an early age, and the law's expectation that many parents would do so. Before the twentieth century, the parental right was meaningful because many poor families often depended on their children's earnings. Indeed, when Hammer v. Dagenhart (S.Ct.1918) struck down an early federal child labor act for exceeding Congress' commerce power, the plaintiff father prevailed on the contention that the act deprived him of his vested right to his two sons' earnings from working under harsh conditions in a North Carolina cotton mill.

Few children help support their families nowadays, and most children work to save for higher education or to purchase clothes, automobiles or other consumer goods. The parents' right to their children's earnings nonetheless survives in many states in common law or by statute. Some states, however, have abolished the parental right.

d.   International Child Labor

Dissenting in Hammer v. Dagenhart in 1918, Justice Holmes wrote that "if there is any matter upon which civilized countries have agreed ... it is the evil of premature and excessive child labor." Worldwide conditions of child labor, however, remain an issue in the 21st century.

The International Labor Organization has called child labor "the single most important source of exploitation and child abuse in the world today." ILO, Child Labour: Targeting the Intolerable (1996). The ILO estimates that in developing countries alone, at least 120 million children between five and fourteen work full-time; the estimate of workers in this age group is 250 million if part-time workers are counted. Working conditions are frequently deplorable. The organization describes "many millions of children ... trapped in forced labor, debt bondage, prostitution, pornography, and other kinds of work which cause lasting damage and immediate dangers."

American companies directly or indirectly employ many of these children, and Americans purchase many of the goods manufactured by child labor abroad, frequently at prices that would be considerably higher without such labor.

2.   STATE REGULATION

a.   Coverage

Many state child labor acts impose general regulations on employment of children under eighteen. Some states, however, end general regulation at a lower age. Some child labor acts expressly exempt children who are or have been married, who are parents, or who have graduated from high school or vocational or technical school. Other states exempt children who have been emancipated by operation of law or by court order, or authorize administrative exemption on a case-by-case basis.

b.   Hazardous Occupations

Even where general child labor regulation ends before majority, state law typically prohibits employment of children under eighteen in "hazardous occupations." These occupations may be enumerated in the child labor act itself, in rules and regulations promulgated under the act, or in other statutes (such as ones regulating sale and use of fireworks, explosives or firearms).

Michigan regulations, for example, prohibit employment of minors in a number of occupations, including construction work such as

roofing, excavation and demolition; manufacturing or storing of explosives; occupations involving
exposure to hazardous substances; occupations
involving use of power-driven bakery machines or
power-driven meat-processing machines; and
occupations requiring "operation of a motor
vehicle on any public road or highway, except
when such operation is occasional and incidental
to the minor's primary work activities." Mich. R.
408.6208.

c. "Work," "Employment" or "Labor"

Child labor acts typically prohibit or
regulate "work," "employment" or "labor" without
defining these critical terms, which do not necessarily have the same meaning. See, e.g., Gabin v.
Skyline Cabana Club (N.J. 1969) ("labor" includes
more than compensatory employment, and "work"
has broader meaning than "employment"). The
acts frequently exempt such activities as agricultural work, work for parents or guardians, or
work in family-owned or family-operated businesses. Performance as a child actor or model
may also be exempted.

Only a handful of child labor acts state
whether children may perform as "volunteers"
without promise, expectation or receipt of
remuneration. The matter is important to scout-
ing, youth sports, and similar groups whose

fundraising projects frequently encourage or require children to sell cookies, raffle tickets, candy or similar products. In states with acts silent about volunteerism, fundraising can raise thorny questions. In 1978, for example, questions were raised about whether volunteer clean-up activities performed by children as part of civic conservation projects in Pennsylvania state parks and forests constituted "work" in violation of the state child labor act, which did not define the term. After concluding that the proposed activities did not violate the FLSA because the children's efforts would introduce no product into interstate commerce, the attorney general also concluded that the activities did not offend the state act, whose "penal provisions cannot be extended by interpretation to include those activities of children which are not essentially 'work' in its ordinarily accepted meaning, or which cannot fairly be said to tend to the exploitation of the labor of children for commercial or other remunerative purposes." 1978 Op. Atty. Gen. No. 22 (Pa.).

d. Hours and Working Conditions

Child labor acts regulate the maximum number of hours children may work weekly and the late hours they may work on school nights during the school term. Several state acts also regulate children's working conditions, frequently providing greater protections than adults would enjoy in the same workplace under generally applicable federal and state workplace safety legislation. Michigan's act, for example, provides: "A minor shall not be employed for more than 5 hours continuously without an interval of at least 30 minutes for a meal and rest period. An interval of less than 30 minutes shall not be considered to interrupt a continuous period of work." Child labor acts also typically authorize a state agency to conduct periodic inspections of places where children are employed.

e.   Work Permits

Most child labor acts require children to secure work permits or certificates, usually from a school official. The applicant must present proof of age and a description of the prospective employment. In most states, a physician must sign the permit to indicate the child is fit for the anticipated employment. Frequently the prospective employer must sign the description. The school official may also be required to certify that the applicant regularly attends school and is performing satisfactorily in the classroom, though school officials generally do not withhold permits for poor academic performance. The child's parent or guardian frequently must provide written consent to the prospective employment.

A person who employs a child without receiving the required permit or certificate commits a criminal offense. The employer must retain the permit or certificate on file throughout the employment. Several states specify that in actions alleging child labor act violations, the work permit or certificate is conclusive proof of the child's age, protecting employers against proceedings under the act for employing children who misrepresent their age to secure employment.

The Fair Labor Standards Act does not require that children secure a work permit or certificate. When federal authorities question the lawfulness of a child's employment, however, the Act requires the employer to prove the child is employed in accordance with the Act and Department of Labor regulations. The Department accepts state-issued work permits and certificates as proof of age. Where the state does not issue permits or certificates meeting standards established in federal regulations, the Department issues age certificates on request.

f.   Criminal and Civil Penalties

Child labor acts impose criminal or civil penalties on employers. Some states also impose criminal or civil penalties on parents or guardians who permit their child to work in violation of the act. Where the child labor act does not sanction parents, a parent may nonetheless face sanction under compulsory school attendance laws where unlawful employment leads the child to miss school. Where unlawful employment harms the child physically or emotionally, the parent might also face sanction under criminal endangerment or civil neglect statutes.

State child labor enforcement is generally lax because budget cutbacks have reduced the ranks of enforcement agents. Where enforcement is sought, the employer normally may not defend by asserting that the minor or parent consented to the otherwise unlawful employment, that the child or the family needed the child's wages to avoid hardship, or that the child was saving for a worthwhile purpose such as college tuition. Only a few states permit exemptions where employment of children is needed to support the family.

Virtually no child labor acts impose criminal punishment on the child for working in violation of the act. The evident policy consideration is that the child is a victim of child labor, rather than a wrongdoer.

g.   Professional and Occupational Licensing

State licensing statutes establish the minimum ages at which persons may practice any of a number of professions and occupations. The

age is usually eighteen, but some licensing
statutes establish a higher or lower minimum age.
The statutes effectively prohibit employment in
the covered professions and occupations by most
children. Statutes and court rules, for example,
typically establish eighteen as the minimum age
at which a person may be licensed to practice law.
Other covered professions and occupations vary
from state to state, but frequently include the
following: barber, certified public accountant,
chiropractor, beautician, dental hygienist, dentist,
emergency medical technician, insurance agent or
broker or adjuster, marriage or family or child
counselor, physician, nursing home administrator, optometrist, pharmacist, physical therapist,
podiatrist, psychologist, real estate agent or
broker or appraiser, and veterinarian.

3.   FEDERAL REGULATION

a.   The Fair Labor Standards Act of 1938

General federal employment safety
standards, such as those of the Occupational
Safety and Health Administration (OSHA), govern
establishments employing children and adults.
The child labor provisions of the Fair Labor
Standards Act of 1938, and its regulations,
provide children enhanced federal protection.

The FLSA operates against "oppressive

child labor." With enumerated exceptions, the
term means employment of a child under sixteen
(except by a parent or a person standing in the
parent's place employing his own child, or a child
in his custody, in an occupation other than
manufacturing or mining or an occupation found
by the Secretary of Labor to be "particularly
hazardous.") The term also means employment of
a child between sixteen and eighteen in any
occupation the Secretary of Labor by regulation
finds "particularly hazardous." 29 U.S.C. § 203.

The FLSA permits some employment of
younger children: "[T]he employment of employees
between the ages of fourteen and sixteen years in
occupations other than manufacturing and
mining shall not be deemed to constitute
oppressive child labor if and to the extent that the
Secretary of Labor determines that such
employment is confined to periods which will not
interfere with their schooling and to conditions
which will not interfere with their health and well-
being." Id. § 203(l). The Act also contains broad
exemptions permitting farm work by children,
including children under twelve. Id. § 213(c).

The Secretary of Labor has designated a
number of occupations "particularly hazardous."
The designation includes manufacturing explosives; working in coal and other mining; working

with various power-driven machinery; working in slaughtering and meat packing establishments and rendering plants; roofing; and excavation. 29 C.F.R. § 570.120. The effect of the Secretary's designation is to raise to eighteen the minimum age of employment in the occupations covered.

b.   Remedies for Violation

The FLSA prohibits employers from employing "oppressive child labor in commerce or in the production of goods for commerce or in any enterprise engaged in commerce or in the production of goods for commerce." 29 U.S.C. § 212(c). The Act also prohibits producers, manufacturers, or dealers from shipping or delivering for shipment in commerce any goods produced by "oppressive child labor." Id. § 212(a). The Act creates criminal and civil remedies on behalf of the Secretary of Labor. Id. § 216(a), (e). Federal child labor enforcement, like state enforcement, however, has generally been inadequate.

4.   PRIVATE ENFORCEMENT

The FLSA does not create an express private right of action for violation of its child labor provisions, and most courts have refused to imply such a right. Without a private federal remedy, children and parents seeking private

relief against employers for child labor violations
are left to state remedies. Most states, however,
bar tort suits under the "exclusive remedy" provisions of workers' compensation acts, which
prohibit employees from suing employers outside
the acts.

Most state workers' compensation acts
cover minors lawfully and unlawfully employed. If
the minor was employed in violation of the child
labor law, many acts award an enhanced remedy,
ranging from 150% of the ordinary rate to double
or even triple the ordinary rate. Enhancement is
ordinarily awarded even to minors who secured
the employment by misrepresenting their age.

Even with enhancement, workers' compensation acts may provide only meager recovery for
death or serious injury suffered by unlawfully
employed children. In Henderson v. Bear (Colo.Ct.
App.1998), for example, the parents of a 15-year-
old electrocuted while working illegally at a car
wash received only a $4000 funeral benefit and
reimbursement for medical expenses from the
workers' compensation fund. Even if the award
had been doubled or trebled, recovery would have
seemed inadequate compensation for the boy's
death.

Plaintiffs like the Hendersons, however,

are not necessarily foreclosed from suit outside the workers compensation laws. These laws generally provide the exclusive remedy against the employer, but permit the employee or his or her estate to sue a non-employer allegedly responsible for the employee's injury or death, such as the manufacturer of equipment involved in the accident.

Where the workers' compensation act is silent about child employees, the exclusive-remedies provision may not bar private tort suits against employers. If a minor is killed or injured by employment that violates the child labor act, some states permit the minor or the estate to choose between workers' compensation and other remedies.

Where a private tort suit is permitted, the defendant employer generally may not assert that the child was contributorily or comparatively negligent, or that the child's parents consented to the unlawful employment. Most decisions also deprive the employer of the affirmative defense that the child assumed the risk of the employment, or misrepresented his or her age to secure employment.

B. ALCOHOL REGULATION

1. THE MINIMUM DRINKING AGE

a. Recent History

After the Twenty-first Amendment repealed national Prohibition and left alcohol regulation to the states in 1933, nearly all states set twenty-one as the minimum drinking age. The age caused little stir until the late 1960s, when many states lowered the drinking age (and the general age of majority). Second thoughts about the newly lowered minimum drinking age began surfacing by the mid-1970s, when studies suggested that it had contributed to an increase in fatal motor vehicle accidents among older teens. The Presidential Commission on Drunken Driving recommended that states raise their minimum drinking ages to twenty-one, but nearly half the states appeared to ignore the recommendation.

In response to foot-dragging by the states, Congress in 1984 enacted the National Minimum Drinking Age Act, 23 U.S.C. § 158. The Act sought to encourage a uniform national minimum drinking age by withholding percentages of otherwise allocable federal highway funds from any state "in which the purchase or public possession ... of any alcoholic beverage by a person who is less that twenty-one years of age is lawful." In South Dakota v. Dole (S.Ct. 1987), the Court upheld section 158 as a proper exercise of Congress' spending power. All states now set the minimum drinking age at twenty-one.

b. Exemptions

Many state alcohol control laws exempt parents who provide alcohol to their underage children, clergy who provide alcohol to underage children as part of a religious service or ceremony, or physicians who prescribe alcohol in their professional practices. The parental exemption defers to family autonomy generally, and reflects debate about whether children should abstain from use of alcohol until they reach the minimum drinking age, or whether children should be encouraged to develop responsible drinking habits through exposure to alcohol under adult supervision in family settings.

Even where alcohol control statutes permit parents to provide their children alcohol, the parent may face civil liability at common law or, as discussed below in section 3, under a dram shop or social host act if the child becomes intoxicated and causes injury to himself or personal or property damage to someone else. Parents also remain subject to the endangerment and other criminal abuse and neglect statutes. In People v. Garbarino (N.Y.App.Div. 1989), for exam-

ple, the mother and stepfather encouraged the
15-year-old to consume at least 25 ounces of
alcohol as the family sat at the kitchen table of
their home. The intoxicated boy, with a blood
alcohol level of .41%, began vomiting and later
died of cardiopulmonary failure due to "aspiration
of gastric contents." The appellate court permitted
prosecution of the parents for criminally negligent
homicide, reckless endangerment, and endangering the welfare of a child.

c.   "Zero Tolerance" Laws

In 1995, Congress enacted a nationwide
"zero tolerance" statute. To combat underage
drinking, the lawmakers encouraged states to
enact and enforce legislation that "considers an
individual under the age of 21 who has a blood
alcohol concentration of 0.02 percent or greater
while operating a motor vehicle in the State to be
driving while intoxicated or driving under the
influence of alcohol." 23 U.S.C. § 161(a)(3). States
failing to comply with the mandate faced loss of a
portion of their federal highway funds.

The congressionally mandated 0.02% cap
is roughly equivalent to one glass of beer or wine.
(A true zero-tolerance measure was deemed
unworkable because some prescription and over-
the-counter drugs, and even some foods, contain
alcohol or other substances that might register on

a drug test.) In most states, drivers over 21 are not legally drunk unless they test more than .10% blood alcohol content; in some states, the adult level is .08%.

State zero-tolerance legislation has been upheld against equal protection challenges as rationally related to the legitimate state purposes of reducing the number of teenage driving fatalities and of protecting the public. See, e.g., Barnett v. State (Ga.1999).

d. Identification
Statutes frequently specify the identification young people, wishing to purchase or be served alcohol, must show to establish that they are over eighteen. Generally acceptable are a drivers' license, military identification card, or passport. To help prevent use of false or altered drivers' licenses, a number of states issue minors special color-coded licenses, or licenses with distinctive photographs or special wording or characters. For possessing or presenting a false or altered license, states generally provide criminal penalties, suspension or revocation of the offender's license, or postponement of the right to apply for a license.

2. DANGERS AND ENFORCEMENT
DIFFICULTIES

The American Academy of Pediatrics
reports that the leading cause of death among 15-
to-24-year-olds is alcohol-related motor vehicle
crashes, that thousands each year survive these
crashes with serious and sometimes permanent
injuries, that alcohol is implicated in the majority
of other unintentional deaths of children such as
drownings and fatal falls, that many child suicide
and homicide victims have elevated blood alcohol
levels, and that a history of suicide attempts is
more prevalent among adolescents in alcohol and
drug treatment facilities. See American Acad. of
Pediatrics, Alcohol Use and Abuse: A Pediatric
Concern, 95 Pediatrics 439 (1995). Teenage drinking is also associated with such high-risk
behavior as assaults and sexual activity. Teenage
alcoholism is also a major problem. Despite these
dangers, enforcement of the underage drinking
laws remains spotty in most places.

3. DRAM-SHOP AND SOCIAL-HOST
LIABILITY

Persons who provide or serve alcoholic
beverages to underage drinkers may face tort
liability in private suits alleging injury or death

caused by the drinker's ensuing conduct. Typically the young drinker consumes liquor provided on the defendant's premises, then drives off in an automobile and has an accident killing or seriously injuring himself or others. Providers often make alluring defendants because they may be better able to pay a judgment than the young drinker, who may be without significant resources and either uninsured or underinsured. Liability now sometimes extends beyond bars, convenience stores and other businesses, to such providers as social hosts and colleges.

Common law decisions disagree about the defenses the provider may assert. Where the underage consumer or the consumer's estate sues the provider, some courts deny recovery based on the underage consumer's contributory negligence, assumption of risk, or willful misconduct. Other courts, however, deny these defenses on the ground that the alcohol laws seek to protect underage persons from their own improvidence. In any event, these defenses would not defeat a third party's suit. Where the defendant provided alcoholic beverages to an underage consumer over eighteen, the defendant may not avoid liability on the ground that the consumer was an adult responsible for his or own conduct.

More than thirty-five states have enacted

"dram shop" acts or social host acts, which may displace or augment the common law. Dram shop acts define circumstances in which providers incur strict liability, without regard to contributory or comparative negligence or assumption of risk, for death or injury proximately caused by an underage or visibly intoxicated drinker. Some dram shop acts specifically limit liability to providers that hold liquor licenses, while other acts also reach social hosts and other providers. Suit may ordinarily be maintained only by third parties, and not by the consumer or his estate, or by members of the consumer's family seeking derivative damages.

A few states disallow dram shop liability, except where the commercial provider knew or should have known the consumer was underage or intoxicated at the time of provision. A few states prohibit dram shop liability altogether.

For their part, social host acts generally permit recovery by family members and injured third-persons against persons who provide alcohol gratuitously to an underage or intoxicated drinker. A few states, however, reject or strictly limit social host liability.

C. TOBACCO REGULATION

1. CHILDREN AND SMOKING

Teenage smoking has been called a "pediatric disease" because adolescents face serious health risks from smoking. The younger a person is when he or she begins smoking, the more difficult it is to quit. If a person does not start smoking as a child, he or she is unlikely to ever start. Early adolescent smokers are more likely to smoke for the rest of their lives, to smoke heavily, and to suffer and die prematurely from smoking-related disease. Smokeless tobacco (moist oral snuff and chewing tobacco) also poses serious health risks.

Because of these health risks, Congress in 1992 required states to enact legislation restricting sale and distribution of tobacco products to minors as a condition of receiving federal substance abuse prevention and treatment block grant funds. In the wake of the congressional mandate, all states now prohibit the sale of tobacco products to persons under eighteen. Despite minimum-age legislation, how-ever, cigarettes remain accessible to children because enforcement of no-sale legislation has been lax and penalties are often minimal.

Efforts to curb tobacco advertising that targets children have run afoul of the First Amendment. In Lorillard Tobacco Co. v. Reilly (S.Ct.2001), for example, the Supreme Court struck down most aspects of Massachusetts regulations that, among other things, prohibited outdoor advertising of tobacco products "in any location within a 1,000 foot radius of any public playground, playground area in a public park, elementary school or secondary school." The Court held that the outdoor advertising regulations were preempted by federal legislation (as to cigarettes) and violated the First Amendment (as to smokeless tobacco and cigars).

2. SANCTIONS AND LICENSING

In some states, sanctions for unlawfully providing tobacco to minors are less than sanctions for unlawfully providing alcohol. The tobacco statutes usually provide only a small fine for first violations.

Most states license retailers that sell tobacco products and penalize licensees that sell to children. Several of the states provide for license suspension or revocation, but only a handful of the states have designated an agency to enforce the delicensing provisions. The rationale for licensing is that the specter of suspension or revocation may be a greater deterrent than modest fines because many retailers receive substantial revenue from tobacco sales to adults. Lax enforcement, however, may compromise deterrence.

3.   THE NATIONAL TOBACCO SETTLEMENT

In November, 1998, the tobacco industry settled damage actions brought by the attorneys general of more than forty states seeking reimbursement for medical costs of treating sick smokers. The settlement produced a sizeable monetary recovery for the states and imposed restrictions on the industry. The settlement reaches a number of matters related to children. Among other things, the settlement:

- requires the industry each year for ten years to pay $25 million to fund a charitable foundation that will support the study of programs to reduce teen smoking and substance abuse and the prevention of diseases associated with tobacco use;

- bans use of cartoons in the advertising, promotion, packaging or labeling of tobacco products;

- prohibits the industry from targeting youth in advertising, promotions, or marketing;

- bans industry actions aimed at initiating, maintaining or increasing youth smoking;
- regulates specified advertising practices (it bans all outdoor advertising of tobacco products, including advertising on billboards, signs and placards in arenas, stadiums, shopping malls, and video game arcades; limits advertising outside retail establishments to 14 square feet; bans transit advertising of tobacco products; and allows states to substitute, for the duration of billboard lease periods, alternative advertising that discourages youth smoking);
- beginning July 1, 1999, bans tobacco companies' distribution and sale of apparel and merchandise with brand-name logos (caps, T-shirts, backpacks, etc.);
- prohibits brand name sponsorship of events with a significant youth audience or team sports (football, basketball, baseball, hockey or soccer); prohibits sponsorship of events whose paid participants or contestants are underage; limits tobacco companies to one brand name sponsorship per year (after current contracts expire or after three years -- whichever comes first); and bans tobacco brand names for stadiums and arenas;

- bans distribution of free samples except in facilities or enclosed areas where the operator ensures no underage person is present;
- bans gifts based on purchases of tobacco products without proof of age; and
- prohibits tobacco companies from opposing proposed state or local laws or administrative rules that are intended to limit youth access to and consumption of tobacco products.

See http://www.wa.gov/ago/tobaccosettlement/ summary.html. The settlement does not ban sales of tobacco products from vending machines, or mandate minimum federal standards for licensing retailers that sell tobacco products directly to consumers, or for suspending or revoking the license for selling to minors. Most states, however, regulate vending machines that dispense tobacco products.

4. FOREIGN EXPORT OF U.S. TOBACCO PRODUCTS

In the United States during the past three decades, the overall consumption of tobacco products has fallen significantly while the rate of teen smoking has generally increased. Major American tobacco companies have moved to establish markets overseas, first in Africa, Latin America and western Europe and more recently in Asia and eastern Europe. United States tobacco companies have been accused of targeting children overseas, assisted by U.S. government trade policy. "Free cigarette samples are distributed in video parlors, discos, and bars. The sponsorship of rock concerts of groups popular with teens is particularly effective. In Taiwan, R. J. Reynolds sponsored a local concert featuring a popular teen idol, charging five empty packets of Winston cigarettes for admission. Firms also create demand by selling paraphernalia targeted at children: children's notebooks, school supplies, shirts, jeans, jackets, and kites with cigarette logos such as Marlboro Gear and Winston House. Finally, they advertise in comic books popular with elementary school pupils, heavily push vending machines, which permit young people to buy cigarettes, and attract first-time smokers through menthol filters and blends that are easier to smoke." Heidi S. Gruner, The Export of U.S. Tobacco Products to Developing Countries and Previously Closed Markets, 28 Law and Pol'y in Int'l Bus. 217 (1996).

D. DRIVING PRIVILEGES

1. AGE RESTRICTIONS

All states establish a minimum age at which persons may secure licenses to drive various types of motor vehicles on public roads. Of greatest interest to most teenagers is the minimum age for securing a standard operator's license, which is usually between fifteen and seventeen. Statutes typically establish higher minimum ages for licenses to drive such specialized vehicles as school buses, other buses, commercial vehicles, taxis, and chauffeured vehicles.

Because motor vehicle-related crashes are the leading cause of death in youths between sixteen and twenty and a leading cause of disability, a growing number of states have instituted graduated licensing, which enables children to secure a standard operator's license only after proceeding through stages designed to help encourage them to develop the experience, ability and maturity to drive safely. Pennsylvania's formula, for example, proceeds from a learner's permit to a restricted junior drivers license (for 16– and 17–year olds), to a regular drivers license at 18 (or at 17 if the applicant is accident-free and has compelled a drivers education course). See 75 Pa. Cons. Stat. §§ 1503, 1505.

2.   PARENTAL PERMISSION AND PARENTAL LIABILITY

In several states, minors may secure drivers licenses only where a parent, custodian or other adult signs the license application as a sponsor. To provide a measure of public protection, the adult assumes liability, generally joint and several with the minor, for the minor's negligent or intentional conduct behind the wheel. Some statutes impose liability on the adult only where proof of financial responsibility is not deposited by the minor or by someone on his or her behalf. In more than thirty states, parents may avoid liability by requesting the motor vehicle department to revoke their children's licenses.

In the absence of statute, the mere existence of a parent-child relationship does not make a parent liable for the child's negligent operation of a motor vehicle, even if the parent owns the vehicle or otherwise provided it to the child. Parents may be liable for damages, however, where they entrust a vehicle to a child they know is an incompetent, inexperienced or reckless driver. Parents and other adults have also been held liable where they provided the motor vehicle to a minor who is below the minimum licensing age or is otherwise unlicensed, or where the parent and child were engaged in a joint venture or held a principal-agent or master-servant relationship.

A number of states apply the common law "family purpose" doctrine. Where a motor vehicle owner maintains the vehicle for the family's pleasure use, the doctrine imposes liability on the owner for damages arising from negligent operation by any family member who uses the vehicle with the owner's express or implied consent for that purpose, including the owner's children. The doctrine treats the operator as the owner's agent or servant. A number of states have rejected the doctrine, though many achieve similar results with statutes imposing liability on the owner for damages caused by anyone operating the vehicle with the owner's express or implied consent.

3. "ABUSE AND LOSE" LAWS

In recent years, many states have enacted so-called "abuse and lose" laws that seek to influence minors' behavior not occurring behind the wheel. Recognizing the importance most teenagers attach to drivers' licenses, these laws provide for denying, suspending or revoking licenses of minors who commit specified crimes or other misbehavior not directly related to driving. If the minor does not yet have a license, abuse-and-lose laws typically provide for postponement of the minor's right to apply for one. Courts have generally upheld the constitutionality of these laws as rationally related to a legitimate state interest in deterring juveniles from committing crimes and other misconduct.

In several states, children subject to the compulsory school attendance act may secure or hold a driver's license only if they show satisfactory educational attendance and performance. Some states deny licenses to habitual truants, students who have been expelled from school, or students who have quit school without graduating for reasons other than financial hardship. More than half the states suspend or revoke licenses of persons under twenty-one convicted of possessing or using drugs or alcohol, even if possession or use does not occur while driving. A few states suspend or revoke the licenses of minors convicted of purchasing or attempting to purchase tobacco products. A few states target graffiti.

E. CHILD HIGHWAY SAFETY

All states require that particularly young

children be restrained in a child-restraint system
(a "car seat") when riding on public roadways.
Coverage, however, does not necessarily extend to
all vehicles. See, e.g., Colo. Rev. Stat. § 42-4-236
(only privately owned noncommercial passenger
vehicles and vehicles operated by child care
centers).

Federal highway funds may be withheld
from states that do not have legislation making it
unlawful to operate a passenger vehicle when a
person in the front seat (other than a child
secured in a child restraint system) is not wearing
a safety belt. 23 U.S.C. § 153. In several respects,
however, the congressional mandate allows states
to provide older children less than adequate
protection:

Primary vs. secondary enforcement. Most
states permit only secondary enforcement of child
restraint and child safety belt laws. Secondary
enforcement permits a police officer to stop a
vehicle only if the officer sees a violation other
than the unprotected child; primary enforcement
permits the officer to stop the vehicle solely
because the officer sees a violation of the
passenger restraint or seat belt requirements.

Primary enforcement produces higher
compliance rates. The ten states with the highest

rates of safety belt usage have primary enforcement laws; of the nine states with the lowest rates
of usage, one (New Hampshire) has no adult
safety belt law and eight have secondary
enforcement laws. See National Safety Council,
Mired in Mediocrity: A Nationwide Report Card on
Driver and Passenger Safety (May 2001).

   Rear-seat passengers. Some states do not
require rear-seat passengers to wear safety belts,
even though children disproportionately occupy
the rear seat of motor vehicles. Rear-seat
legislation assumes greater importance because
safety professionals recommend that children ride
in rear seats to avoid dangers associated with
front-seat air bags. Air bags have saved many
adult lives, but have caused the deaths of some
infants and young children in front seats.

   Truck exemption. In a few states, safety
belt legislation creates a blanket exemption for
trucks. This exemption removes any requirement
that passengers, including children over the age
for child restraint systems, be restrained by a
safety belt while riding in the front seat or any
other seat of a truck.

   Cargo areas. Only a few states have
legislation prohibiting children from riding
unrestrained in the open cargo areas of pickup

trucks. Most passengers thrown from a vehicle in
a crash die or suffer serious physical injury, even
if the vehicle is traveling at a relatively moderate
speed. Most cargo area passengers, and most
cargo area fatalities, are children.

F. GAMBLING

Teenage compulsive gambling appears to
be a growing problem. According to a 1999 study,
approximately 2-5% of adults in the United States
are compulsive and problem gamblers. By contrast, 6-12% of 13-17-year-olds have serious
gambling problems. See Adolescent Compulsive
and Problem Gamblers, 6 Prevention Researcher
(Winter 1999), available at http//:www.integres.
org/prevres.

A number of states prohibit gambling by or
with minors generally. Most states also prohibit
the offer or sale of state lottery tickets or shares to
persons under eighteen, though adults generally
may make gifts of lottery tickets to persons under
eighteen. If a child wins a lottery prize, the prize
ordinarily must be paid to the child's parent or
guardian, or to another adult member of the
child's family for the child's benefit. States may
also prohibit children from engaging in riverboat
gambling, wagers at horse races, bingo and other
types of gambling. By constitution or statute,

some states also regulate raffles, a favorite
fundraising activity of youth groups. In some
states, raffles are not regulated by name, but fall
within general regulation of "games of chance" or
some similar designation.

G.   FIREARMS

1.   GENERAL PROHIBITIONS AND
RESTRICTIONS

The Violent Crime Control and Law Enforcement Act of 1994 restricts juveniles' access
to firearms. The Act prohibits persons under
eighteen (with exceptions relating to farming,
hunting and other specified uses) from knowingly
possessing handguns or ammunition suitable for
use only in handguns. The Act also prohibits
persons from selling or otherwise transferring
these weapons to someone they know or have
reason to believe is under eighteen. 18 U.S.C. §
922(x). The Act further prohibits licensed
importers, licensed manufacturers, licensed
dealers or licensed collectors from selling or
delivering a firearm or ammunition to an
individual the licensee knows or has reason to
believe is under eighteen (or, if the firearm or
ammunition is other than a shotgun or rifle, to an
individual the licensee knows or has reason to
believe is under twenty-one). Id. § 922(b)(1). The

Act also permits states to detain in secure
facilities juveniles arrested or convicted for
possessing handguns in violation of section 922(x)
or of any similar state statute. 42 U.S.C. §
5633(a)(12)(A).

All states prohibit or restrict juveniles'
possession and use of firearms or handguns.
Nearly half the states prohibit firearms possession
for some period of time by adjudicated delinquents, at least ones adjudicated for acts that
would be felonies if committed by an adult.

Legislation typically also prohibits persons
from selling or otherwise providing firearms to
juveniles. Some states permit sale, provision or
possession where the juvenile's parent or
guardian consents, or where the seller or provider
is the parent or guardian. States typically also set
the minimum age at which a person may secure a
license or permit to carry a firearm. See, e.g., Ga.
Code § 16-11-129 (twenty-one; pistol or revolver).
Possession statutes normally do not operate
against juveniles who use the firearm to hunt
with a valid hunting license.

2.   "GUN-FREE SCHOOLS" AND "SAFETY ZONES" ACTS

The federal Gun-Free Schools Act, which took effect March 31, 1994, provides that local educational agencies receiving federal funds must have a policy requiring expulsion for not less than a year of any student who brings a firearm to school; the local agency, however, may modify the expulsion requirement on a case-by-case basis. See 20 U.S.C. § 8921(b)(1). A second federal Gun-Free Schools Act, enacted in October 1994, requires local agencies to implement a policy of "referral to the criminal justice or juvenile delinquency system of any student who brings a firearm or weapon to a school served by such agency." Id. § 8922(a).

More than forty states prohibit possession of firearms by students and others on or near school grounds. In many of these states, the prohibition extends to school grounds, school owned vehicles, and school sponsored activities. Students who violate these provisions are typically subject to expulsion and delinquency proceedings or criminal prosecution.

3.   SAFE STORAGE AND CHILD ACCESS PREVENTION STATUTES

Several states prohibit persons from leaving firearms unattended in places where children may gain access to them. Most of the statutes require persons to take reasonable precautions to prevent child access, but permit prosecution only where the child uses the firearm to cause death or serious physical injury to himself or someone else. Some states, however, permit prosecution regardless of the use the child makes of the weapon. Some statutes specify that reasonable precaution includes keeping the firearm in a securely locked box or container or securely locking the firearm with a trigger lock.

H. OTHER REGULATED CONDUCT

States have regulations in a number of other areas affecting minors' health and well-being. These include prohibiting or limiting minors' access to fireworks and explosives, excluding minors from poolhalls and from fighting in professional boxing and wrestling matches, and limiting tattooing and body piercing.

I.   JUVENILE CURFEWS

1.   HISTORY AND THE CONTEMPORARY LANDSCAPE

Curfews have had a long, and not always noble, history in the United States. Before the Civil War, many localities imposed curfews prohibiting slaves or free blacks from being on the streets during specified hours. Toward the end of the nineteenth century, states and localities began enacting curfews directed solely at juveniles. The juvenile curfews received their first substantial boost when President Benjamin Harrison called them "the most important municipal regulation for the protection of children of American homes, from the vices of the street." By the turn of the century, about 3000 villages and municipalities had enacted curfews, which were frequently seen as measures to help control immigrant children.

In the early twentieth century, interest in juvenile curfews diminished until World War II, when they were seen as helpful to control children while their parents were in the armed forces or employed in war industries, frequently on night shifts. A Presidential executive order imposed a curfew in military zones against Japanese-Americans of all ages (most of whom were United

States citizens). Curfews were also imposed on more than a half million undocumented Italian immigrants. The Supreme Court upheld the executive order as a valid exercise of the federal war power in an emergency, but the episodes are now viewed with general embarrassment. See, e.g., Hirabayashi v. United States (S.Ct.1943).

With the end of the War, the focus once again shifted away from juvenile curfews, which remained on the books in many jurisdictions but were rarely enforced. Indeed, curfews went unmentioned in the crime-fighting recommendations made in the final report of the Katzenbach Commission's Juvenile Delinquency Task Force in 1967.

Since the early 1990s, juvenile curfews have proliferated in reaction to violent juvenile crime and gang activity. Most juvenile curfews are enacted by local governments pursuant to their general police powers. According to a 1997 survey of 347 cities with a population over thirty thousand, 276 of the cities had a nighttime juvenile curfew. Twenty-six percent had daytime curfews which, with enumerated exceptions, required school-age children to be off the streets during the hours when schools are in session during the academic year. See U.S. Conference of Mayors, A Status Report on Youth Curfews in

America's Cities (Dec. 1997).

Courts have upheld a variety of local curfew-like ordinances designed to regulate children's public activities. See, e.g., Rothner v. City of Chicago (7th Cir.1991) (ordinance that prohibited children under seventeen from playing video games in commercial establishments during school hours on days when school is in session did not violate First Amendment); Lutz v. City of York (3d Cir.1990) (ordinance that prohibited "cruising," driving repeatedly around a loop of major roads through the heart of the city, did not violate constitutional right to travel).

Chicago's Gang Congregation Ordinance, on the other hand, did not survive a court challenge. The ordinance provided that "[w]hen-ever a police officer observes a person whom he reasonably believes to be a criminal street gang member loitering in any public place with one or more other persons, he shall order all such persons to disperse and remove themselves from the area." The Supreme Court held that the ordinance was void for vagueness. See City of Chicago v. Morales (S.Ct.1999) (plurality opinion).

2. A REPRESENTATIVE JUVENILE
CURFEW ORDINANCE

In Hutchins v. District of Columbia
(D.C.Cir.1999) (en banc), the court upheld the
District's juvenile curfew ordinance, whose
provisions are typical of those found in such
ordinances throughout the nation. Based on
detailed statistics documenting the prevalence of
local juvenile crime, the District's ordinance
prohibits juveniles sixteen and under (except
emancipated or married juveniles) from being in a
public place unaccompanied by a parent, or
without equivalent adult supervision, from 11:00
p.m. on Sunday through Thursday to 6:00 a.m.
on the following day and from midnight to 6:00
a.m. on Saturday and Sunday.

The District ordinance provides that a
parent or guardian commits an offense by
knowingly permitting, or through insufficient
control allowing, the juvenile to violate the curfew.
Owners, operators, or employees of public
establishments violate the curfew by knowingly
allowing the juvenile to remain on the premises,
unless the juvenile has refused to leave and the
owner or operator has notified the police.

The District ordinance has eight "defenses." The curfew is not violated if the juvenile

is (1) accompanied by the juvenile's parent or
guardian or any other person 21 or older
authorized by a parent to be the juvenile's
caretaker; (2) on an errand at the direction of the
juvenile's parent, guardian, or caretaker, without
any detour or stop; (3) in a vehicle involved in
interstate travel; (4) engaged in specified
employment activity, or going to or from employment, without any detour or stop; (5) involved in
an emergency; (6) on the sidewalk that abuts the
minor's or the next-door neighbor's residence, if
the neighbor has not complained to the police; (7)
attending an official school, religious, or other
recreational activity sponsored by the District, a
civic organization, or another similar entity that
takes responsibility for the juvenile, or going to or
from, without any detour or stop, such an activity
supervised by adults; or (8) exercising First
Amendment rights, including free exercise of
religion, freedom of speech, and the right of
assembly.

If, after questioning an apparent offender
to determine his age and reason for being in a
public place, a police officer reasonably believes a
curfew violation has occurred without a defense,
police will detain the juvenile and release him into
the custody of a parent, guardian, or an adult
acting in loco parentis. If no one claims response-
bility for the juvenile, the juvenile may be taken

either to his residence or placed into the custody of the Family Services Administration custody until 6:00 a.m. the following morning. Juveniles violating the curfew may be ordered to perform up to 25 hours of community service for each violation, while parents who allow a juvenile to violate the curfew may be fined up to $500 or required to perform community service, and may be required to attend parenting classes. Businesses violating the curfew may be fined.

3. CONSTITUTIONALITY OF JUVENILE CURFEWS

Courts generally agree that in the absence of an emergency, states may not constitutionally impose a general curfew on adults. See, e.g., Bykofsky v. Middletown (cert. denied S.Ct.1976); Ruff v. Marshall (M.D.Ga.1977). Curfews reaching adults and children alike, however, are generally upheld where they are limited in duration and narrowly tailored to help insure public safety during specific emergencies such as natural disasters. See, e.g., Smith v. Avino (11th Cir.1996) (upholding county curfew imposed after Hurricane Andrew).

As the number of general juvenile curfew statutes and ordinances has increased nationwide, constitutional challenges by juveniles and

their parents has also increased. Challengers
have alleged numerous violations, including
violation of parents' due process right to direct
their children's upbringing without unreasonable
government interference, denial of the right of free
movement and the right to travel, denial of equal
protection, invalid search and seizure and void-
for-vagueness. The Supreme Court has not ruled
on the constitutionality of juvenile curfews, and
the lower courts remain split. See, e.g., Schleifer
v. City of Charlottesville (4th Cir.1998) (upholding
juvenile curfew); Nunez v. City of San Diego (9th
Cir.1997) (striking down juvenile curfew).

Appellate courts ordinarily uphold the
authority of juvenile and criminal courts to
impose particularized curfews on juveniles adjudicated as delinquents or sentenced as adults. Also
ordinarily upheld are particularized curfews
imposed on juveniles as part of informal,
negotiated dispositions or plea bargains. Curfews
imposed on juveniles as a sanction for committing
a particular offense do not implicate the constitutional questions raised by blanket curfews that
operate against juveniles generally regardless of
prior individual behavior.

J. STATUS OFFENSES

1. THE NATURE OF STATUS
OFFENSE JURISDICTION

A status offense is conduct sanctionable only where the person committing it is a juvenile. (Delinquency, on the other hand, alleges that the juvenile has committed an act that would be a crime if committed by an adult.) This section treats the three quintessential status offenses -- ungovernability, truancy, and runaway behavior. Also sometimes labeled status offenses are various other acts sanctionable only when committed by a juvenile, such as underage purchase, possession or consumption of tobacco or alcohol, and curfew violations. Because these other acts are often proscribed by criminal statutes, however, violators may appear in juvenile court under delinquency jurisdiction rather than status offense jurisdiction.

Alleged status offenders may be referred to the juvenile court by law enforcement agents, parents, school authorities, social service agencies or others. Law enforcement agencies make nearly half of all status offense referrals, but a signify-cant percentage of referrals are made each year by the child's parents themselves. Nomenclature varies from state to state, but a status offender is

typically called a PINS (person in need of supervision), a CHINS (child in need of supervision), a
MINS (minor in need of supervision), or an unruly
child.

Broad frontal attacks on the constitutionality of the juvenile court's status offense jurisdiction have generally failed. Among other things,
challengers have unsuccessfully asserted that the
jurisdiction is void for vagueness, constitutes
cruel and unusual punishment, and violates
equal protection and substantive due process.

2. UNGOVERNABILITY

The juvenile court may find a child
ungovernable (or incorrigible) if the child habitually refuses to obey the parents' reasonable
commands and thus is beyond their control.
Critics charge that ungovernability jurisdiction
frequently sanctions children for their parents'
failings because many status offenders are victims
of abuse and neglect that may not surface when
the court adjudicates a status offense petition.
On the other hand, parents may feel genuine need
for ungovernability jurisdiction when the child is
truly beyond their control, endangering himself
and perhaps others and threatening violent
behavior. An ungovernability petition may be a
desperate preventive measure for parents seeking

court action before the child commits a crime, perhaps one that would produce a hefty prison term.

3. TRUANCY

Truancy is the habitual absence from school of a youth subject to the compulsory school act. A child is truant only where the fault for missing school lies with the child and not with the parents.

Where a child is habitually absent from school, truancy might indicate present or future distress, such as abuse or neglect, gang membership, drug and alcohol abuse or delinquency. Many child welfare workers also believe that truants often have undiagnosed learning disabilities and attention deficit disorders but are labeled as discipline problems without ever receiving special education. Truants may be depressed or angry or both. Their families may also suffer from unemployment, serious illness, parental discord, alcoholism, or other serious problems.

4. RUNAWAYS

a. The Scope of the Problem

More than a million children each year run

away from home and live on the streets,
frequently to escape persistent physical, emotional or sexual abuse, alcoholic or drug addicted
parents, divorce, sickness, poverty or school
problems. The cause is ongoing family dysfunction more often than one precipitating event.
Precise accountings of runaway children are
unavailable because many children who leave
their families, foster homes or group homes are
not reported.

Many runaways (more than a fifth and as
many as 46%, depending on the study) are more
aptly labeled "throwaways" because they are
directly told to leave the household, because they
have been away from home and a caretaker has
refused to allow them back, because they have
run away but the caretaker makes no effort to
recover them or does not care whether they
return, or because they are abandoned or
deserted. Throwaways come from all social
classes, generally come from households without
both natural parents, and are generally left
destitute by their families.

Some runaway children receive help in
shelters funded by the federal or state governments or by private caregivers. Many others find
shelter with friends or relatives. Many, however,
live on the streets, frequently turning to

prostitution, pornography, panhandling and
crimes against persons or property for survival.
Some street children land in jail before
encountering a shelter.

        Many runaways and throwaways return
home after a brief period. For many, however,
ongoing family dysfunction makes returning home
impossible or undesirable. Some are repeat
runaways because they try to return home, only
to encounter the same domestic circumstances
that led them to leave in the first place. Many
runaways and throwaways report that they do not
even know their parents' whereabouts.

        Without family care and support,
runaways and throwaways on the streets are
much more likely than other children to suffer
malnutrition, inadequate hygiene, respiratory
infections, depression, mental illness, suicidal
ideation, drug and alcohol abuse, unwanted
pregnancies, and HIV and other sexually
transmitted diseases resulting from prostitution
and other high-risk sexual conduct and drug
abuse with shared needles. Even if runaways and
throwaways overcome fear or ignorance to seek
medical treatment, they may face imposing legal
barriers. Ordinarily they cannot consent to
treatment because they have not reached
majority. They also lack documentation to qualify

for entitlement programs and cannot use private insurance without parental consent. Most employment remains unavailable to them because of the child labor laws and their lack of skills. Some barriers may be overcome with a judicial order of emancipation, but such an order is unlikely at best because runaways normally lack counsel and cannot qualify as economically and emotionally self-sufficient.

b.   Federal and State Legislation

The Supreme Court has evidently put to rest any sustained argument that runaway and throwaway children have constitutional rights to government-provided care and treatment. See, e.g., DeShaney v. Winnebago County Dep't of Soc. Servs. (S.Ct.1989) (holding that an abused or neglected child has "no affirmative right to governmental aid, even where such aid may be necessary to secure life, liberty, or property interests of which the government itself may not deprive the individual"); Jefferson v. Hackney (S.Ct.1972) (holding that the state's formula for dividing a fixed pool of welfare funds did not violate Fourteenth Amendment); Lindsey v. Normet (S.Ct.1972) (holding that "the need for decent shelter" is not a fundamental interest under the Constitution); Dandridge v. Williams (S.Ct.1970) (holding that the Constitution does not "empower the Supreme Court to second-guess" state officials' allocation of welfare funds).

Despite the absence of a federal constitutional imperative, Congress and several states have forged initiatives to assist runaway, throwaway and unaccompanied homeless children. The major federal initiative designed to assist state and local efforts is the Runaway and Homeless Youth Act (RYHA), 42 U.S.C. § 5700 et seq. Among other things, the RYHA authorizes grants to states, localities and community-based agencies that operate existing or proposed local shelters for runaway and homeless youth outside the law enforcement system, the child welfare system, the mental health system and the juvenile justice system. Some children seek shelter on their own initiative; most, however, are referred to shelters by child welfare and protective services agencies, juvenile law enforcement officers, or school personnel.

5.   GENDER AND RACE

In 1995, the U.S. General Accounting Office analyzed six years of national data (1986-91) and found "only relatively small differences in the percentages of female and male status offenders detained, adjudicated, and placed." Minimal Gender Bias Occurred In Processing Noncriminal Juveniles (1995). Race, however,

predicts differences in treatment. Case rates for
status offenses are similar for white and minority
children, but minority children are more likely to
receive detention or probation.

6. THE DEINSTITUTIONALIZATION
MANDATE

a.   The Nature of the Mandate
     The Juvenile Justice and Delinquency
Prevention Act of 1974, as amended, 42 U.S.C. §
5601 et seq., enables state and local governments
to secure federal formula grant funds for projects
and programs related to juvenile justice and
delinquency. To secure these funds, a state must
satisfy several mandates. The "deinstitutionalization" mandate requires states to prohibit detention of status offenders (and also of such
nonoffenders as dependent, abused or neglected
children) in secure detention facilities or secure
correctional facilities. A secure facility is one the
juvenile may not leave without permission, such
as a jail, police lockup, juvenile detention center,
or training school.

     Under a 1980 amendment to the Act, a
state may authorize its courts to order secure
detention of status offenders who violate valid
court orders. See id. § 5633(a)(12)(A). Where a
status offender violates a court order mandating

treatment, this authorization permits the court to
hold the status offender in criminal contempt and
confine him in secure detention for a limited
period. By alleging an act that would be a crime if
committed by an adult, the contempt charge
alleges delinquency, which is outside the deinstitutionalization mandate. The 1980 amendment
was enacted on findings that the mandate had
compromised the courts' ability to protect some
at-risk juveniles, particularly chronic runaways or
chronic truants, but many states have not
conferred on their courts the authority approved
by the amendment.

By rule, the U.S. Office of Juvenile Justice
and Delinquency Prevention has created an
exception to the deinstitutionalization mandate to
permit secure placement of accused status
offenders for a maximum of twenty-four hours,
excluding weekends and holidays, to permit
identification, investigation, release to parents, or
transfer to a nonsecure facility or to court.   A
second 24-hour period may follow an initial court
contact. In 1992, Congress specified that a status
offender who violates a court order may be held in
secure detention only if before entry of the
violated order, (1) the offender was brought before
a judge and given full due process rights, and (2)
it was determined that all dispositions (including
treatment) other than placement in a secure

detention or correctional facility were exhausted
or clearly inappropriate. Id. § 5603(16).

b.   The Overlap Between Status Offense and Delinquency Jurisdiction

Authorities seeking to impose secure
detention on a juvenile may avoid the deinstitutionalization mandate by charging a minor
criminal offense rather than (or in addition to) a
status offense, even when the facts would
reasonably support only a status offense petition.
The juvenile may then be processed as a
delinquent, free from the mandate.

The overlap between status offense and
delinquency jurisdiction would also permit
authorities to invoke the former jurisdiction
against juveniles suspected of criminal behavior
that might be difficult or impossible to prove in a
delinquency or criminal proceeding. For several
reasons, fairness questions would arise.

For one thing, accused status offenders
are less likely than delinquents to be represented
by counsel. Proof of the status offense need not
meet the beyond-a-reasonable-doubt standard
that In re Winship (S.Ct.1970) mandates in
delinquency proceedings, and the juvenile is not
constitutionally entitled to other procedural
protections mandated for delinquency cases by In

re Gault (S.Ct.1967) and later decisions. Because more than half of adjudicated delinquency petitions result in probation as the most restrictive sanction, a status offense petition may produce the same sanction as a delinquency petition would, even though the sanction might be based on proof insufficient to sustain a delinquency petition.

c.   The Deinstitutionalization Controversy

Without necessarily arguing for a return to widespread secure detention of status offenders, several commentators argue that the deinstitutionalization mandate has had unintended effects inconsistent with its salutary purpose. The U.S. Attorney General's Advisory Board on Missing Children, for example, charged that the mandate deprives police in many states of "all authority to deal with runaway and homeless children," who are "permitted to walk out of police stations or runaway shelters and resume their flight," despite the evident dangers of life on the streets, including prostitution, rape, disease, malnutrition and murder. See America's Missing and Exploited Children: Their Safety and Their Future (OJJDP 1986). Some commentators also charge that the deinstitutionalization man-date has led to unnecessary commitment of many troubled youth to secure mental health and drug treatment facilities.

7. THE FUTURE OF STATUS OFFENSE
JURISDICTION

In 1967, the Katzenbach Commission
recommended that status offense jurisdiction
should be repealed or "substantially circumscribed so that it ... comprehends only acts that
entail a real risk of long-range harm to the child."
President's Commission on Law Enforcement and
Administration of Justice: The Challenge of Crime
in a Free Society 85 (1967). Seven years later, the
National Council of Crime and Delinquency
advocated outright repeal because noncriminal
juvenile conduct "should be referred to social
agencies, not to courts of law." National Council
of Crime and Delinquency, Jurisdiction Over
Status Offenses Should Be Removed from the
Juvenile Court, 21 Crime and Delinq. 97 (Apr.
1975).

In 1990, the National Council of Juvenile
and Family Court Judges assumed a middle-
ground position. The Council advocated a strong
role for schools and community-based social
service agencies in status offense cases involving
ungovernability, truancy and runaways alike.
But the National Council also urged continuation
of status offender jurisdiction for the "few children
... who simply will not or cannot seek help on a

voluntary basis, or who will continue a course of self destructive behavior unless and until forceful intervention occurs." National Council of Juvenile and Family Court Judges, A New Approach to Runaway, Truant, Substance Abusing, and Beyond Control Children, 41 Juv. & Fam. Ct. J. (1990).

A few states have repealed status offense jurisdiction, though dependency or neglect jurisdiction may now reach former status offenses in some of these states. See, e.g., 42 Pa. Cons. Stat. § 6302 (stating that "dependent child" includes a child who is truant, without proper parental care or control, or incorrigible). The move from status offense jurisdiction to dependency or neglect jurisdiction, however, concerns more than mere labeling. Repeal of status offense jurisdiction ends the juvenile court's quasi-criminal control over juvenile conduct that would not expose adults to criminal sanction, and eliminates the possibility that the juvenile court adjudication will be used against the juvenile in a later delinquency or criminal proceeding. Where family dysfunction appears as a root cause, dependency or neglect jurisdiction also focuses on the parents rather than on the child. By making child protective agencies primarily responsible for wayward juveniles not processed as delinquents or tried as adults, dependency jurisdiction

identifies such juveniles as needing treatment and
not as quasi-criminals.

CHAPTER 10

DELINQUENCY

A "delinquent" act is one that would be a crime if committed by an adult. (By contrast, chapter 9 treated status offenses, conduct that would constitute no crime if committed by an adult but is sanctionable when committed by a juvenile.) Delinquency jurisdiction reaches most acts that would be felonies or misdemeanors, though states frequently exclude some relatively minor offenses, such as traffic violations not involving driving while intoxicated.

A. A BRIEF LOOK AT JUVENILE CRIME IN AMERICA

1. OVERVIEW

Juvenile crime has held the national attention in recent years. The lion's share of the attention has focused on violent crime (murder and nonnegligent manslaughter, forcible rape, robbery, and aggravated assault). In 1989, the juvenile violent crime arrest rate reached its highest level since the 1960s, the earliest period for which comparable data are available. The rate continued to climb each year until it reached a peak in 1994. The rate rose 62% between 1988 and 1994, a period when the violent crime arrest rate increased for all age groups, including adults.

Examining increases in violent juvenile crime for much of the prior decade, experts in the early 1990s warned of a "coming blood bath" and a "crime time bomb" because the number of males in the crime-prone 14–to–17–year-old cohort would grow by 23 percent by 2005.

The experts were wrong. Violent crime in America fell each year from 1994 to 2000. According to Federal Bureau of Investigation crime data, the rate of violent juvenile crime in 2000 was lower than at any time in the previous two decades. During these six years, the juvenile crime rate fell even faster than the adult rate. See Jeffrey Butts and Jeremy Travis, The Rise and Fall of American Youth Violence: 1980 to 2000 (Urban Institute 2002).

2. JUVENILE RECIDIVISM

Most youths who come in contact with the juvenile justice system apparently do so only once. In 1999, the U.S. Justice Department reported that 54% of males and 73% of females who come in contact with the juvenile justice

system never return to juvenile court on a new
referral. See Juvenile Justice: A Century of
Change (1999).

Recidivism is not necessarily an accurate
barometer of persistent criminality because
absence of rearrest may simply mean that the
offender has learned how to reoffend without
being caught, and because rearrest may result
from heightened surveillance by police or
probation officers arising from the prior arrest.
Nevertheless, several studies have found that a
relatively small number of chronic offenders
commit a large percentage of juvenile crime. A
1988 Arizona-Utah study, for example, found that
16% of youths referred to juvenile court had four
or more referrals, accounting for 51% of all
juvenile court referrals, including a disproportionate share of serious referrals: 70% of motor
vehicle thefts, 67% of robberies, 67% of
burglaries, 66% of forcible rapes, 64% of murders
and 61% of aggravated assaults.

Youth gang members are responsible for a
disproportionate share of violent and nonviolent
offenses. See Howard N. Snyder and Melissa
Sickmund, Juvenile Offenders and Victims: 1999
National Report (1999) ("1999 National Report").
Youth gangs affect communities of all sizes.
According to a 2001 report, 3700 localities (about

2550 cities, towns and villages and 1150 counties) reported gang problems by the late 1990s. The report found "a striking increase in the growth of gang problems in the Nation's smaller cities, towns, and villages." The Growth of Youth Gang Problems in the United States, 1970-98 (OJJDP 2001). In recent years, females have accounted for a significant number of gang members (between 8% and 38%, depending on the survey). See Joan Moore and John Hagedorn, Female Gangs: A Focus on Research (OJJDP 2001).

3. GENDER AND RACE

Most juvenile offenders are males, but the percentages of females arrested have steadily increased in recent years. In 1997, males were involved in 77% of delinquency cases. The delinquency case rate for males was more than three times greater than the rate for females, but the male rate had been four times greater in 1988. (The case rate is the number of cases disposed per 1,000 juveniles in the population.) See Charles Puzzanchera et al., Juvenile Court Statistics 1997 (May 2000) ("Juvenile Court Statistics 1997"). The delinquency system is struggling to develop programs and staff for dealing with the influx of female delinquents.

Minorities are overrepresented in the juvenile justice system from arrest forward. In 1997, for example, 15% of the nation's juveniles were black, but black youths were involved in 26% of juvenile arrests, including 44% of juvenile violent crime arrests and 27% of property crime arrests. See 1999 National Report.

In 2000, researchers with the National Council on Crime and Delinquency found that "[m]inority youth are more likely than white youth to become involved in the [juvenile justice] system with their overrepresentation increasing at each stage of the process." See Eileen Poe-Yamagata and Michael A. Jones, And Justice For Some: Differential Treatment of Minority Youth in the Justice System (2000). Another group of researchers concludes that minority overrepresentation may be partly related to differences in the rates of offenses by black and white youths, but that these differences alone do not "explain the disparity." The researchers reported that "two-thirds of existing studies found that racial and/or ethnic status influenced decision makers within the juvenile justice system. ... [D]iscriminatory effects occur at every stage of the judicial process, but they were most pronounced at the earlier stages, at the time of arrests and referrals to juvenile court." See Howard N. Snyder and Melissa Sickmund, Juvenile Offenders and

Victims: A National Report (1995) ("1995 National Report").

B. THE JUVENILE COURT AS AN INSTITUTION

1. THE JUVENILE COURT'S ORIGINAL CONCEPTION

Within a few years after Illinois enacted the first juvenile court act in 1899, all other states created juvenile courts. The prevailing view is that juvenile court legislation climaxed an essentially humanitarian nineteenth-century reform movement that sought to help dependent children, and to extricate delinquent children from the harshness of the adult criminal process and adult punishment. At common law, children were subject to incarceration with hardened adult criminals and to severe sentences, sometimes including hanging during the colonial period. Reformers sought to substitute rehabilitation for criminal sanction because science no longer viewed children merely as miniature adults, but rather as persons with developing moral and cognitive faculties. The reformers perceived children both as less responsible than adults for antisocial behavior and as more amenable than adults to rehabilitation. Judge Julian W. Mack, a prominent leader of the juvenile court movement, said the court would "treat these juvenile offenders, as we deal with the neglected children, as a wise and merciful father handles his own child whose errors are not discovered by the authorities." Julian W. Mack, The Juvenile Court, 23 Harv. L. Rev. 104 (1909).

The prevailing view of the nineteenth-century reform impulse dissatisfies some revisionist historians. These writers have asserted that while many reformers undeniably perceived the juvenile court as a moral imperative, the reformers also perceived the court as a heavy-handed vehicle for imposing traditional agrarian values on an increasingly urban nation, and particularly on poor immigrant children. Early juvenile court acts defined delinquency broadly to include both conduct that would be crimes if committed by adults and other antisocial behavior that today would be status offenses. "It was not by accident," writes revisionist Anthony M. Platt, "that the behavior selected for penalizing by the child savers – drinking, begging, roaming the streets, frequenting dance-halls and movies, fighting, sexuality, staying out late at night, and incorrigibility – was primarily attributable to the children of lower-class migrant and immigrant families." The Child Savers: The Invention of Delinquency (2d ed. 1977).

Regardless of the motives that energized the juvenile court movement throughout the nineteenth century, the court's delinquency jurisdiction was marked by five characteristics that distinguished it from the criminal justice system -- individualized rehabilitation and treatment, civil jurisdiction, informal procedure, confidentiality, and incapacitation of children separate from adults. These characteristics help shape juvenile court practice today.

a. Individualized Rehabilitation and Treatment

Without necessarily overlooking rehabilitation and treatment of prisoners who will someday return to the general population, the criminal law imposes sanctions defined primarily by the nature of the act committed. Each crime carries a sanction or sanction range (usually imprisonment, fine or both) prescribed by statute or sentencing guidelines. The court may have discretion to impose a sanction calibrated after considering the defendant's condition, but the sanction must remain within the range defined by the nature of the defendant's act.

By contrast, delinquency sanctions were based not on the nature of the act committed, but on the juvenile's condition. Acting in effect as a quasi-welfare agency, the juvenile court held broad discretion to fashion a disposition after examining not only such factors as the juvenile's attitude, school performance, standing in the community, and mental health but also the family's stability and supportiveness.

The aim of individualized justice was to treat and rehabilitate the juvenile, much as a benevolent social services provider would. The result – a sanction grounded in the delinquent's condition – could be more or less severe than the sanction a court would impose on an adult convicted of the same act. For example, in In re Gault (S.Ct.1967), which is discussed in section D.6.b below, the juvenile court found that the fifteen-year-old delinquent had made lewd telephone calls to a neighbor. The court assigned the boy to the state industrial school for as long as six years (until he reached majority, unless released earlier); an adult committing the same offense could have received no more than two months' imprisonment or a fine of five to fifty dollars. If young Gault had committed first-degree murder, the juvenile court could have institutionalized him for no more than the same six-year maximum, though the criminal court could have sentenced an adult to life imprisonment or worse.

b. Civil Jurisdiction

Juvenile courts exercised only civil jurisdiction. This jurisdiction raised no eyebrows in abuse and neglect cases because the child, whose condition was the focus of these proceedings, was a victim rather than a wrongdoer and deserved no punishment. Civil proceedings also did not preclude criminal court prosecution of adults responsible for the condition.

Civil delinquency jurisdiction was a greater conceptual challenge because it displaced criminal jurisdiction and could deprive children of liberty. Civil jurisdiction appeared entirely defensible, however, because the parens patriae doctrine likened juvenile courts to the English chancery court, which had protected children in civil matters by tempering law with mercy for centuries.

c. Informal Procedure

Because delinquency jurisdiction sought to rehabilitate rather than punish, informal procedure became the juvenile court's hallmark. Due process was seen to impede rehabilitation because the court acted "not as an enemy but as a protector, as the ultimate guardian" of the child. "The child who must be brought into court should, of course, be made to know that he is face to face with the power of the state, but he should at the same time, and more emphatically, be made to feel that he is the object of its care and solicitude. The ordinary trappings of the court-room are out of place in such hearings. The judge on a bench, looking down upon the boy standing at the bar, can never evoke a proper sympathetic spirit. Seated at a desk, with the child at his side, where he can on occasion put his arm around his shoulder and draw the lad to him, the judge, while losing none of his judicial dignity, will gain immensely in the effectiveness of his work." Mack, supra, 23 Harv. L. Rev.

Informal procedure quickly produced a distinct vocabulary laden with euphemisms. The juvenile offender was an alleged "delinquent" who had committed an "act of delinquency," not an accused criminal who had committed a crime. The juvenile was "taken into custody," not arrested. The juvenile court proceedings began with a "petition of delinquency," not a complaint, indictment or charge, and with a "summons," not a warrant. The juvenile proceeded to an "initial hearing," not to arraignment. The juvenile might be "held in detention," but was not jailed. If matters proceeded further, the court would conduct a "hearing," not a trial. An "adjudication," a "finding of involvement" or a "finding of delinquency" might follow, not a conviction. The court would enter a "disposition," not an order of conviction or acquittal. The juvenile might be "placed" in a "training school," "reformatory," or "group home," not convicted and sent to a prison. "Aftercare," not parole, might follow.

The juvenile court's procedural informality created little need for lawyers, and assured a role for non-lawyer judges. "Lawyers were unnecessary -- adversary tactics were out of place, for the mutual aim of all was not to contest or object but to determine the treatment plan best for the child. That plan was to be devised by the increasingly popular psychologists and psychiatrists; delinquency was thought of almost as a disease, to be diagnosed by specialists and the patient kindly but firmly dosed." President's Commission on Law Enforcement and Administration of Justice, Task Force Report: Juvenile Delinquency and Youth Crime 3 (1967). In 1967, a quarter of all juvenile court judges had no law school training.

d. Confidentiality
To enhance prospects for rehabilitation and treatment, juvenile court proceedings were normally closed to the public. Juvenile court records and dispositions were sealed or expunged to protect the juvenile's privacy, and delinquency adjudications did not leave the juvenile with a criminal record.

e. Separate Incapacitation

Juvenile court reformers sought to segregate confined delinquents from hardened adult criminals. The institutions to which juvenile courts sent delinquents before or after adjudication were frequently as inhospitable as prisons that housed adults, but reformers believed that the ultimate success of treatment and rehabilitation depended on protecting children from adult criminal influences and from assaults by adult inmates.

2. THE JUVENILE COURT TODAY

The five characteristics that marked the juvenile court's traditional rehabilitative model have been strained in the past few decades as the public has grown increasingly impatient with juvenile crime, particularly violent crime. Public pressure has led state legislatures to embrace a more punitive model that resembles the adult criminal process in significant respects. The federal Office of Juvenile Justice and Delinquency Prevention has also moved away from rehabilitation, placing greater emphasis on he need to hold juvenile offenders accountable and ensure community safety.

Scarce resources have also challenged the rehabilitative ideal. In 1967, the Katzenbach

Commission found that juvenile court hearings often lasted only 10 to 15 minutes. In many jurisdictions, the situation is not much different today. In 1998, for example, the President of the American Bar Association reported that "[i]n many cities an overworked juvenile court judge's average disposal rate for a case is less than 10 minutes. Sometimes the juvenile and family members have not even met their lawyer before they appear in court." Jerome J. Shestack, What About Juvenile Justice?, 84 A.B.A.J. 8 (May 1998).

3. FEDERAL DELINQUENCY JURISDICTION

This chapter primarily concerns state delinquency proceedings, which adjudicate the vast majority of delinquency cases nationwide. In 1997, state courts with juvenile jurisdiction handled about 1,755,100 delinquency cases. See Bureau of Justice Statistics, Sourcebook of Criminal Justice Statistics 1999 (Nov.2000) ("1999 Sourcebook").

Federal courts, however, also hear delinquency cases. In 2000, 230 delinquency proceedings were commenced in the federal district courts. See http://www.uscourts.gov/judbus2000.appendices/d02set00.pdf. These proceedings charged acts committed by children under eighteen that would be federal crimes if committed by an adult because they were committed on military bases, or other federal lands or Indian reservations, or because they violated federal drug laws or other federal criminal statutes.

Federal delinquency cases are subject to the Juvenile Delinquency Act, 18 U.S.C. § 5031 et seq., which sharply limits federal delinquency jurisdiction. Section 5032 creates blanket federal authority to prosecute misdemeanors committed by juveniles within the "special maritime and territorial jurisdiction of the United States," such as national parks. Other federal offenses by juveniles, however, are not processed in the district court unless the Attorney General certifies to the court (1) that the juvenile court or other appropriate state court does not have jurisdiction or refuses to assume jurisdiction, (2) that the state does not have available programs and services adequate for juveniles' needs, or (3) that the offense charged is a crime of violence that is a felony or an offense under specified federal drug or firearms possession laws, and that "there is a substantial Federal interest in the case or the offense to warrant the exercise of Federal jurisdiction." Where the Attorney General does not make this certification, federal authorities must surrender the juvenile to state authorities.

Aspects of the federal Juvenile Delinquency Act are treated in relevant sections throughout the remainder of this chapter.

C. THE CONTOURS OF DELINQUENCY

1. THE MINIMUM AND MAXIMUM AGES OF DELINQUENCY JURISDICTION

About fifteen states have a statutory minimum age of original delinquency jurisdiction, usually ten. All states have statutes defining the maximum age of that jurisdiction. In most states the juvenile court has delinquency jurisdiction over persons who were under eighteen at the time of the offense, arrest, or referral to court. The maximum age is sixteen in ten states and fifteen in three states (Connecticut, New York and North Carolina).

Many states have statutory exceptions to the maximum age, which accelerate the criminal court's original jurisdiction. The exceptions relate to the minor's age, alleged offense, and court history. In some states, a combination of the youth's age, offense and court history place the minor under the original jurisdiction of both the juvenile court and the criminal court; the prosecutor has authority to determine which court initially handles the case.

2. THE INFANCY DEFENSE

The common law conclusively presumed that children under seven were without criminal capacity, created a rebuttable presumption of criminal incapacity for children between seven and fourteen, and held children over fourteen to adult capacity. The prosecutor could rebut the presumption by demonstrating that the child knew what he was doing when he committed the act, and knew the act was wrong.

Where a juvenile is transferred to criminal court for trial and sentencing as an adult, the infancy defense applies in its common law form or as codified in the criminal code. States disagree, however, about whether an infancy defense is available in delinquency proceedings. Some states withhold the defense on the grounds that delinquency proceedings are civil in nature and that their dispositions are rehabilitative rather than punitive. Other states recognize the infancy defense in delinquency proceedings on the grounds that confinement or other sanction is inherently punitive, and that a juvenile should not suffer a delinquency sanction without proof a crime was committed.

In states that recognize the infancy defense in delinquency proceedings, courts weigh various factors to determine whether the juvenile knew the wrongfulness of the acts, including "(1) the nature of the crime; (2) the child's age and maturity; (3) whether the child showed a desire for secrecy; (4) whether the child admonished the victim not to tell; (5) prior conduct similar to that charged; (6) any consequences that attached to the conduct; and (7) acknowledgment that the behavior was wrong and could lead to detention." State v. J.P.S. (Wash. 1997).

As a practical matter, some defense counsel report that they rarely challenge the juvenile's competency because an incompetency finding may make things worse, rather than better, for the client. If the court finds the juvenile incompetent, it may commit him to state custody and deprive him of significant control over his life, perhaps through foster placement, psychiatric commitment or court monitoring. Delinquency sanctions normally do not include removal from the home.

3. THE INSANITY DEFENSE

Under the so-called M'Naghten test, an accused is insane, and thus not criminally responsible, if, when he committed the charged act or omission, (1) he was suffering from such a mental disability that he did not know the act or omission was wrong and could not distinguish right from wrong, or (2) he was suffering from such a disability of reason or disease of the mind that he did not understand the nature or consequences of the act or omission. See, e.g, Castro v. Ward (10th Cir.1998).

Some state juvenile codes or rules permit invocation of the insanity defense. Where the code and rules are silent, however, courts disagree about whether the defense is available in juvenile court as an essential element of due process. See, e.g., Commonwealth v. Chatman (Va.2000) (defense not available); Matter of Two Minor Children (Nev.1979) (defense available).

4. TRANSFER

a. Transfer Statutes

Ever since the 1899 Illinois juvenile court act, juvenile courts have held authority to transfer to criminal court older juveniles charged with serious crimes. Today every state has "transfer" or "waiver" statutes, which authorize trial and sentencing of some juveniles as adults in criminal court.

Amid fears of violent juvenile crime in recent decades, public pressure has produced legislation authorizing transfer of an increasing number of juveniles. This expansion of transfer graphically demonstrates not only erosion of public confidence in the juvenile court's traditional rehabilitative model, but also belief that some juveniles deserve the sort of criminal punishment that may be imposed on adults. Expansion also reflects public belief that criminal courts will be harsher than juvenile courts on children who commit crime, though research casts some doubt on the accuracy of this belief, particularly in cases involving property offenses and other less serious crimes.

For the juvenile, high stakes are involved in the decision whether to proceed by criminal court prosecution rather than delinquency adjudication. The juvenile justice system may impose confinement or other sanction for a few years, usually until majority or shortly thereafter. Transfer exposes the juvenile to the full range of criminal court sanctions, which may be lengthier and more severe.

Amid growing public pressure in the past few years, most states have lowered minimum transfer ages, expanded the range of crimes for which transfer is available, or reduced the factors the juvenile court must consider before ordering transfer. In most states the minimum age is now fourteen or younger. In some states children of any age may be transferred, at least when they are accused of one or more of the most serious crimes; as a practical matter, the minimum age is then set by the infancy defense, which at common law would permit prosecution of children as young as seven.

Some transfer statutes reach beyond violent crime. Several states permit transfer of juveniles for any felony, violent or otherwise. Some states require or permit adult prosecution of juveniles for misdemeanors, ordinance violations, and summary statute violations such as fish and game violations. Courts, however, evidently do not transfer alleged nonviolent offenders in large numbers.

Traditionally the transfer decision rested with the juvenile court, acting in its discretion on the prosecutor's motion. For some serious felonies, however, most states now also authorize the prosecutor to make the transfer decision without resort to the court. Other states have enacted mandatory transfer statutes, which divest the court of discretion and require transfer where the juvenile is charged with one or more of the serious felonies enumerated in the statute, such as murder, rape or armed robbery. Proceedings begin in juvenile court, whose only role is to conduct a preliminary hearing to determine whether the mandatory-waiver requirements are satisfied. If the answer is affirmative, transfer to criminal court follows as a matter of law.

Mandatory transfer must be distinguished from "statutory exclusion" provisions, which prevail in more than half the states for particularly serious crimes by older juveniles. Where the legislature has excluded a particular crime from juvenile court jurisdiction, juvenile court jurisdiction never attaches and the juvenile is processed directly in criminal court.

More than half the states permit the juvenile court to grant the prosecutor's transfer motion only if it finds probable cause to believe that the juvenile committed the offense charged. The court generally must also consider (and in some states, must make findings concerning) factors enumerated in the transfer statute. These factors typically relate to the nature and seriousness of the offense; the juvenile's maturity, sophistication, prior record and amenability to treatment and rehabilitation; and the public's need for protection. A few states add other factors. Arizona courts, for example, must also consider the victim's views and whether the juvenile was involved in a gang. See Ariz. Rev. Stat. § 8-327. Missouri courts must also consider "racial disparity in certification" of juveniles for criminal trial. See Mo. Rev. Stat. § 211.071.

The court generally may order discretionary transfer only where its propriety is established by the ordinary civil "preponderance of the evidence" standard, though a handful of states impose the higher "clear and convincing evidence" standard in some or all cases. Most states impose the burden of proof on the prosecutor, though a few states require some older juveniles to demonstrate that transfer should be denied.

Transfer statutes ordinarily grant the juvenile court broad discretion. Frequently the transfer decision emphasizes public safety rather than rehabilitation, giving considerable weight to the seriousness of the offense and the juvenile's prior record. A serious violent offense, without more, for example, may support transfer. See, e.g., Carroll v. State (Ark. 1996). Transfer may be appropriate even when one or more of the statutory factors point in the juvenile's favor. See, e.g., State v. Stephens (Kan. 1999). As a practical matter, the court weighing the various statutory factors usually may order transfer in any case that alleges a serious act of violence, concerns a prominent victim, or receives widespread press coverage.

Where a transferred juvenile is tried in criminal court, most states require that any future proceedings alleging an offense by the juvenile also be heard in criminal court. This "once an adult, always an adult" requirement generally applies only where the earlier transfer resulted in a conviction.

b. The Transfer Hearing

In Kent v. United States (S.Ct.1966), the Court held that a juvenile may not be transferred to criminal court pursuant to a discretionary transfer statute "without hearing, without effecttive assistance of counsel, without a statement of reasons." The transfer hearing "must measure up to the essentials of due process and fair treatment," but the court is not bound by the rules of evidence or procedure. States may take a stricter approach, but most states do not bind courts to the rules of evidence or procedure in transfer hearings. Courts generally may admit hearsay such as reports by psychologists, psychiatrists, child welfare personnel or law enforcement officers. Courts disagree about whether the right to confrontation is an "essential of due process" that must be accorded the juvenile in transfer hearings. See, e.g., In re

P.W.N. (N.D.1981) (yes); State v. Wright (Iowa 1990) (no).

The state need not prove the juvenile's guilt in the transfer hearing. The court need determine only that the statutory factors make discretionary transfer appropriate. The juvenile's counsel must have access to the social records and probation or similar reports that are before the court. Some states require the court to consider a pre-hearing investigative report on the juvenile, prepared by the juvenile probation office or other agency. States differ on the question whether a transfer order is final, and if not, whether an interlocutory appeal may be taken.

c. Some Ramifications of Transfer
Loss of juvenile protections. A juvenile transferred to criminal court receives only the rights afforded adult defendants in that court. The juvenile court act's protections and rules of procedure no longer apply. The transferred juvenile loses such rights as the right to a finding of delinquency rather than criminality, the right to confidentiality rather than a public proceeding and disposition, and the right to a juvenile disposition rather than adult sentencing. In some states, juveniles convicted of felonies in criminal court are among the persons barred for life from voting.

Lesser included offenses. Where transfer to criminal court is mandatory for a serious crime, the court may also try the youth for any lesser non-mandatory crimes arising from the same act. See, e.g., State v. Behl (Minn.1997). States disagree, however, about whether the criminal court may sentence a juvenile acquitted of the mandated crime, but convicted of a lesser crime that alone would not have mandated transfer. Oregon, for example, specifies that the case must be returned to the juvenile court for disposition. Or. Rev. Stat. § 419C.361. Other states authorize the criminal court to impose an adult sentence on the juvenile for the lesser crime, without further juvenile court proceedings.

Confining juveniles in adult prisons. Pursuant to a mandate in the federal Juvenile Justice and Delinquency Prevention Act of 1974, states may not incarcerate delinquents in adult prisons before or after disposition. The mandate stems from studies demonstrating that children in adult prisons face increased risk of assault, rape, abuse by staff and suicide. The 1974 Act imposes no such mandate, however, when a juvenile is tried and sentenced as an adult. Some states indeed incarcerate juveniles in adult prisons pending criminal court trial and after conviction. In other states, juveniles sentenced as adults are

505 DELINQUENCY Ch. 10

placed in separate facilities for younger adult convicts. In some states, juveniles begin their sentences in juvenile facilities and are moved to adult facilities for the remainder of their sentence when they reach a particular age.

A jury of one's peers? In the federal system and in forty-six states, eighteen is the minimum age for jury service in civil and criminal cases. The minimum age is higher in only Alabama (nineteen), Mississippi (twenty-one), Missouri (twenty-one) and Nebraska (nineteen).

Courts have rejected claims that the Sixth Amendment or due process guarantees juveniles the right to trial by a jury that includes juveniles. See, e.g., United States v. McVean (5th Cir. 1971); Matter of Welfare of J.K.B. (Minn.Ct.App.1996). Rejection is normally grounded in the Supreme Court's pronouncement that "the Constitution does not forbid the States to prescribe relevant qualifications for their jurors. The States remain free to confine the selection to ... persons meeting specified qualifications of age." Carter v. Jury Comm'n (S.Ct.1970).

d. Race and Transfer

In 1999, 0.7% of petitioned delinquency cases involving white youths were waived to criminal court, as compared to 1.1% of cases

involving black youths. See Bureau of Justice
Statistics, Sourcebook of Criminal Justice
Statistics 2001 ("2001 Sourcebook"). From 1990
to 1994, 63% of juveniles transferred to criminal
courts were black males, 29% were white males,
3% were black females and 2% were white
females. See Bureau of Justice Statistics, Juvenile
Felony Defendants in Criminal Courts (1998).

Several studies have found that disproportionate numbers of minority youth are transferred to criminal court. A 1995 report, for
example, found that 73% of Maryland cases in
which the juvenile court waived jurisdiction
involved black youth while 27% of the state's
population is black. See Human Rights Watch,
No Minor Matter: Children in Maryland's Jails
(1999).

The National Coalition for Juvenile Justice
argues that despite enumerated statutory factors
the court must consider on discretionary transfer
motions, discrimination may infect the transfer
process. When deciding whether a youth is
"amenable to treatment in the juvenile system,"
for example, the court may rely on subjective
factors, may be influenced if the prosecutor
charges a more serious rather than a less serious
crime, or may order transfer more readily if the
juvenile lives in a depressed area far from

treatment facilities. See Coalition for Juvenile Justice, No Easy Answers: Juvenile Justice in a Climate of Fear (1994).

e. Transfer to Juvenile Drug Courts

In 1994, Congress authorized the Attorney General to make grants to state and local jurisdictions to create "drug courts." 42 U.S.C. §§ 3796ii-3796ii-8. These courts hear cases against non-violent adults and juveniles, who are often first-time offenders and are usually charged with possessing drugs or with committing minor drug-related crimes. Grantee courts may not adjudicate cases involving violent offenders. 28 C.F.R. § 93.4.

Drug courts focus on treatment rather than incarceration. Some courts use a deferred prosecution approach, under which an offender agrees before trial to enter a court-monitored treatment and counseling program. The charges are dismissed if the offender completes the program, but failure to complete the program returns the offender to court for criminal processing. Most courts, however, use a post-adjudication approach because they have greater supervisory authority after adjudication than at the diversion stage. The offender may enter the treatment program only after conviction and sentencing, but sentence is suspended during treatment and reinstated only if the offender fails to complete the treatment program. In either event, judges, prosecutors, attorneys, treatment providers, law enforcement officials and others use the court's coercive power to compel abstinence and change behavior through intensive judicial supervision, escalating sanctions, mandatory drug testing, treatment, and aftercare programs.

f. Transfer Under the Federal Juvenile Delinquency Act

Unlike state systems, the federal system does not have a separate juvenile or family court; federal delinquency hearings are heard in district court by a district judge or magistrate judge. Where the case remains in federal court, § 5032 of the Juvenile Delinquency Act provides that the government may use a delinquency proceeding or may seek to "transfer" the juvenile to adult status. For most offenses, a delinquency proceeding ensues unless the juvenile requests, in writing on advice of counsel, to be processed as an adult. The Attorney General may move to prosecute as an adult, however, where a juvenile fifteen or older is charged with committing specified acts of violence, specified offenses involving sale or importation of drugs or firearms, or handgun possession; the minimum transfer age is thirteen for a few specified serious offenses such as murder, robbery or bank robbery or if the juvenile possessed a firearm while committing a violent crime.

When seeking to transfer a juvenile to adult status in federal court, the government must rebut the statutory presumption of juvenile treatment. The court after a hearing may grant the motion to prosecute as an adult if it finds, by a preponderance of the evidence, that "transfer would be in the interest of justice" according to factors enumerated in § 5032. The court must make written findings concerning each factor, which (like the factors recited in most state transfer statutes) relate generally to the nature of the alleged offense and the juvenile's circumstances, condition and prior record.

Transfer to adult status is automatic for some repeat offenders sixteen or older charged with specified crimes of violence, or drug or firearms possession crimes. An order transferring a juvenile to adult status is immediately appealable under the collateral order exception to the final judgment rule, but § 5032 ordinarily gives the district court broad discretion to strike a balance between rehabilitation and public protection, which the court of appeals reviews only for abuse of discretion.

D. THE ADJUDICATORY PROCESS

1. ARREST AND CUSTODY

a. "Arraignment"

The delinquency process begins when a juvenile is referred to the juvenile court. In 1997, 85% of delinquency cases were referred by law enforcement authorities, frequently after discretionary screening and informal adjustment by the police on the street and in the stationhouse. The remainder were referred by such sources as social service agencies, schools, parents, probation officers or victims. See Juvenile Court Statistics 1997.

A juvenile taken into custody must be brought before the juvenile court within a short time, normally about twenty-four hours. The court informs the juvenile of the charges, explains applicable constitutional rights, appoints counsel where necessary, and determines the conditions for release or orders preventive detention pending the adjudicatory hearing. If the juvenile denies the allegations, the court also sets a hearing date.

b. Fingerprints, Photographs and Lineups

Consistent with the juvenile court's rehabilitative focus, many states traditionally prohibited police or juvenile authorities from taking fingerprints or photographs ("mug shots") of juvenile suspects, at least unless necessary to the investigation or otherwise approved by the court. States also typically required law enforcement to turn over this evidence to the juvenile court, which would treat it in accordance with general confidentiality statutes and statutes providing for sealing or expunging the record.

The recent juvenile justice trend toward punishment and accountability has changed the landscape considerably. For juveniles charged with only less serious offenses or for particularly young juveniles, some states still prohibit fingerprinting or photographing without court approval. Most states, however, permit authorities to fingerprint or photograph juvenile suspects without application to the court, at least where the child has reached a specific age or is charged with a serious felony. See, e.g., Conn. Gen. Stat. § 46b-133(a) (any crime). Indeed many states now require fingerprinting and photographing of juvenile suspects in some or all circumstances. See, e.g., Fla. Stat. § 985.212 (juveniles charged with felonies and other enumerated serious offenses); N.C. Gen. Stat. § 7B-2102(a) (juveniles ten or older).

Several states still provide for destruction of fingerprints or photographs where no charge is

filed or where the juvenile court determines the
juvenile did not commit the offense charged.
Otherwise fingerprints and photographs normally
become part of the juvenile court record, and thus
remain subject to sealing or expungement
statutes.

Where a juvenile is transferred to criminal
court for trial and sentencing, the juvenile may be
fingerprinted and photographed in accordance
with the criminal statutes and rules. See, e.g.,
Kan. Stat. § 38-1611(a)(3)(A).

Only a few state juvenile codes have
provisions relating to lineups. The provisions
normally require a court order before authorities
may place an alleged delinquent in a lineup.

**c. Arrest Under the Federal Juvenile
    Delinquency Act**
Where an alleged delinquent is taken into
federal custody, the arresting officer must
immediately advise the juvenile of his legal rights
"in language comprehensive [sic?] to a juvenile,"
and must immediately notify the juvenile's
parents, guardian or custodian of the custody, the
alleged offense and these rights. The juvenile
must be taken before a magistrate "forthwith." 18
U.S.C. § 5033. Where the government makes a
good faith, though unsuccessful, effort to locate

and notify the adult, the government satisfies the latter requirement and may introduce the juvenile's otherwise admissible statements.

2. SEARCH AND SEIZURE

a. New Jersey v. T.L.O. (1985)

In New Jersey v. T.L.O. (S.Ct.1985), the Supreme Court held that the assistant vice principal's search of the student's purse in his office did not violate the Fourth Amendment. The Court held that the Amendment's prohibition on unreasonable searches and seizures applies to searches conducted by public school officials, but that school officials need not obtain a warrant before searching a student who is under their authority.

T.L.O. held that the legality of a school official's search of a student depends not on probable cause, but "simply on the reasonableness, under all the circumstances, of the search."   Reasonableness, in turn, depends on a two-part inquiry: Was the search "justified at its inception," and was the search as actually conducted "reasonably related in scope to the circumstances which justified the interference in the first place"?   Ordinarily a search of a student by a teacher or other school official is justified at its inception when "there are reasonable grounds for suspecting that the search will turn up evidence that the student has violated or is violating either the law or the rules of the school." The search is permissible in scope when "the measures adopted are reasonably related to the objectives of the search and not excessively intrusive in light of the age and sex of the student and the nature of the infraction."

T.L.O. determined only the student's Fourth Amendment rights. A search that passes muster under the federal Constitution might nonetheless violate state constitutional guarantees.

b. Age and Sex
T.L.O. said that the constitutionality of a school official's search depends in part on "the age and sex of the student." The Court, however, did not offer guidance helpful to lower courts that must apply these factors.

Does the burden on a school official seeking to justify the reasonableness of a search of the person increase or decrease the older the student? An argument can be made that a search of the person would be more traumatic to elementary school students than high school students; an argument can also be made that high school students are more sensitive about

their personal privacy than elementary school
students.

   Where a search does not involve examination of the person, *T.L.O* did not discuss
whether searches of boys' property should be
judged by different standards than searches of
girls' property, or whether the standards should
vary according to the child's age.

c. Acting In Concert With Police
   T.L.O. left unresolved a number of
questions, which the remainder of this section 2
explores. First, the Court did not decide whether
the reasonable suspicion standard applies to
searches conducted by school officials "in
conjunction with or at the behest of law
enforcement agencies."

   Whether a principal or other school official
conducted the search as a police agent depends
on the circumstances.   See, e.g., People in re
P.E.A. (Colo.1988). Lower courts generally apply
T.L.O.'s reasonableness standard to searches and
seizures done by school officials, even when the
officials later turn over the fruits of the search to
law enforcement authorities. Courts are alert to
the prospect that law enforcement officers might
try to avoid Fourth Amendment strictures by
having a school official conduct a search or make

a seizure that would be unlawful if done by the police themselves. School officials, however, have a duty to take reasonable measures, including searches and seizures, to detect and prevent crime that might compromise student safety.

On the other hand, courts have required probable cause where police conduct the search at the school, e.g., In re Thomas B.D. (S.C.Ct.App. 1997), or sometimes where school officials call police before conducting the search, Picha v. Wielgos (N.D.Ill.1976).

d. Individualized Suspicion
Because *T.L.O.* concerned the search of a particular student suspected of criminal activity, the Court reserved the question whether reasonableness can ever be established without individualized suspicion of wrongdoing by the student searched. The Court answered the question in Acton v. Vernonia School District (S.Ct.1995) and Board of Education v. Earls (2002), which are discussed in chapter 1. *Vernonia* held that the defendant school district's random suspicionless urinalysis drug testing program for interscholastic athletes comported with the Fourth Amendment. *Earls* extended the ruling to students engaged in any school-sponsored extracurricular activity.

e. The Exclusionary Rule in School Searches

T.L.O. declined to decide whether the Fourth Amendment exclusionary rule applies in delinquency proceedings, which are civil proceedings that since *Gault* have carried some criminal due process protections. The Court has not addressed the issue since, but lower court delinquency decisions have consistently applied the rule. See, e.g., In re A.C.C. (Utah Ct.App. 2000).

Application of the exclusionary rule to school disciplinary proceedings would appear foreclosed by Pennsylvania Bd. of Probation and Parole v. Scott (S.Ct.1998), which refused to apply the rule to proceedings other than criminal trials.

f. Locker Searches

T.L.O. did not decide whether public school students have a legitimate expectation of privacy with respect to their lockers, which may hold intimate personal effects but which may also be convenient hiding places for weapons, drugs and other contraband. Most lower courts have held that as a general matter, students have a reasonable expectation of privacy in their lockers and their contents. See, e.g., Commonwealth v. Snyder (Mass.1992). Some courts, however, have specified that the expectation is only minimal, at least where written school policy states that the student's possession of the locker is not exclusive as against the school, or that lockers may be searched without warning on reasonable suspicion that the contents threaten student health, welfare and safety. See, e.g., Commonwealth v. Cass (Pa.1998). Some courts have held that students have no reasonable expectation of privacy at all where a statute or the school district's written policy states that lockers are not private property. See, e.g., In re Patrick Y. (Md.2000).

Even where a reasonable privacy expectation is found, courts ordinarily uphold the reasonableness of locker searches, including blanket searches of school locker searches in the absence of individualized suspicion, by weighing the students' privacy interest with school officials' duty to maintain safety and discipline.

g.   Metal Detectors

T.L.O. did not concern metal detectors (magnetometers), which had become common fixtures in airports, courthouses, and some other public buildings even before the September 11, 2001 terrorist attacks. These devices have also appeared in many schools concerned about students who bring drugs or concealed guns, knives and other weapons to the campus. Hand-held or walk-through metal detectors may screen all persons who enter the school, or these devices may be directed only at particular persons at entrances or other places in the building.

Use of the metal detector constitutes a Fourth Amendment search. See, e.g., McMorris v. Alioto (9th Cir. 1978). Courts have consistently upheld the constitutionality of general metal detector screening in public schools, however, because "[t]he prevalence and general acceptance of metal scanners in today's society underscores the minimal nature of the intrusion." In re F.B. (Pa. 1999). Where school officials use a hand-held detector, the search's validity is not upset because a walk-through detector assertedly would be less intrusive.

Even in the absence of individualized suspicion, courts have also upheld the constitutionality of metal detector scans against particular students, which may lead to a pat-down or other further search if the detector is activated. Whether the metal detector screen is general or particular, courts have rejected contentions that school screening is unreasonable under the Fourth Amendment because students, unlike citizens entering most other public buildings, cannot withhold consent to search because compulsory education statutes leave them no choice but to attend school.

h. Sniff Searches

School officials sometimes use trained drug-sniffing dogs to examine students' persons or their lockers, bookbags or other property. In the absence of Supreme Court resolution, lower courts have disagreed on the threshold question whether a dog-sniff of a student's person is a search. See, e.g., B.C. v. Plumas Unified School District (9th Cir.1999) (yes, because "close proximity sniffing of the person is offensive whether the sniffer be canine or human"); Doe v. Renfrow (7th Cir.1980) (no, because of the diminished expectation of privacy in public schools, the school's in loco parentis duty to supervise students, and the minimal intrusion involved). The Supreme Court has not resolved the question, but *Vernonia* and *Earls* would seem to establish that a dog-sniff of a student's person is a search.

Once a dog-sniff of a student's person is held to be a search, the court proceeds to determine whether (under *T.L.O.*) the search is reasonable under all the circumstances. In *B.C.*, for example, school authorities seeking evidence of drug use conducted a random suspicionless sniff search of the persons and property of an entire class. The Ninth Circuit found the search "highly intrusive" and held it unreasonable because the record showed no drug crisis or even drug problem at the school.

The Supreme Court has held that dog sniffs of personal property in a public place are not Fourth Amendment searches, thus seemingly disposing of the constitutional question when dogs sniff only student lockers, backpacks or other property. See United States v. Place (S.Ct. 1983).

i. Strip Searches

A strip search requires a person to remove all or most clothes to reveal areas of the body, including areas normally covered by under-clothes. Strip searches, sometimes called nude searches, have been termed "the greatest personal indignity" the state can impose on a person. Bell v. Wolfish (S.Ct.1979) (Stevens, J., dissenting).

T.L.O. did not address public school strip searches, but left the door open to their use by stating that a search's "intrusiveness" is only one factor to weigh in determining reasonableness. Reasonableness, however, may be an imposing barrier to strip searches because "as the intrusiveness of the search of a student intensifies, so too does the standard of Fourth Amendment reasonableness. What may constitute reasonable suspicion for a search of a locker or even a pocket or pocketbook may fall well short of reasonableness for a nude search." Cornfield v. Consolidated High School District (7th Cir.1993).

At a minimum, strip searches must be done by school officials of the same sex as the student. The sex issue aside, most decisions have found strip searches of students unreasonable under the Fourth Amendment. In Konop v. Northwestern School District (D.S.D.1998), for example, the court held that strip searches of two eighth grade students were unreasonable because school officials did not have reasonable basis for believing that either student had stolen the $200 the officials sought. *Konop's* survey of strip search precedent yielded three "clear" rules: "(1) a strip search is not justified absent individualized suspicion unless there is a legitimate safety concern (e.g. weapons); (2) school officials must be investigating allegations of violations of the law or school rules and only individual accusations justify a strip search; and (3) strip searches must be designed to be minimally intrusive, taking into account the item for which the search is conducted."

Press reports suggest that public school strip searches still occur periodically, and that many ensuing damage actions result in out-of-court settlements, sometimes with sizeable payments to the searched students. Most state education acts are silent about strip searches by school authorities, but some prohibit them.

3. INTERROGATION AND CONFESSION

a. **Miranda v. Arizona (1966) and Fare v. Michael C. (1979)**

In Miranda v. Arizona (S.Ct.1966), an adult criminal proceeding, the Court held that "the prosecution may not use statements, whether exculpatory or inculpatory, stemming from custodial interrogation of the defendant unless it demonstrates the use of procedural safeguards effective to secure the [Fifth Amendment] privilege against self-incrimination." The Court required these now-familiar safeguards:

> Prior to any questioning, the person must be warned that he has a right to remain silent, that any statement he does make may be used as evidence against him, and that he has a right to the presence of an attorney, either retained or appointed. The defendant may waive effectuation of these rights, provided the waiver is made voluntarily, knowingly and intelligently. If, however, he indicates in any manner and at any stage of the process that he wishes to consult with an attorney before

speaking there can be no questioning.
Likewise, if the individual is alone and
indicates in any manner that he does not
wish to be interrogated, the police may not
question him. The mere fact that he may
have answered some questions or volunteered some statements on his own does
not deprive him of the right to refrain from
answering any further inquiries until he
has consulted with an attorney and
thereafter consents to be questioned.

Gault held that the privilege against
compulsory self-incrimination and the right to
counsel apply, as essentials of due process, in
delinquency proceedings. In Fare v. Michael C.
(S.Ct.1979), the Court assumed without deciding
that *Miranda* principles are "fully applicable" in
these proceedings, but held that the juvenile's
request for his probation officer was not a per se
invocation of the right to remain silent because a
probation officer's role is fundamentally different
from an attorney's. *Fare* also held that the
totality-of-the-circumstances approach is "adequate" to determine whether a juvenile has
knowingly and intelligently waived the privilege
against self-compulsory incrimination and the
right to counsel. The juvenile court must evaluate
all circumstances surrounding the interrogation,
including the alleged delinquent's age, experience,

education, background, and intelligence.

In Dickerson v. United States (S.Ct.2000), the Court rejected a broad challenge to *Miranda* and held that the earlier decision had announced a constitutional rule that may not be abrogated or abridged by statute. In light of *Gault's* earlier application of the Fifth Amendment privilege to delinquency proceedings, *Miranda's* application to these proceedings would now seem assured. Counsel representing alleged delinquents must remain abreast of Miranda decisions in criminal prosecutions, which help shape the contours of the juvenile right.

b.   "Juvenile Miranda" and the States
        By statute, court rule or constitutional directive, a state may provide alleged delinquents greater protection than *Fare's* totality-of-the-circumstances approach. Some states have enacted "juvenile Miranda" statutes or rules, which typically permit waiver only where the juvenile is informed of the right to communicate with a parent, relative, lawyer or other adult interested in his welfare, or to have the adult present during questioning. A few statutes mandate heightened protection only for younger juveniles. See, e.g., Wash. Rev. Code § 13.40. 140(10) (where the juvenile is under twelve, waiver of Miranda rights may be made only by the

parent or guardian).

Without a statute or rule, the absence of a parent or other interested adult may be a factor to consider but is generally not dispositive. In re E.T.C. (Vt.1982), however, the court held that the state constitution permits a juvenile to waive the rights to remain silent and to counsel only after he is given the opportunity to consult with a parent, guardian or other fully informed adult interested in the juvenile's welfare and not associated with the prosecutor. A few courts have distinguished between older and younger juveniles. In Commonwealth v. A Juvenile (Mass. 1983), for example, the court held that a juvenile under fourteen cannot waive Miranda rights unless a parent or interested adult is present, understands the warnings, and has the opportunity to explain them to the juvenile; where the juvenile is fourteen or older, however, waiver is valid without such a consultation where the juvenile has "a high degree of intelligence, experience, knowledge, or sophistication."

Oddly enough, a parent's presence before and during interrogation may not help, and may indeed hurt, a child with no attorney. Professor Thomas Grisso has found that parents often heighten the coercive effect because they are "almost as scared as the child" and sometimes even urge the child to confess. Only about 2% of parents tell their children not to talk without an attorney present, about 16% of parents encourage their children to talk, and 71% of parents say nothing and thus allow the child to talk. When parents encourage or permit their children to talk, children may confess in error to satisfy their parents.

c. Who Are "Law Enforcement Officers"?

Miranda applies to custodial interrogation by law enforcement officers. Where a juvenile is suspected of criminal behavior, interrogation is frequently conducted by persons not employed by the police department. The interrogator may be a principal or other school administrator, a juvenile officer, or an employee of a juvenile treatment facility. Where the custodial interrogation is not conducted by a police officer, *Miranda* nonetheless applies where the interrogator acts as an agent or instrument of the police. See, e.g, Commonwealth v. A Juvenile (Mass.1988) (suppressing juvenile's confession to assistant director of home for troubled adolescents, who had a duty to report crime to police).

Principals and other school administrators, however, are generally not required to give Miranda warnings before questioning students about infractions on school grounds during school hours. Courts generally find that these officials do not act as police agents because they can fulfill their duty to protect the student body only when they have leeway to question students about violations of the law or of school rules. This rule prevails even where the school official intends to report any evidence of crime to the police.

d. When Is a Juvenile "In Custody"?

Miranda applies where the suspect has been "taken into custody or otherwise deprived of his freedom of action in any significant way." The suspect is in custody if under all the circumstances, a reasonable person in the defendant's position would have understood himself to be in custody or under restraints comparable to those associated with a formal arrest. See Berkemer v. McCarty (S.Ct.1984). Some courts have applied a "reasonable juvenile" test, which considers "whether a reasonable person in child's position -- that is, a child of similar age, knowledge and experience, placed in a similar environment -- would have felt required to stay and answer all of [the officer's] questions." State ex rel. Juvenile Dep't v. Loredo (Or.Ct. App.1993).

When juveniles are questioned away from police headquarters, the facts of the case determine whether the interrogation was custodial. In *Loredo*, for example, the court held that the police officer was not required to give Miranda warnings to a junior high school student he questioned for twenty minutes in the school principal's office about an alleged rape. The officer, not in uniform and displaying no firearm, identified himself as a police officer but told the juvenile he was not under arrest, did not have to speak and could leave if he wished. On the other hand, in State ex rel. Juvenile Dep't v. Killitz (Or.Ct.App.1982), the court granted the suppression motion of a junior high school student questioned in the principal's office by an armed, uniformed police officer who did not tell the student he was free to leave, and who said and did nothing "to dispel the clear impression communicated to defendant that he was not free to leave."

e. When Does "Interrogation" Occur?

Interrogation takes place "whenever a person in custody is subjected either to express questioning or to its functional equivalent." For *Miranda* purposes, the term "interrogation" refers to any words or action by the police, other than those normally attendant on arrest and custody, that the police should know are reasonably likely to elicit an incriminating response from the suspect. See Rhode Island v. Innis (S.Ct.1980).

f. Use of a Juvenile's Statement In Criminal Proceedings

In State v. Ouk (Minn. 1994), the juvenile was tried as an adult and convicted on two counts of first-degree murder and two counts of attempted first-degree murder committed when he was 15 years old. He received consecutive life sentences on the murder convictions and consecutive 180-month sentences on the attempt convictions. Applying the totality-of-the-circumstances approach, the state supreme court held that the 15-year-old knowingly and intelligently waived his Miranda rights while he was in juvenile custody, even though the police did not inform him that any statement he gave might be used against him in a criminal proceeding. The court held that the defendant was of suitable intelligence and maturity to waive these rights because he had received Miranda warnings at least three times previously and knew how to act on them. The court acknowledged that juvenile suspects were "routinely not being informed" of the possibility of adult prosecution.

Ouk's approach is not the unanimous view. Some decisions hold that where a juvenile is questioned about an act that could produce transfer to criminal court, any purported waiver of Miranda rights is per se invalid unless the juvenile has been advised of that possibility. See, e.g., State v. Benoit (N.H.1985).

g. Voluntary, Knowing and Intelligent Waiver

It appears that the vast majority of unrepresented juveniles waive their right to remain silent, and that they do so even more often than adult suspects. One study, for example, found that unrepresented juveniles under fifteen virtually never refused to talk, that only 12-14% of 15 to 16 year-olds refused, but that the adult refusal rate was more than 40%. See Thomas Grisso and Carolyn Pomicter, Interrogation of Juveniles: An Empirical Study of Procedures, Safeguards, and Rights Waiver, 1 Law and Hum. Behav. 321 (1977).

Empirical studies have indicated that most children under fifteen cannot understand the nature and significance of the rights to remain silent and to have counsel appointed. Professor Grisso's study of 10- to 16-year-olds also found that older juveniles generally understand their rights as well as adults do, though the study did not test the capacity of these juveniles to waive their rights under the stress of actual police questioning. Thomas Grisso, Juveniles' Capacity to Waive *Miranda* Rights: An Empirical Analysis, 68 Cal. L. Rev. 1134 (1980). One study suggested that high juvenile waiver rates stem at least in part from the beliefs of many juveniles that police may try to dissuade a person from remaining silent, or that the judge may later revoke the person's right to remain silent. Research also indicates that many juveniles do not understand defense counsel's role, are afraid to confide in their lawyer because they believe the lawyer must assist the court rather than maintain the client's confidences, or feel they have more in common with their probation officers than with defense counsel unfamiliar to them.

Many doubts about the voluntariness of juvenile confessions might be removed by videotaping interrogations, perhaps a prudent practice even where it is not required. In In re Doe (Idaho Ct.App.1997), for example, the court held that when evaluating a police officer's credibility at a juvenile suppression hearing, the court may draw a negative inference from the absence of a videotape when the officer conveniently could have made one.

h.   "Terry Stops"
A police officer may briefly detain a person and make reasonable inquiries when the officer observes unusual conduct that leads him to reasonably suspect in light of experience that the person is engaged in, or about to engage in,

criminal activity. The officer may frisk a person he reasonably believes may be armed and presently dangerous to the officer or others. See Terry v. Ohio (S.Ct.1968). "Terry stops" are generally not subject to *Miranda* because the detainee is not "in custody." A valid stop, however, "can ripen into an illegal detention for Miranda purposes if events transpire sufficient for a reasonable person in the defendant's position to consider himself or herself to be in custody." In re Eric J.D. (Wis.Ct.App.1998).

4. INTAKE AND DIVERSION

a. The General Process

In the criminal justice system, the prosecutor determines whether to invoke the judicial process by charging a person with a crime. In delinquency cases, however, the decision whether to invoke the judicial process traditionally has been made by the juvenile probation department or other members of the court staff itself during "intake." The intake officer examines the probable strength of the evidence and meets with the juvenile and the parents, and sometimes also the victim. The officer then decides whether to "divert" the case by dismissing the charges or fashioning an "informal adjustment," or whether to authorize the filing of a petition seeking formal adjudication.

534 DELINQUENCY Ch. 10

Informal adjustment may result in a "consent decree" outlining specific conditions the juvenile must satisfy for a specified period, frequently supervised by a probation officer. The conditions typically concern victim restitution, community service, school attendance, drug or alcohol counseling, or a curfew. Generally a juvenile may be offered an informal disposition only after admitting the charge. The court ultimately dismisses the case if the juvenile satisfies the conditions, but formally processes the juvenile if he fails.

Under the traditional juvenile court rehabilitative model, the intake decision focused largely or entirely on the juvenile's needs, circumstances and record. Some states, however, now limit intake officers' discretion, at least in some circumstances. In Virginia, for example, officers may not divert the case, and must file a petition, where conduct constituting a violent felony is charged or where the juvenile was previously diverted or adjudicated a delinquent or status offender. See Va. Code § 16.1-260.

The prosecutor now may play a central intake role by statutory authorization, informal practice, or both. At one extreme, a prosecutor may be limited to reviewing petitions filed by the intake officer to determine their accuracy and legal sufficiency. At the other extreme, the prosecutor may receive all law enforcement referrals, with authority to determine whether to charge the case without consulting the intake officer. Between the extremes, the intake officer may consult the prosecutor on felony cases and dismiss or divert a case only with the prosecutor's approval; the intake officer's decisions may be subject to the prosecutor's approval; or the prosecutor may receive felony cases, with the intake officer handling only other cases.

b. Teen Courts

In more than half the states, some local jurisdictions provide for diversion to "teen courts" or "youth courts." A juvenile who has admitted guilt or responsibility, usually a first-time misdemeanor offender, may consent to appear before a teenage "jury" for disposition within a fixed range, generally community service, counseling or restitution. A volunteer attorney typically serves as judge, and a juvenile officer serves as bailiff. The American Bar Association encourages creation of these courts as a way to discourage criminal behavior by offenders and jurors alike through positive peer pressure and reinforcement.

c. Discrimination In Police Encounters and Intake

Some research indicates that police are more likely to detain and arrest minority youth than white youth, even when the research controls for offense seriousness and prior offenses. Some commentators also allege that the broad discretion permeating intake and diversion may result in discriminatory treatment. "[S]chool performance, demeanor, family situation, prior record, degree of contrition, and other factors will come into play, with many of these reflecting race, ethnicity, or social status." Robert E. Shepherd, Jr., Juvenile Justice, 9 Crim. Just. 42 (Summer 1994).

In 1997 formal handling was used in 62% of cases involving black juveniles, 54% of cases involving white juveniles, and 55% of cases involving juveniles of other races. Racial differences in the likelihood of formal handling were greatest in drug cases: 78% of drug cases involving black juveniles were handled by formal petition, compared with 56% for white juveniles and 55% for juveniles of other races. See Juvenile Court Statistics 1997.

d. Plea Bargaining

In cases not diverted, prosecutors and alleged delinquents frequently engage in plea bargaining driven by interests that resemble the interests that drive criminal plea bargaining. The juvenile may seek adjudication to reduced charges or a disposition with less restrictive restraints (for example, probation rather than institutionalization, or the shortest possible probationary period). The prosecutor may seek to assure a result for the state (much as prosecutors of adult defendants may seek to create the highest possible conviction record), may seek to spare witnesses the ordeal of unpleasant testimony, may seek to conserve the office's resources by clearing a backlog, and may even seek to spare the juvenile adjudication on serious charges. Plea bargaining may serve the court's interest in moving the docket, assuring that the juvenile will receive necessary treatment not available after acquittal or dismissal, and assuring that the juvenile receives treatment quickly. Some courts also believe a juvenile's plea bargain may amount to an acknowledgment of responsibility that enhances prospects for rehabilitation.

Analogies between plea bargaining in delinquency and criminal cases can break down, however, when the delinquency system's rehabilitative, rather than punitive, goal is emphasized. In re Jimmy P. (Cal.Ct.App.1996), for example, the court held that the criminal court rule precluding a sentencing court from

considering charges dismissed as part of plea
bargain is inapplicable when the juvenile court
determines the proper placement for a delinquent
after a plea bargain. *Jimmy P.* explained that the
court must consider all available social and
behavioral evidence bearing on the juvenile's
fitness.

5. PREVENTIVE DETENTION

a. Due Process Considerations
In Schall v. Martin (S.Ct.1984), the Court
held that pretrial detention under New York's
Family Court Act did not violate Fourteenth
Amendment due process. The Court concluded
(1) that preventive detention of juveniles under
the Act did not constitute punishment, but served
a legitimate state objective of protecting the
community and the juvenile from the hazards of
pre-hearing crime, and (2) that the pre-hearing
procedures the Act afforded the detained juvenile
amply protected against erroneous and unnecessary deprivations of liberty. For example, juveniles
were entitled to notice, a hearing and a statement
of facts and reasons before detention, and a
formal probable cause hearing shortly afterwards;
detention was strictly limited in time; detained
juveniles were entitled to an expedited factfinding
hearing. Absent exceptional circumstances,
juveniles could not be detained in a prison or

lockup where they might be exposed to adult criminals.

Today states authorize preventive detention where the juvenile is a fugitive from another jurisdiction, would be a danger to himself or others if released, would be likely to flee the jurisdiction if released, has no parent or other adult to assume supervision, or has been charged with a serious crime such as murder. The national rate of preventive detention has so increased that many juvenile detention facilities are filled beyond capacity, leading to recommendations that criteria be developed to help limit detention to dangerous youth and those most likely to flee, and development of alternatives, such as electronic monitoring, for other juveniles.

b. Preventive Detention's Effect on Disposition

A 1989 study found that preventive detention has a "substantial impact" on delinquency dispositions because the very fact of detention fuels a perception that the detainee is dangerous to himself or the community, and thus warrants more severe sanction. Barry C. Feld, The Right to Counsel in Juvenile Court: An Empirical Study of When Lawyers Appear and the Difference They Make, 79 J. Crim. L. & Criminol. 1185 (1989). The impact of preventive detention is likely to be especially profound where, as is often the case, the judge who ordered the detention later presides at the adjudicatory hearing and imposes the disposition.

In 1999, 18.3% of white alleged delinquents and 25.3% of black alleged delinquents were detained at some point between referral and disposition. See 2001 Sourcebook. Some researchers conclude that racial disparities in preventive detention are a major cause of racial discrimination in delinquency sanctions.

c. Bail

The Eighth Amendment provides that "[e]xcessive bail shall not be required." The Amendment "says nothing about whether bail shall be available at all," United States v. Salerno (S.Ct.1987), and "fails to say all arrests must be bailable." Carlson v. Landon (S.Ct.1952). The Supreme Court has not determined whether juveniles have a constitutional right to bail in delinquency cases, but lower courts have held that they do not.

In the absence of a federal constitutional right, states disagree about whether a detained juvenile is entitled to release on bail pending the adjudicatory hearing or an appeal. Some juvenile court acts authorize bail and others preclude it.

In the absence of a statute authorizing bail in
delinquency cases, state constitutional provisions
guaranteeing the right to bail in criminal cases
provide little help to juveniles because delinquency proceedings are civil in nature. Where the
juvenile code is silent about entitlement to bail,
most courts have held that the code's express
safeguards obviate the need for it.

Where the juvenile is transferred to
criminal court, the juvenile thereafter enjoys the
same right to bail held by adult defendants.
Courts, however, have rejected claims that a
constitutional right to bail attaches where an
alleged delinquent is confined in juvenile
detention under conditions that assertedly
resemble the conditions that mark preventive
detention of adults.

d. The Juvenile Justice and Delinquency
   Prevention Act of 1974

The 1974 Act, as amended, establishes
four mandates relating to juvenile detention,
including preventive detention. States must
comply with the mandates as a condition for
receiving formula grant funds under the Act.
Chapter 9 discussed one mandate, deinstitutionalization of status offenders and nonoffenders.

The second mandate -- "sight and sound

separation" -- provides that juveniles may not have regular contact with adults who have been convicted of a crime or who are awaiting trial on criminal charges. 42 U.S.C. § 5633(a)(13). States must assure that juvenile and adult inmates cannot see each other and that no conversation between them is possible. The major aims are to prevent adult prisoners from committing assault (including sexual assault) on juveniles, and to prevent juveniles from being infected with the criminal culture of adult prisons. (The Violent Crime Control and Law Enforcement Act of 1994 permits secure detention of juveniles charged with or convicted of possessing handguns or ammunition in violation of federal law or any similar state statute.)

The "jail and lockup removal" mandate requires states to provide that juveniles charged with delinquency "shall not be detained or confined in any institution in which they have contact with adult [inmates]." The mandate has a few exceptions. An arrested juvenile, for example, may be held in a lockup for only a short period (usually up to six hours). Juveniles charged in criminal court with a felony may be detained in a secure adult facility. Id. § 5633(a)(14).

Finally a 1992 amendment creates the "disproportionate confinement of minority youth" mandate, which requires states to determine whether such disproportion exists and, if so, to demonstrate that they have undertaken efforts to reduce it. Id. § 5633(a)(23).

6. THE ADJUDICATORY HEARING

a. Introduction
    If the intake staff decides to process the case formally, the staff files a petition and the case is placed on the calendar for an adjudicatory hearing. The overwhelming majority of juvenile court petitions are resolved when the juvenile admits the alleged facts; less than 10% require a full hearing.

    If the petition proceeds to an adjudicatory hearing and the state fails to prove delinquency beyond a reasonable doubt, the court enters judgment for the juvenile. If the juvenile admits delinquency or if delinquency is proved, the case normally proceeds to the disposition hearing. Sometimes, however, the case is dismissed or continued in contemplation of dismissal if the juvenile takes action the court recommends, such as paying restitution or entering into substance abuse treatment.

    The Supreme Court first wrestled with delinquency procedure in Kent v. United States

(S.Ct.1966). *Kent* invalidated the District of
Columbia juvenile court order that had transferred the teenager to criminal court. The
Supreme Court found that the juvenile court had
deprived the teenager of a hearing, had denied his
counsel access to the social and probation reports
prepared about him, and had failed to enter a
statement of reasons for waiver. Writing for the
five-member majority, however, Justice Fortas left
it somewhat unclear whether the decision was
grounded thoroughly in constitutional mandate.
Kent held that the rights in question were
"required by the [D.C. Juvenile Court Act] read in
the context of constitutional principles relating to
due process and the assistance of counsel."

Less than fourteen months later, with
Justice Fortas again writing for the majority, In re
Gault (S.Ct.1967), removed doubt and established the Constitution as the ultimate source of
procedural rights in delinquency cases.

b. In re Gault (1967)
For nearly seven decades before *Gault*, the
law perceived juvenile authorities as protectors
rather than prosecutors of the child, and due
process as an impediment to rehabilitation and
treatment. Some observers reported that
adjudicatory and dispositional hearings were
frequently hollow formalities because the outcome

was a forgone conclusion even before the juvenile
court heard witnesses. Juveniles and their
families ordinarily stood alone because few were
represented by counsel.

Gault reversed the juvenile court order
that had found the unrepresented 15-year-old
delinquent for making lewd or indecent telephone
calls to a woman neighbor, and had committed
him to the state industrial school until 21, unless
discharged sooner. Attacking the procedural
shortcomings that preceded the boy's commitment, the Court stated forcefully that "neither the
Fourteenth Amendment nor the Bill of Rights is
for adults alone," and that "the condition of being
a boy does not justify a kangaroo court."

Gault held that in any delinquency
proceeding in which the juvenile may be
committed to a state institution, due process
requires (1) that the juvenile and his or her
parents or guardian be given written notice,
stating the charges with particularity, at the
earliest practicable time, and in any event
sufficiently in advance of the hearing to permit
reasonable opportunity to prepare, (2) that the
juvenile and his or her parents be notified of the
juvenile's right to be represented by retained
counsel, or that counsel would be appointed to
represent the juvenile if they cannot afford

counsel, (3) and that the juvenile enjoy the Fifth
Amendment privilege against self-incrimination,
and the rights to confrontation and cross-
examination. *Gault* did not decide whether due
process requires a state to grant a right to appeal
from delinquency determinations or to provide a
transcript or recording of the juvenile court
hearing.

Gault highlights delinquency's sometimes
uneasy status as a hybrid jurisdiction. A
delinquency proceeding remains civil in nature.
Delinquency practice now resembles criminal
practice in important respects, however, because
Gault and later decisions have held many federal
constitutional criminal law guarantees applicable
in delinquency proceedings as essential to "fundamental fairness" under due process.

Gault has been called "the charter of
juvenile justice." In Memoriam Honorable Abe
Fortas (S.Ct.1982). A generation after the land-
mark decision, however, the law on the books
does not always resemble the law in practice. In
many states, less than half of the juveniles
adjudicated delinquent receive assistance of
counsel. See Barry C. Feld, Justice For Children:
The Right to Counsel and the Juvenile Courts
(1993). Several explanations are offered for low
representation rates -- parents may be unwilling

to retain counsel for the juvenile, public defender legal services may be scarce outside urban centers, and juvenile courts may pressure juveniles and their parents to waive the right to counsel.

c. The Role of Counsel

As noted above, *Gault* clearly gives alleged delinquents the right to counsel during the adjudicatory phase. The Court stated that the alleged delinquent "needs the assistance of counsel to cope with problems of law, to make skilled inquiry into the facts, to insist upon regularity of the proceedings, and to ascertain whether he has a defense and to prepare and submit it. The child 'requires the guiding hand of counsel at every step in the proceedings against him.'"

Debate continues, however, about counsel's appropriate role and whether counsel is required at other stages in a delinquency proceeding. Generally attorneys for alleged delinquents are expected to take direction from their child clients as they would from adult clients. The IJA/ABA Standards Relating to Counsel for Private Parties, for example, provide that counsel for the respondent in a delinquency proceeding "should ordinarily be bound by the client's definition of his or her interests with respect to admission or denial of the facts or conditions alleged. It is appropriate and desirable for counsel to advise the client concerning the probable success and consequences of adopting any posture with respect to those proceedings." The comment to the Standard states that:

> [E]ven a youthful client will be mature enough to understand, with advice of counsel, at least the general nature of the proceedings, the acts with which he or she has been charged, and the consequences associated with the pending action. On this basis a juvenile client can decide whether to accede to or contest the petition. That, in essence, is what is required of the defendant in criminal proceedings and should suffice for juvenile court purposes. Although counsel may strongly feel that the client's choice of posture is unwise, and perhaps be right in that opinion, the lawyer's view may not be substituted for that of a client who is capable of good judgment.

The client-directed attorney role is endorsed more strongly at the adjudicatory stage, however, than at the disposition stage. See, e.g., In the Interest of K.M.B. (Ill.App.Ct.1984) (holding that thirteen-year old delinquent was not denied constitutional right to counsel when attorney recommended out-of-home placement despite the child's express wish to remain at home).

d.   Juvenile Waiver of the Right to Counsel

A few states prohibit juvenile waiver of the right to counsel. Most states, however, permit juveniles to waive the right voluntarily and intelligently, though many states require particular formalities designed to help assure that the juvenile and his parents understand the significance of the waiver decision.

A former American Bar Association president reports that "[t]housands of juveniles are urged or cajoled into waiving their rights without adequate representation, without a full vetting of their charges and without a complete and detailed understanding of their rights." N. Lee Cooper, Conveyor Belt Justice, 83 A.B.A. J. 6 (July 1997). An ABA Juvenile Justice Center report states that "[w]aivers of counsel by young people are sometimes induced by suggestions that lawyers are not needed because no serious dispositional consequences are anticipated -- or by parental concerns that they will have to pay for any counsel that is appointed. These circumstances raise the possibility -- perhaps the likelihood -- that a substantial number of juvenile waivers are not 'knowing and intelligent.'" A Call For Justice: An Assessment of Access to Counsel

and Quality of Representation in Delinquency
Proceedings (1995).

e. Competency to Participate In the Proceeding

A criminal defendant may stand trial only
if he "has sufficient present ability to consult with
his lawyer with a reasonable degree of rational
understanding -- and ... a rational as well as
factual understanding of the proceedings against
him." Dusky v. United States (S.Ct.1960). The
issue of alleged delinquents' competency does not
have a long pedigree because the issue did not
normally arise before *Gault* imposed due process
constraints on the juvenile court. The issue has
arisen with increased frequency in recent years as
juvenile court sanctions have grown more punitive, conditions of juvenile confinement have
remained harsh in many places, and juveniles
have faced greater likelihood of transfer to
criminal court.

In some states, statutes or rules define
competency in delinquency proceedings. In other
states, courts may hold that due process requires
application of the criminal law competency
standard and prohibits adjudication of juveniles
who fail to satisfy the standard. These courts
reject arguments that juvenile court dispositions
are rehabilitative rather than punitive, and thus

that the court may proceed with a lower level of competency than the criminal court would require. See, e.g., In re D.D.N. (Minn.Ct.App. 1998).

Adults' competency has generally focused on mental illness or retardation. In juvenile or criminal court, however, a juvenile's competency might also be questioned based on developmental immaturity. Behavioral research has begun to indicate that children below fourteen are considerably less able than older children or adults to understand the meaning of a trial, to assist counsel, and to make decisions. Some courts have found particularly young children incompetent even when they do not suffer from any mental illness or retardation. See, e.g., In re Charles B. (Ariz.Ct.App. 1998) (11-year-old boy charged with aggravated assault).

f. Discovery
Discovery is generally available in delinquency cases. Some states apply criminal discovery rules in delinquency cases. In other states, juvenile court rules define disclosure obligations in delinquency cases, generally in considerable detail.

In the absence of express authority, juvenile courts sometimes exercise inherent authority to order discovery. Some delinquency decisions apply Brady v. Maryland (S.Ct.1963), which held in an adult criminal trial that "suppression by the prosecution of evidence favorable to an accused upon request violates due process where the evidence is material either to guilt or to punishment, irrespective of the good faith or bad faith of the prosecution."

g. Admitting the Petition's Allegations

In Boykin v. Alabama (S.Ct.1969), the Court held that before accepting a criminal defendant's guilty plea, due process requires the trial judge to address the defendant personally in open court. The judge must inform the defendant of, and determine that he understands, the nature and consequences of the plea and the rights the plea waives. The court must also determine that the plea is voluntary and not the result of force or threats or promises apart from a plea agreement.

The Supreme Court has not decided whether *Boykin*'s due process holding applies in delinquency proceedings. State statutes or rules, however, generally require juvenile courts to determine after a colloquy in open court that the juvenile's admission to the petition's allegations are knowing and voluntary. Some states require only substantial adherence to *Boykin* in delinquency proceedings. See, e.g., In re John D. (R.I.1984). Even where no statute or rule requires adherence to *Boykin,* juvenile courts tend to adhere anyway.

Alleged delinquents may withdraw their plea and proceed to adjudication for reasons analogous to those that would support withdrawal in criminal cases. Juvenile withdrawal has been permitted, for example, (1) where the state does not comply with the terms of the plea bargain that produced the plea, (2) where the plea colloquy did not comply with statutory or rule requirements, for example because the juvenile court did not inform the alleged delinquent of the right to counsel, or (3) where the record demonstrates doubt that the juvenile understood the charges and knowingly and voluntarily waived the right to counsel.

The alleged delinquent is not permitted to withdraw the plea merely because the court refuses to accept the prosecutor's sentencing recommendation. Courts disagree about whether the delinquent may withdraw a plea merely on a showing that withdrawal would be in the best interests of the child. See, e.g., In re Bradford (Pa.Super.Ct.1997) (yes); In re J.E.H. (D.C.Ct.App. 1996) (no).

h. Speedy Trial

The Sixth Amendment guarantees that "[i]n all criminal prosecutions, the accused shall enjoy the right to a speedy ... trial." The Supreme Court has not determined whether an alleged delinquent holds a federal due process right to a speedy trial, and lower courts are divided on the question. See, e.g., In re Benjamin L. (N.Y.1999) (state constitution guarantees alleged delinquents a speedy trial). In more than half the states, however, statutes or court rules guarantee a speedy trial by imposing time standards for processing and determining petitions.

The National District Attorneys Association recommends that no more than sixty days pass between police referral and disposition for juveniles held in secure detention, and no more than ninety days for juveniles not detained. A significant percentage of delinquency cases nationwide, however, do not reach disposition within these deadlines, including nearly half the cases pending in large jurisdictions.

In a delinquency proceeding in federal district court, the federal Juvenile Delinquency Act grants the right to a speedy trial where an alleged delinquent is held in preventive detention. If the detainee "is not brought to trial within thirty days from the date upon which such detention was begun, the information shall be dismissed on motion of the alleged delinquent or at the direction of the court, unless the Attorney General shows that additional delay was caused by the juvenile or his counsel, or consented to by the juvenile and his counsel, or would be in the interest of justice in the particular case. Delays attributable solely to court calendar congestion may not be considered in the interest of justice. Except in extraordinary circumstances, an information dismissed ... may not be reinstituted." 18 U.S.C. § 5036.

i. Jury Trial

In McKeiver v. Pennsylvania (S.Ct.1971), just four years after *Gault*, the Supreme Court held that due process does not require a jury trial in delinquency proceedings. As juvenile justice has moved from a largely rehabilitative model in the years since *McKeiver*, alleged delinquents have unsuccessfully sought to overcome the decision and establish a constitutional right to a jury trial. In State v. J.H. (Wash.Ct.App.1999), for example, the court rejected the contention that recent juvenile justice code amendments had made delinquency proceedings so much less rehabilitative and more punitive as to require a jury trial right under the federal and state constitutions.

Absence of the jury trial right, however,

may limit the juvenile court's authority to impose incarceration in an adult facility. In In re C.B. (La.1998), for example, the court invalidated under the state constitution's due process clause a statute which, without affording the right to a jury trial in juvenile court, required transfer of juveniles at age seventeen to adult penal institutions, where they would be confined at hard labor like adult felons for as much as four years. The court held that the challenged statute "sufficiently tilted the scales away from a 'civil' proceeding, with its focus on rehabilitation, to one purely criminal."

j. Rules of Evidence
In the juvenile court's early years, the rules of evidence did not apply or were relaxed because they, like formal procedure, were seen as impediments to rehabilitation. Since *Gault*, however, states have applied the criminal rules of evidence in the adjudicatory phase of delinquency proceedings. Subject to due process constraints, however, statutes or rules generally permit the court at the dispositional phase to consider all information relevant to the circumstances of the delinquent and the family.

k. The Parents' Role
Juvenile codes typically make the alleged delinquent's parent, guardian or custodian a

party to the proceedings, thus giving them an absolute right to attend. Indeed many states require their attendance. The juvenile and the adults are entitled to be heard, to present material evidence, and to cross-examine witnesses.

Where the adult will testify, courts disagree about whether the trial judge may exclude the adult from a portion of the hearing pursuant to an order excluding prospective witnesses until their testimony. See, e.g., In re J.E. (Ill.App.Ct.1996) (yes); In re L.B. (Ind.Ct.App.1996) (no).

1. Standard of Proof

In In re Winship (S.Ct.1970), the Court held that due process requires application of the criminal beyond-a-reasonable-doubt standard in delinquency proceedings. Some question remains, however, about the decision's practical impact in some cases. Some observers suggest that juvenile court judges sometimes find juveniles delinquent on less evidence than would satisfy the beyond-a-reasonable-doubt standard in criminal cases, presumably because the judge believes that adjudication and the ensuing disposition are for the juvenile's own good, or knows that needed treatment is unavailable without a finding of delinquency.

m. Double Jeopardy

In Breed v. Jones (S.Ct.1975), the juvenile was convicted in criminal court after the juvenile court had found that he had violated a criminal statute but that he was unfit for treatment as a juvenile. *Breed* unanimously held that jeopardy attached when the juvenile court began hearing evidence, and thus that the later criminal prosecution violated the Fifth Amendment Double Jeopardy Clause, as applied to the states through the Fourteenth Amendment.

Before *Gault* imposed due process constraints on the juvenile court, the conceptual basis for a double jeopardy claim was not at all clear because non-criminal delinquency proceedings created no jeopardy. Like *Gault* and *Winship,* however, *Breed* refused to treat delinquency proceedings as purely civil because the Court noted "a gap between the originally benign conception of [the juvenile court] system and its realities."

The Court distinguished *Breed* in Swisher v. Brady (S.Ct.1978). *Swisher* challenged Maryland procedures which, designed to cope with heavy juvenile court caseloads, provided that delinquency petitions would often be heard by masters, who would make proposed findings and recommendations to the juvenile court judge. The judge was empowered to accept, modify or reject the findings and recommendations and had sole authority to enter a final order. Where the state filed objections to the master's recommendation of non-delinquency, the court could rule on the objections based only on the record made before the master and on any additional relevant evidence to which the parties did not object. The juvenile contended that the state thus had the opportunity to convince two factfinders of his guilt, and that the state had the functional equivalent of appealing an incipient acquittal (the recommendation of non-delinquency). *Swisher* held that the state's right to file objections did not violate the Double Jeopardy Clause.

Today about half the states allow juvenile court masters or referees to conduct adjudicatory hearings, with only a judge authorized enter final judgments. Some states do not require the master or referee to be a lawyer or do not require the juvenile's consent before a master or referee may sit.

A juvenile expelled, suspended or otherwise disciplined by school authorities may thereafter be the subject of a delinquency proceeding (or a criminal trial) arising from the same conduct that gave rise to the expulsion. Double jeopardy is not implicated because the expulsion is a civil administrative action and not a judicially imposed criminal punishment.

n. Race and Delinquency Adjudication
     A 1990 survey found that "differences in the adjudication rates for minority v. non-minority groups do not appear significant, and one may conclude that the judiciary relies on the evidence in making an adjudicatory judgment." See Minority Youth in the Juvenile Justice System: A Judicial Response, 41 Juv. & Fam. Ct. J. (No. 3A 1990). In 1999, 67.0% of white alleged delinquents and 62.5% of black alleged delinquents were adjudicated. See 2001 Sourcebook.

     Some researchers have found, however, that once the adjudication decision is made, minority youth may receive harsher sanctions than white youth for similar offenses.

o. The Hearing Under the Federal Juvenile Delinquency Act
     Delinquency proceedings in federal court resemble state delinquency proceedings. The beyond-a-reasonable-doubt standard of proof applies; the juvenile has a right to counsel; the hearing is closed to the public; and the juvenile has no right to a jury trial. The proceeding is civil rather than criminal, and a delinquency adjudi-

cation does not constitute a criminal conviction.

7. JUVENILE COURT CONFIDENTIALITY

To help enhance prospects for rehabilitating youth, delinquency proceedings and records were traditionally confidential and closed to the public. The public could not attend delinquency proceedings. Delinquency records, including the disposition, were sealed at the conclusion of the proceedings, subject to release only on court order, and expunged after a period of time. Juvenile court confidentiality stood in sharp contrast to practice in general criminal and civil courts, whose proceedings and records (with rare exceptions) were generally open to the public by constitutional and statutory mandate.

a. Proceedings and Records

Responding to public desire for greater juvenile accountability, most states in the 1990s enacted legislation that modified or removed traditional juvenile court confidentiality provisions to make delinquency proceedings more open. Some states have even replaced closed delinquency proceedings with a presumption of open proceedings, at least in cases involving older juveniles or juveniles charged with specified serious crimes.

Juvenile codes in at least forty-seven
states have provided for release of information
contained in juvenile court records to at least one
of the following: the prosecutor, law enforcement,
social agencies, schools, the victim and the
public.

Barriers to release of records have fallen in
part because prosecutors and courts applying
broad transfer statutes need information about
the juvenile. Social agencies need information to
help fashion treatment alternatives, and schools
need information to protect students from violent
classmates. Some states make delinquency
records available to victims, sometimes with the
proviso that the victim may not make further
disclosure of the record. Victims remain informed
of their case's status, and they may use the
records in a later damage action arising from the
offense. In about half the states, juvenile court
records are now also open to the public in at least
some circumstances, usually where a serious
violent crime is charged or adjudicated. In several
states, the court must release the identity of
juveniles who are adjudicated delinquent for
serious offenses or who commit repeated offenses.

b. Confidentiality and the Media

As a matter of self-restraint based on
cooperation with juvenile court personnel, the

media normally do not reveal the identities of
accused juveniles, at least unless the crime is
serious or unless the juvenile is transferred to
criminal court. In more than forty states, the
names of juveniles involved in delinquency
proceedings may be released to the media in some
or all cases. Even where confidentiality is
mandated, however, neither the court nor the
legislature may restrain or prohibit the press from
reporting an alleged delinquent's name that the
press learns through a leak, community disclosure or otherwise. A media report naming the
offender in effect becomes a permanent record
that may come back to haunt him in later life,
regardless of statutes providing for confidentiality
or for sealing or expunging the record.

In Oklahoma Publishing Co. v. District Ct.
(S.Ct.1977), the Court struck down an injunction
that prohibited the news media from publishing
the name or photograph of an eleven-year-old boy
who was the subject of a delinquency hearing.
The juvenile court had permitted reporters and
other members of the public to attend a hearing
in the case, and then had attempted to halt
publication of information obtained from that
hearing. The Supreme Court held that once
truthful information was "publicly revealed" or "in
the public domain," the First Amendment
prohibited the juvenile court from restraining its

dissemination.

In Smith v. Daily Mail Publishing Co.
(S.Ct.1979), the Court struck down a state statute
that made it a crime for a newspaper to publish,
without the juvenile court's written approval, the
name of a youth charged as a juvenile offender.
The Court held that where a newspaper lawfully
obtains truthful information about a matter of
public significance, the state may not constitutionally punish publication of the information,
absent a need to further "a state interest of the
highest order." The Court rejected the state's
contention that the challenged statute, which
concededly imposed a prior restraint on speech,
nonetheless passed constitutional muster
because the state held an interest in protecting
the identity of juveniles to aid their rehabilitation.

E. DISPOSITION

1. FASHIONING THE DISPOSITION

a. Introduction

At the dispositional hearing after
delinquency is admitted or proved, the court has
broad discretion to determine the sanctions it will
impose on the juvenile. In recent years,
delinquency dispositions have faced criticism from
many quarters. Juvenile courts have been

criticized for enabling many offenders to develop lengthy "rap sheets" before ever holding them truly accountable for their conduct. Juvenile courts have been criticized for imposing unduly lenient sanctions that amount to little more than "slaps on the wrists" that "coddle" persistent offenders and compromise public safety. But juvenile courts have also been criticized for imposing harsh sanctions that place punishment ahead of rehabilitation, without jury trials and other constitutional rights available in criminal court. Finally juvenile courts have been criticized for allowing racial and gender bias to infect dispositions.

Because the cost of housing a child in a detention facility for a year typically exceeds $30,000, many commentators argue that prevention programs, such as after-school care and recreation programs, are the most cost effective way to deal with delinquency.

b. The Duration of the Disposition
In more than thirty states, the juvenile court may impose a disposition – such as probation or confinement in a juvenile facility -- that extends beyond the maximum age of the court's exclusive original delinquency jurisdiction. In most states, the maximum age of that jurisdiction is eighteen, though a few states have

enacted maximum ages between fifteen and
seventeen. The maximum dispositional age, for
example, is twenty-four in California, Montana,
Oregon and Wisconsin. In some states, the
extended dispositional age may apply only to
particular offenses or particular juveniles, such as
violent crimes or habitual offenders. Where the
juvenile has committed a serious crime such as
murder, the swiftly approaching maximum
dispositional age may lead the court to transfer
the juvenile to criminal court for trial and
sentencing as an adult.

c. Pre-Disposition Information

If the court adjudicates the juvenile a
delinquent, the probation staff prepares a social
history (or predisposition report) describing the
condition and circumstances of the child and
family, and recommending an appropriate disposition, which may include treatment and other
support services. To aid in preparation, the court
may order mental health and medical professionals to examine the juvenile. The prosecutor
and the juvenile may also make recommendations
to the court. After reviewing all recommendations,
the court enters its disposition. The social history
is persuasive because the juvenile court follows
the probation staff's recommendations more than
90% of the time.

d. The Interstate Compact On Juveniles

Interstate relations may become an issue at the disposition stage or afterwards if the juvenile committed crimes outside the state of residency or if the family moves to a new state. States have responded with the Interstate Compact on Juveniles, which authorizes, among other things, (1) supervision of a juvenile on probation by a state other than the state that adjudicated the juvenile, (2) return to the home state of escaped delinquents, and (3) pooling of funds by states to create cooperative facilities to treat delinquents.

2. THE RANGE OF DISPOSITIONS

a. Graduated Sanctions

According to the U.S. Office of Juvenile Justice and Delinquency Prevention (OJJDP), "[f]or intervention efforts to be most effective, they must be swift, certain, consistent, and incorporate increasing sanctions, including the possible loss of freedom." "As the severity of sanctions increases, so must the intensity of treatment. At each level, offenders must be aware that, should they continue to violate the law, they will be subject to more severe sanctions and could ultimately be confined in a secure setting, ranging from a secure community-based juvenile facility to a training school, camp, or ranch." John J.

Wilson and James C. Howell, Serious and Violent
Juvenile Crime: A Comprehensive Strategy, 45
Juv. & Fam. Ct. J. (No. 2 1994)

From the least severe to the most severe,
the range of delinquency sanctions normally
includes reprimanding or warning the juvenile;
placing the juvenile on probation; ordering the
juvenile or parent, or both, to attend counseling
or mental health treatment; ordering the juvenile
to pay a fine, make restitution or perform
community service; placing the juvenile in a group
home, foster home or similar residential facility;
committing the juvenile to a secure institution
(that is, an institution the juvenile may not leave
without permission); or committing the juvenile to
an outside agency or mental health program. As
discussed above in section B.1, federal and state
law precludes incarcerating adjudicated delinquents with adults.

b. Probation

Probation is the sanction most frequently
imposed in the juvenile justice system. In 1997,
55% of adjudicated delinquents nationwide
received probation as the most severe disposition.
See Juvenile Court Statistics 1997. In 1999,
61.9% of adjudicated white delinquents and
60.90% of adjudicated black delinquents received
probation. See 2001 Sourcebook.

Probation may be voluntary (where the juvenile agrees to comply rather than proceed to adjudication), or may be imposed by the court after adjudication. A probation order may include such requirements as participation in drug counseling, community service or payment of restitution to the victim. Probation conditions must be reasonably related to the juvenile's rehabilitation or to the offense committed, but courts take a generous view of reasonableness. In In re McDonald (N.C.Ct.App.1999), for example, the court upheld a juvenile court probation order that prohibited the delinquent from watching television for one year. The order was based on a determination that television contributed to her delinquency because she had watched television program on Charles Manson and then spray painted "Charles Manson rules" on the walls of a private boathouse.

The court may hold periodic hearings to review the juvenile's compliance with the terms of probation, and to consider probation staff reports. The court terminates the case when the juvenile has fully complied. If the juvenile does not fully comply, the court may revoke probation and consider stricter sanctions. The petition for revocation must reasonably describe the time, place and manner in which the violation occurred,

and the juvenile is entitled to notice and a
revocation hearing with the right to counsel.

c. Parental Responsibility

In a growing number of states, the juvenile
court may require the delinquent's parents to
participate in the disposition, for example by
attending parenting classes or by contributing to
restitution paid to the victim. Courts have upheld
the constitutionality of these statutes as rationally
related to the legitimate state purposes of casting
the burden of loss on delinquents' parents rather
than on innocent victims, and of encouraging
parents to guide their children's upbringing. A
number of states have enacted statutes requiring
parents to pay reasonable costs of maintaining
their child in a state institution pursuant to a
delinquency disposition.

d. Victims' Rights Measures

All states now grant victims rights in the
delinquency process. Victims may be entitled, for
example, to notice of juvenile court proceedings
involving the alleged offender, to attend proceedings otherwise closed to the public, to be heard
throughout the proceedings, to make a statement
the court must consider in determining the
disposition, to participate in compensation
programs available to crime victims generally, to
learn the names and addresses of the offender

and his or her parents, and to receive notice of
the offender's release from custody. Legislation
may permit child victims to have a parent or other
adult present during the victim's testimony.

e. Serious and Habitual Juvenile Offender Statutes

Criminal sentences, grounded primarily in
the nature of the act rather than in the offender's
condition, are generally determinate, that is
defined by a minimum and maximum number of
years. Juvenile sanctions, grounded in the
offender's condition, have traditionally been
indeterminate, that is, lasting until the age at
which the juvenile court's dispositional authority
ends but terminable sooner if the court finds that
the offender has been rehabilitated.

A number of states now provide for
determinate delinquency sanctions in at least
some circumstances, for example where the
offender has committed repeated violent offenses.
Several codes include serious and habitual
offender provisions, which may (1) impose
mandatory minimum sentences or sentencing
ranges for listed offenses, (2) authorize the
juvenile court to impose a determinate sentence
for specified offenses; (3) authorize the juvenile
court to impose a longer period of incarceration,
up to a statutory maximum, for some serious

offenses; (4) authorize the juvenile court to impose
harsher dispositions on youths who commit
specified crimes; (5) extend juvenile court
jurisdiction over serious offenders to a later age
than is permitted for delinquents generally; or (6)
authorize the juvenile court to place serious or
habitual offenders in an adult facility or juvenile
boot camp. Most serious and habitual juvenile
offender statutes reach only older juveniles, but
some do not distinguish based on age.

f.   "Restorative Justice"

Many states authorize juvenile courts to
order "restorative justice," that is, sanctions that
produce the least restrictive disposition for the
juvenile while enhancing the juvenile's accountability for the offense, providing relief for the victim
and protecting the community. A range of
sanctions are available:

Restitution imposes punishment at less
cost than incarceration or extended probation,
provides some compensation for the victim's loss,
and may be more likely than incarceration to
encourage rehabilitation and discourage recidivism. The court may order the delinquent to
perform services or pay full or partial restitution,
depending on the juvenile's age, physical and
mental condition, and reasonable earning
capacity. To avoid reprisals by an angry juvenile,

payment of money is usually made to a court
officer rather than directly to the victim.

Statutes sometimes authorize courts to
order a delinquent's parents to pay restitution in
an amount the parent can reasonably pay, at
least where the offense was intentional or
malicious. Courts have rejected contentions that
such orders impose liability without fault, holding
instead that the orders reasonably encourage
parental supervision while compensating victims.
The parent, however, holds a due process right to
notice and opportunity to be heard before entry of
the restitution order.

Community service may be an attractive
way to try to rehabilitate the delinquent,
particularly where the service is related to the
wrongdoing. Courts have upheld community
service orders against contentions that they
violate the Thirteenth Amendment, which
prohibits "slavery [or] involuntary servitude,
except as a punishment for crime whereof the
party shall have been duly convicted." See, e.g., In
re Erickson (Wash.Ct.App.1979) (community
service order constituted "punishment for crime"
because delinquent act is one that "would
constitute a crime if it was committed by an
adult").

Juvenile victim-offender mediation enables victims of property crimes and minor assaults to meet with a mediator and describe to the offender how the offense affected them and how the offender may assume responsibility and provide restitution. Victim-offender mediation sessions may result in signed restitution agreements, though victims may find the agreements less important than the opportunity to discuss the offense with the offender and reach an accommodation. Some juvenile courts have also used other alternative dispute resolution mechanisms such as arbitration and conferencing to bring victim and offender together.

g. Blended Sentences

More than a third of the states authorize imposition on juveniles of "blended sentences," which combine delinquency sanctions and criminal court sanctions. Blended sentencing permits efforts at rehabilitation while also introducing punishment into the formula.

Minnesota, for example, provides for "extended jurisdiction juvenile prosecutions," created by the legislature in part because delinquency dispositions were often too lenient but criminal sentences imposed on children were often too harsh. The juvenile court may impose both a delinquency and a criminal sanction on

older juveniles, with the criminal sanction stayed
pending satisfaction of the delinquency sanction;
the criminal sanction becomes operative only
where the juvenile fails to satisfy the delinquency
sanction or commits a new offense. In a
proceeding contemplating blended sentencing, the
juvenile is entitled to a jury trial. Minn. Stat. §
260B.130.

h. Boot Camps

In a number of jurisdictions, older juvenile
offenders may be assigned to "boot camps," also
known as "shock incarceration programs." These
programs generally serve non-violent first-time
male offenders between seventeen and twenty-
five. The aim is to instill discipline and
self-respect through military drill and ceremony,
physical training, manual labor, academic
education, vocational assessment, drug abuse
education and life skills training. In recent years,
boot camps have won public support because
they appear "tough on crime," but some critics
have questioned their efficacy.

i. Aftercare

When a juvenile is released from an out-of-
home placement, the court may place the juvenile
on supervised aftercare, which is similar to adult
parole. The juvenile must report periodically to
the court or the juvenile office, which monitors

the juvenile's compliance. If the juvenile fails to comply with conditions of aftercare, he or she may be subject to further sanction.

j. Dispositions Under the Federal Juvenile Delinquency Act

If the federal district court adjudicates the juvenile a delinquent, the court must hold a dispositional hearing and may suspend the delinquency findings, order the juvenile to pay restitution, place the juvenile on probation, or commit the juvenile to official detention. 18 U.S.C. § 5037. Section 5039 prohibits incarceration of delinquents in "an adult jail or correctional institution in which he has regular contact with adults incarcerated because they have been convicted of a crime or are awaiting trial on criminal charges." Because the federal Bureau of Prisons does not have its own facilities for delinquents, delinquents receiving confinement are housed in state juvenile corrections facilities under contract with the Bureau.

3. CAPITAL PUNISHMENT

The federal government (both civilian and military) and thirty-eight states authorize the death penalty for some forms of murder. In eighteen of these jurisdictions, the criminal court may impose capital punishment only on persons

who were at least eighteen at the time of the
crime. In five, however, the minimum age is
seventeen. In the other seventeen, the minimum
age is sixteen. See Victor L. Streib, The Juvenile
Death Penalty Today: Death Sentences and
Executions for Juvenile Crimes, January 1, 1973-
December 31, 2003, at http://www.law.onu.edu/
faculty/streib/juvdeath.htm.

In Thompson v. Oklahoma (S.Ct.1988), the
Court set aside a death sentence imposed on a
defendant who was fifteen when he committed the
crime. Justice Stevens' plurality opinion (for
himself and Justices Brennan, Marshall and
Blackmun) concluded that executing a defendant
who was under sixteen at the time of the crime
would constitute cruel and unusual punishment
in violation of the Eighth Amendment, but
declined to establish a firm constitutional rule
prohibiting execution of persons under eighteen
at the time of the crime.

Justice O'Connor concluded in *Thompson*
that "a national consensus forbidding the execution of any person for a crime committed before
the age of 16 very likely does exist," but she
concurred on the ground that Oklahoma's statute
did not express a minimum age. In light of
Thompson, the Eighth Amendment prohibits a
state from imposing the death penalty on a

defendant who was fifteen or younger when he
committed the crime, provided the statute
expresses the minimum age for execution.

In Stanford v. Kentucky (S.Ct.1989), the
Court held that executing a defendant who was
sixteen or seventeen at the time of the crime does
not constitute cruel and unusual punishment. In
Eddings v. Oklahoma (S.Ct.1982), the Court held
that in a capital case, a juvenile's age, mental
condition and maturity must be considered as
important mitigating factors in determining
whether to invoke the death penalty.

Even where a death sentence is within the
constitutional boundaries established by *Thompson* and *Stanford*, the sentence remains open to
challenge under the state constitution. See, e.g.,
Brennan v. State (Fla.1999) (imposition of death
penalty for crime committed when the defendant
was sixteen violates the state constitution's cruel
or unusual punishment clause).

In Atkins v. Virginia (S.Ct.2001), the Court
held that the Eighth Amendment prohibits
application of the death penalty to mentally
retarded persons. The decision, based on
diminished capacity, led to calls to reevaluate the
constitutionality of executing persons for crimes
committed before they turned eighteen. Two

months later, in Patterson v. Texas (S.Ct.2002),
the Court denied a stay of execution and a
petition for a writ of certiorari from a juvenile
offender facing execution; dissenting Justice John
Paul Stevens, joined by Justices Ginsburg and
Breyer, stated that the Court should reconsider
the juvenile death penalty's constitutionality.
Later the same year, Kevin Stanford applied
unsuccessfully for an original writ of habeas
corpus on the ground that he was under eighteen
when he committed his crime two decades earlier.
Justice Stevens (writing for himself and Justices
Souter, Ginsburg and Breyer) dissented from the
Court's denial of certiorari. The four dissenters
stated that the practice of imposing capital
punishment for juvenile crimes is "a relic of the
past and is inconsistent with evolving standards
of decency in a civilized society. We should put an
end to this shameful practice." In re Stanford
(S.Ct.2002).

4.　COLLATERAL USE OF JUVENILE DISPOSITIONS

a.　Expungement and Sealing

States have traditionally provided that
juvenile court records, including the transcript
and exhibits, are sealed at the conclusion of the
proceeding and may be expunged at a future time,
for example when the juvenile reaches majority.

Expungement normally occurs on the juvenile's motion after he reaches the specified age, which may be years after the adjudication, when the juvenile is unrepresented and may not even know of the right. Where the record is expunged, it is deemed never to have existed and the juvenile, may indicate that no record exists. This confidentiality mandate prevails over state open records and open meetings laws, which do not operate against courts engaged in decision-making.

Most sealing and expungement statutes are no longer unconditional. For example, Colorado specifies that expunged records are nonetheless available to any court or probation department for use in sentencing the youth in future juvenile or criminal proceedings. Id. § 19-1-306(5)(a). The state also permits expungement only where (1) the juvenile has been convicted of no further crime and has been adjudicated a delinquent for no further offense, (2) no criminal or delinquency proceeding is pending or being instituted against the juvenile, (3) the juvenile's rehabilitation has been attained, and (4) expungement is in the best interests of the juvenile and the community. Id. § 19-1-306(5)(c). Some states have increased the number of years the juvenile must wait before expungement. In some states, delinquency records may not be expunged where the underlying offense was a violent or other serious felony.

b. The Growth of Collateral Use

Until recently, sealing or expungement often left prosecutors and judges unaware of an offender's delinquency record. The criminal court was sometimes inclined to "go easy" on a defendant it thought was a first-time offender, unaware that the defendant had an extensive juvenile record.

Most states, however, have now enacted "three strikes" laws, other legislation, or sentencing guidelines that permit criminal courts to consider some earlier delinquency adjudications when determining pretrial release or when sentencing an adult or a transferred juvenile. In nearly all states, for example, limitations on the use or disclosure of juvenile court records do not apply to sentencing proceedings following adult convictions, at least where the record concerned an adjudication for a designated felony or where the record is relatively recent. Case law in nearly all jurisdictions has upheld factoring juvenile adjudications into adult sentencing. In a number of states, juvenile adjudications may even be considered in determining whether to impose the death penalty in criminal court. A growing number of states have also enacted provisions permitting use of delinquency adjudications for impeachment in later civil or criminal proceedings, at least where the adjudication was for a serious or relatively recent offense.

Broad collateral use of delinquency adjudications may raise fairness questions. For example, alleged delinquents often appear in juvenile court unrepresented, or represented by counsel who seek to accommodate the court; are often cajoled into admitting responsibility "for their own good" (and without notice that the adjudication may be used against them later); may be adjudicated on less proof than would satisfy the beyond-a-reasonable-doubt standard in criminal court; and do not enjoy the right to a jury trial in most states. Juvenile courts may loosely apply the hearsay rule and other rules of evidence, and may use masters or referees rather than judges to preside at the hearing, affording the state a second opportunity to convince a decisionmaker when the judge decides whether to confirm the initial report. Courts, however, are generally not receptive to claims of constitutional deprivation arising from collateral use of delinquency adjudications.

c. Interagency Sharing of Information

Confidentiality statutes have sometimes led juvenile justice and child welfare agencies to practice "informational territorialism," failing to share with one another information about a troubled juvenile. The failure may stem from such reasons as ignorance about which other agencies are serving the child, interagency mistrust, or fear that information may be misused, altered or released. A consensus has emerged, however, that courts, school officials, law enforcement and child welfare agencies need to share information about troubled and delinquent youth within their care. Lack of information sharing frequently causes wasteful duplication of effort by agencies with limited budgets, and may inhibit effective treatment.

A growing number of states now specify that where a delinquency adjudication is for an offense committed on school property, a serious violent offense, or a drug offense, the disposition must be transmitted to the delinquent's school. The evident purpose is to provide schools information needed to protect students against violent classmates.

5. THE RIGHT TO TREATMENT

Speaking in 1998 about nationwide conditions in juvenile detention facilities, the president of the National Juvenile Detention Association (which represents the heads of the nation's

juvenile jails) said, "The issues of violence against
offenders, lack of adequate education and mental
health, of crowding and of poorly paid and poorly
trained staff are the norm rather than the
exception." See Fox Butterfield, Profits at a
Juvenile Prison Come With a Chilling Cost, N.Y.
Times, July 15, 1998, at A1.

Some juvenile correctional facilities
operate at 200% to 300% of design capacity, even
though overcrowding is associated with higher
rates of institutional violence and suicidal behavior, and with greater reliance by authorities on
short-term isolation. A sizeable number of
delinquents confined in secure facilities nationwide suffer from mental disabilities, ranging from
learning disabilities to mental retardation. In
1998, mental health authorities estimated that
20% of juveniles incarcerated nationwide have
serious mental illnesses, including juveniles who
cannot get mental health treatment outside the
prison system because of budget cuts.

a. Private Litigation
Chapter 4 treated the states' constitutional
obligation to provide a minimal level of care to
foster children and other abuse and neglect
victims in state custody. In the early 1970s,
lawsuits by private plaintiffs began challenging
conditions in secure juvenile correctional facilities

in a number of states. Several federal courts
mandated minimum standards of care and
treatment, sometimes after finding conditions so
harsh as to violate the Eighth Amendment ban on
cruel and unusual punishment. See, e.g., Morales
v. Turman (E.D.Tex.1974) (describing "the widespread practice of beating, slapping, kicking and
otherwise physically abusing juveniles in the
absence of any exigent circum-stances; the use of
tear gas and other chemical crowd-control devices
in situations not posing an imminent threat to
human life or an imminent and substantial threat
to property; the placing of juveniles in solitary
confinement or other secured facilities, in the
absence of any legislative or administrative
limitation on the duration and intensity of the
confinement and subject only to the unfettered
discretion of corrections officers"); Nelson v.
Heyne (N.D.Ind.1972) (describing super-vised
beatings of juvenile inmates with a thick board for
violating institutional rules; the use of major
tranquilizing drugs to control inmates' excited
behavior, without medically competent staff
members to evaluate the inmates before or after
administration, despite the potential for serious
medical side effects; and the use of solitary
confinement for prolonged periods on any staff
member's request); Inmates of Boys' Training
School v. Affleck (D.R.I.1972) (describing dark,
cold solitary confinement room where boys would

be kept for as long as a week, wearing only their underwear, without being provided toilet paper, sheets, blanket, or change of clothes).

In Alexander S. v. Boyd (D.S.C.1995), the court found that conditions in South Carolina juvenile detention facilities violated the detainees' due process right to reasonably safe conditions of confinement, freedom from unreasonable bodily restraint, and minimally adequate training. The decision was unusual because it resulted from final judgment after trial, rather than from a settlement or consent decree without full trial. Consent decrees will be much more difficult to secure after enactment of the Prison Litigation Reform Act of 1995, 18 U.S.C. § 3626, which applies to accused or adjudicated delinquents, and to federal, state or local facilities that incarcerate or detain accused or adjudicated delinquents. Id. § 3626(g)(3), (5).

The 1995 Act provides that "[p]rospective relief in any civil action with respect to prison conditions shall extend no further than necessary to correct the violation of the Federal right of a particular plaintiff or plaintiffs. The court shall not grant or approve any prospective relief unless the court finds that such relief is narrowly drawn, extends no further than necessary to correct the violation of the Federal right, and is the least

intrusive means necessary to correct the violation
of the Federal right." Id. § 3626(a)(1)(A). A court
may not enter a consent decree unless the decree
complies with these three conditions. Id. §
3626(c). A consent decree is thus possible only
where corrections authorities admit violations of
federal rights. Such admissions are unlikely
because they would expose authorities to private
civil damage suits.

b. Federal Enforcement

In 1980, Congress enacted the Civil Rights
of Incarcerated Persons Act, 42 U.S.C. §§ 1997-
1997j (CRIPA), which authorizes the U.S. Department of Justice to sue state and local
governments to remedy "egregious or flagrant"
conditions that deny constitutional rights to
persons residing or confined in public institutions. The covered institutions include ones for
juveniles awaiting trial, receiving care or
treatment, or residing for any other state purpose
(except solely for educational purposes). Id. §
1997(1)(B)(iv). The court may order equitable
remedies that "insure the minimum corrective
measures necessary to insure the full enjoyment"
of these rights. Id. § 1997a(a). The Justice
Department may also sue under a provision of the
Violent Crime Control and Law Enforcement Act
of 1994 that prohibits a "pattern or practice" of
civil rights abuses by law enforcement officers.

Id. § 14141.

CRIPA authorizes the Justice Department to sue only to remedy systemic problems and not to represent individuals. The Act does not create constitutional rights, but provides a cause of action to enforce and effectuate rights otherwise created by constitution or statute. The Department may secure voluntary compliance from investigated facilities, or it may commence litigation seeking minimum corrective measures after exhausting the Act's notice and conciliation provisions designed to permit states to voluntarily remedy deficiencies found by the Department. The Act does not preclude private litigants from filing suit alleging unconstitutional conditions.

As of November 1997, the Justice Department had investigated 73 juvenile detention and correctional facilities. The investigations have led to consent decrees relating to more than thirty such facilities, including ones in Kentucky, New Jersey and Puerto Rico.

The Justice Department sued Georgia in 1998 and Louisiana in 1999. The Department charged that Georgia's juvenile detention facilities were marked by a pattern, among other things, of severe overcrowding, physical abuse by staff, use of pepper spray to restrain mentally ill juveniles, inadequate education, inadequate medical and psychiatric care, inadequate supervision of suicidal inmates, inadequate educational facilities, and guards who pitted inmates against one another for sport and who routinely stripped young inmates and locked them in their cells for days at a time.

To avoid federal takeover of the juvenile correctional system, Georgia swiftly reached an agreement with the Justice Department to appoint an independent monitor and to spend $10 million to hire more teachers, guards and medical personnel. The president of the National Mental Health Association criticized the agreement for lacking an enforcement mechanism and for allowing the state to monitor its own compliance.

The Justice Department charged Louisiana with a pattern of failing to protect confined juveniles from beatings by guards and with providing inadequate education, medical and mental health care at the state's four secure juvenile correctional facilities. The case settled in late 2000.

Federal prosecution of juvenile corrections officers for conduct against inmates remains possible under 18 U.S.C. §§ 241 and 242. Section

241 permits prosecution of persons who conspire to "injure, oppress, threaten, or intimidate" a person in the "free exercise or enjoyment" of a federal constitutional or statutory right. Section 242 permits prosecution of a person who, under color of law, willfully deprives any person of a federal constitutional or statutory right. Conviction under either provision, however, would be difficult because the Justice Department would need to prove that the defendant acted with specific intent to interfere with the federal right and knowingly and willfully participated in the violation. See, e.g., Screws v. United States (S.Ct.1945); United States v. Guest (S.Ct.1966).

c. Reform Efforts

Massachusetts and Missouri are leaders among states that have taken decisive steps to reform their juvenile correctional systems. Massachusetts closed its training schools beginning in the early 1970s. Based on their current crime and their prior record, about 15% of committed youths receive secure detention. The remaining youths are referred to a wide range of community-based programs, including group homes, forestry programs, day treatment programs, outreach and tracking programs, and foster care. The Massachusetts program emphasizes the importance of maintaining small residential facilities and manageable caseloads.

The Massachusetts reforms influenced
other states, including Missouri, which closed its
training schools in the early 1980s. Missouri
reserves secure confinement for violent offenders
and chronic repeaters, and places other youth in
the less restrictive programs. The state stresses
small decentralized facilities, regional management, and expansion of a full range of community
based alternative placements. Residential programs have units housing 10 or fewer youths, and
other secure units hold a maximum of seventy
youths. Most confined youth are placed in
wilderness programs, community group homes,
proctor homes in which youths live with college
students, day treatment programs, or individual
supervision programs.

d. Privatizing Juvenile Corrections

In recent years, some states have assigned
children to secure juvenile detention centers built
and maintained by for-profit corporations. The
nation has more than twice as many privately
operated juvenile correctional facilities as public
facilities, though the public facilities hold more
than twice as many juveniles as the private
facilities.

Critics charge that some of the worst
conditions in juvenile prisons exist in many of

these private facilities. In particular, some private facilities allegedly seek to maximize profits by holding juveniles longer than necessary, permitting dangerous overcrowding, hiring poorly trained guards who fail to protect inmates from violence and often perpetrate or encourage violence, providing inadequate medical and mental health care, and serving inadequate food. Once states contract with a private facility, they often allegedly fail to monitor the facility's conditions.

INDEX

References are to Pages

593

References are to Pages

References are to Pages

References are to Pages

†